TRADING MADE EASY USING CPR INDICATOR

"A PRACTICAL GUIDE TO MARKET STRUCTURE, TIMING, AND EXECUTION"

GOMATHI SHANKAR

(CPR by KGS)

notionpress.com

INDIA • SINGAPORE • MALAYSIA

ISBN
Paperback 979-8-89826-660-8
Hardcase 979-8-89826-925-8

Disclaimer

The authors and publisher do not accept any responsibility for financial losses that readers may incur from trading or investing based on the strategies discussed in this book. All readers are encouraged to consult a qualified financial advisor before making any investment decisions.

This book is intended for educational purpose only.

Dedication

"To my father, Lord Arunachala, and my mother, Goddess Kamatchi.
Without their grace, I would have remained lost.
This book, this life, this journey, everything belongs to them.
Every page here is touched by their blessing."

"My heartfelt thanks to Devi, Pavithran, Gowtam, and Parameshwaran for their unwavering support in helping me complete this book, a dream that had long been waiting on the shelf."

CONTENTS

LIST OF FIGURES & TABLES

Chapter 01

UNPACKING THE LAYERS OF MARKET STRUCTURE

When I began my trading journey, I was eager to take trades and make quick profits. I wasn't thinking about structure or strategy, just entries and exits. One morning, I spotted a clean breakout on my usual 5-minute chart. The setup looked perfect. I jumped into the trade, set a small target, and watched it like a hawk. A few minutes later, my target was hit. I had made a quick profit, and it felt like I had cracked the code. But what came next changed how I looked at trading forever.

Later in the day, I noticed the stock had continued its rally, far beyond my exit point. Out of curiosity, I zoomed out to the weekly timeframe chart and was struck by what I had missed. It was a powerful breakout from a multi-year resistance level. My narrow focus on the short-term chart had caused me to miss a far more significant opportunity.

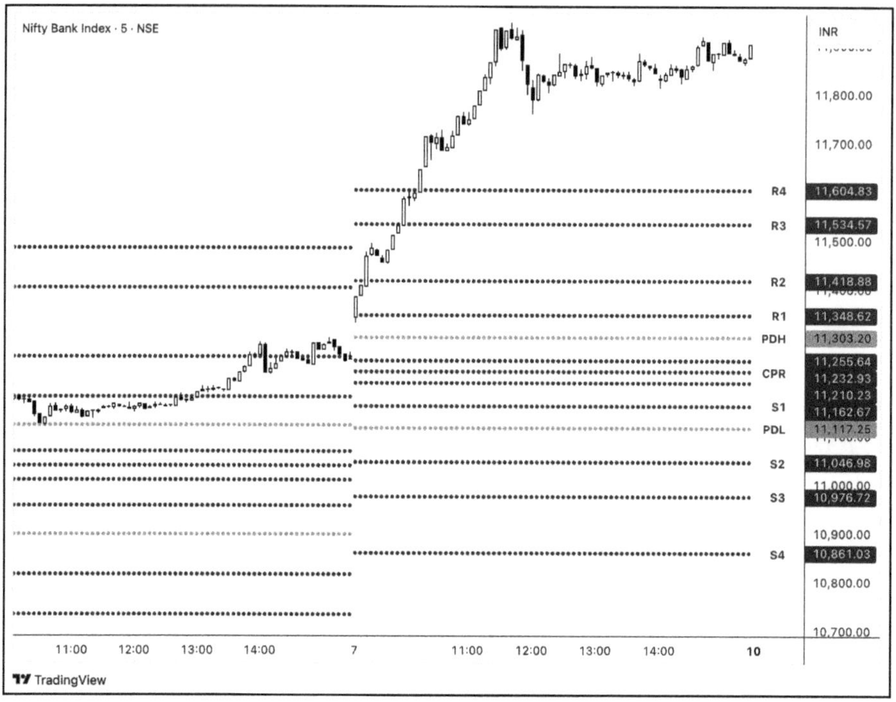

Fig. 1.1: *Quick Entry Above R1, Quick Exit at R2 (5-Minute Timeframe)*

Fig. 1.2: *The Bigger Picture I Missed (Weekly timeframe)*

The real story? I found it only after I switched to a higher timeframe. Here's the weekly chart of Bank Nifty. It clearly shows a major breakout from a multi-year resistance level. This was the real reason behind the strong rally. But I only noticed it after exiting my intraday trade. A perfect example of how a higher timeframe can guide you to stay in the trade longer.

That day changed my perspective. It was no longer just about the trade I exited. It was about the way I had been looking at the market. I realized that two traders can look at the same chart and see completely different things. One sees random moves, noise, and uncertainty. The other sees structure, patterns, and opportunity. What separates them is not luck or a secret indicator.

Fig. 1.3: Confused trader Vs. Smart trader

It is their understanding of market structure. Understanding market structure is not just a theory. It is a practical skill that transforms the way you trade. Most traders get caught in the noise of daily price swings, making impulsive decisions without a clear plan. But when you learn how the market truly moves, you stop reacting. You wait. You act with intent. You exit with clarity. The market stops feeling random, and that is when real growth begins. Now that you understand why market structure matters, this chapter will take you through the key insights and experiences that helped me build that understanding. You can apply them in your own trades with clarity and confidence.

Market Moves in Trend - Dow Theory

One of the oldest and most reliable ways to understand market movement is Dow Theory. Developed by Charles Dow, it laid the foundation for modern technical analysis. At its core, it says that everything known by the market is already reflected in the price, and that price doesn't move randomly. It moves in trends. While Dow Theory has six key principles, in this section, we'll focus on the most practical one for traders. How trends form, how they shift, and how you can spot them early.

Dow Theory helps decode the market's logic. It shows that price doesn't move without reason, and it follows trends shaped by time and volume. Instead of random ups and downs, they follow clear patterns called trends. As seen in Figure 1.4, these trends usually fall into three categories, depending on how long they last and how they behave.

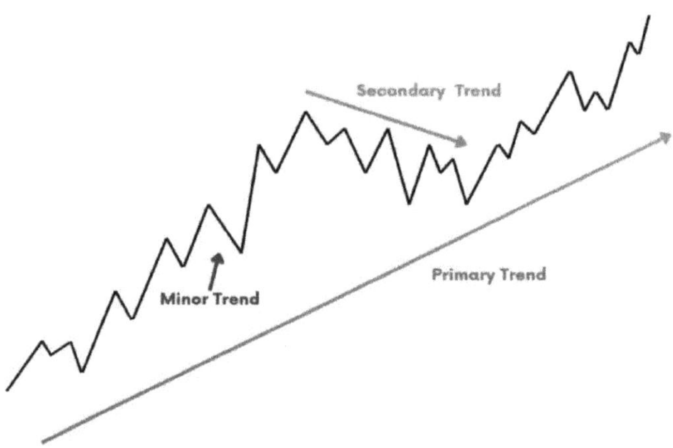

Fig. 1.4: *Market Trend Structure*

The ***Primary trend*** is the main flow of the river. It moves slowly but steadily in one direction. Even if it takes a few turns along the way, it keeps heading toward the sea. That's like a long-term trend in the market. It might take time, but the direction is clear.

Now, sometimes the river meets a bend or flows under a low bridge. It slows down, swirls for a bit, maybe even moves backward slightly before regaining its course. These are like ***Secondary trends***, short-term pullbacks that go against the main flow but don't change its ultimate direction.

And then there are ***Minor trends***, like quick diversions around a rock or the sudden rush under a narrow bridge. They create short bursts of movement, drawing attention but fading just as fast. In the market, they are those sharp price moves driven by news or emotion. They are easy to notice but not always meaningful if you forget the bigger picture.

Fig. 1.5: *Primary, secondary, and minor trends over time using a monthly timeframe*

On a monthly timeframe (see Figure 1.5), the primary trend outlines the overall long-term direction, the secondary trend highlights the corrective swings that occur along the way, and the minor trend captures the short-term price moves driven by news or brief shifts in sentiment. This view helps you see how they interact in real market conditions.

Basics of Market Dynamics (HH, HL, LL, LH)

In an uptrend, the market keeps climbing by forming higher highs and higher lows. Each new high shows that buyers are still in control, and each pullback that holds above the last low signals strong support. This steady climb reflects growing demand and confidence.

Like a mountain trekker climbing uphill. He moves forward, then pauses to catch his breath. But each pause happens a little higher than the last. He might slip a bit, but he doesn't return to the bottom. Step by step, he reaches new heights. That's what an uptrend looks like: progress with pauses, not perfection. Traders who recognize this rhythm don't panic on the dips. They see them as resting spots before the next climb.

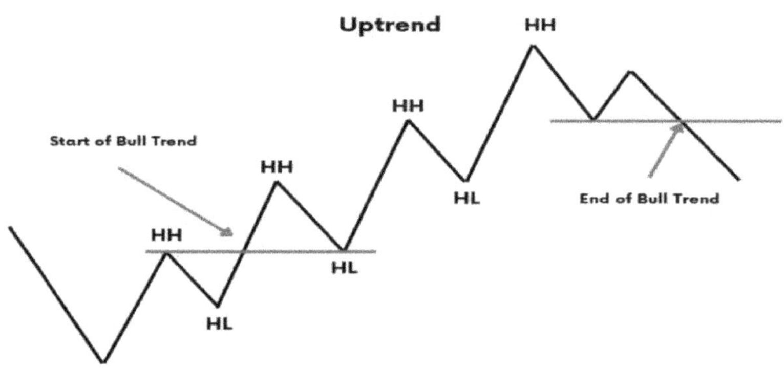

Fig. 1.6: *Structure of an Uptrend*

Figure 1.6 illustrates the anatomy of an uptrend, marked by a series of Higher Highs (HH) and Higher Lows (HL). The Start of the Bull Trend occurs when the price breaks above the previous high, confirming upward momentum. The trend remains intact as long as HHs and HLs persist. The End of the Bull Trend is signaled when the price fails to make a new HH and breaks below a key HL, indicating a possible trend reversal.

Downtrends: Lower Highs and Lower Lows

You can relate this to a ball bouncing down a staircase. Each bounce is weaker than the last, and every drop lands it lower than before. That's how a downtrend unfolds. The market tries to rise, but each attempt falls short of the previous peak, followed by a deeper low. These patterns of lower highs and lower lows signal growing selling pressure and fading buyer strength. Traders who recognize the downtrend early can prepare to short or step aside until the fall slows.

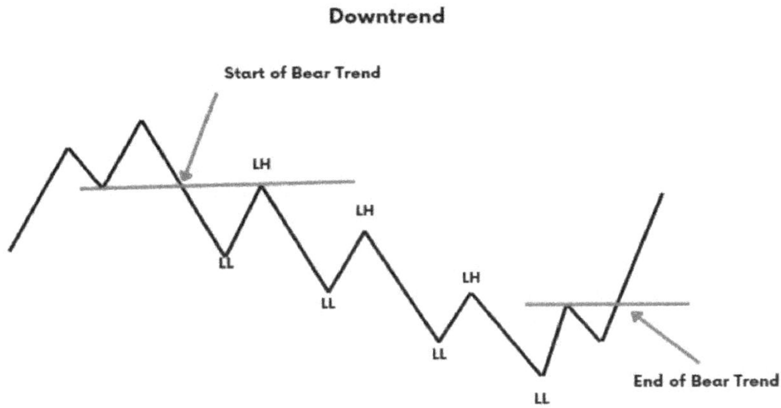

Fig. 1.7: *Structure of a Downtrend*

Figure 1.7 illustrates the anatomy of a downtrend, marked by a series of Lower Highs (LH) and Lower Lows (LL). The start of the bear trend is confirmed when the price breaks below a previous low, signaling building selling pressure. The trend stays intact as long as the market continues forming LLs and LHs. The end of the bear trend is signaled when the price fails to make a new LL and breaks above a key LH, suggesting a possible shift in momentum and a potential trend reversal.

Before diving into trade setups, it's worth pausing to ask a simple question. Why does the price move at all? What makes a stock suddenly rally or collapse? Trends don't begin by chance. They are sparked by something deeper, the market's underlying forces. At the heart of these dynamics lies one simple truth: it all comes down to demand and supply.

The Law of Supply and Demand: The Engine of Price

In the stock market, prices don't just move randomly; they are shaped by the basic economic principle of supply and demand. When buyers drive the demand, prices climb. When the market is flooded with sellers, prices fall. This balance between buyers and sellers plays a crucial role in shaping market trends, and understanding this dynamic is key to making informed trading decisions. This struggle creates constant pressure in the market, and Fig. 1.8 offers a visual of how bulls and bears push prices back and forth during such battles.

Fig. 1.8: *Tug-of-War Between Bulls and Bears*

Reliance Industries: The Jio Effect

Though many people used to see Reliance as just an oil and petrochemical giant, it proved to be much more. In 2016, the company launched Jio, offering free mobile data and calling services. This bold move sparked a revolution in the telecom sector, reshaping the industry and changing consumer expectations. Investors quickly recognized the massive growth potential. As the news spread, interest in Reliance shares soared. The demand skyrocketed, and its stock price surged in response.

Fig. 1.9: *The effect of Jio's launch reflected in Reliance Industries' stock rally on the weekly timeframe*

This chart clearly illustrates how demand played a crucial role in Reliance's price movement (Figure 1.9). Before Jio's entry, the stock was mostly range bound, trading between ₹150 and ₹250 for years, with relatively low demand. But once the market saw the scale of Jio's ambition and its impact, demand for the stock surged, and it began a strong upward trend. By 2020, it had crossed ₹700, driven by strong investor interest and institutional participation. The stock now trades around ₹1,204. This price journey reflects how a powerful business move backed by demand and market structure can trigger long-term stock growth and offer key lessons for traders and investors alike.

Yes Bank: From Investor Darling to Panic Selling

On the other hand, supply overtaking demand can lead to sharp declines. A classic example was Yes Bank in 2019–2020. Once a favorite among investors, Yes Bank faced financial troubles, and concerns about its stability began to spread. As fear took over, investors rushed to sell, creating an oversupply of shares. Banking is a highly competitive space, and when trust is broken in one bank, people quickly move their money to safer alternatives. This dramatic fall shows how negative sentiment, combined with excess supply, can lead to a steep and painful decline in stock value.

***Fig. 1.10:** Yes Bank's collapse from ₹350 to ₹5 during the crisis period, reflected on the weekly chart*

Fig. 1.10 captures the stunning collapse of Yes Bank from its 2018 highs near ₹350 to a shocking low of ₹5 by 2020. What was once a favorite among investors turned into a cautionary tale, driven by excess supply, panic selling, and a total breakdown in confidence.

Key Forces Behind India's Market Movements

We've seen how price responds to shifts in demand and supply, and how investor sentiment can turn a stock into a long-term winner or drive it into a steep fall. But what actually triggers these shifts? Behind every surge in demand or wave of selling, there are larger forces at play. From government policies to global cues, these external drivers shape the market's mood and direction. To truly understand why prices move the way they do, we need to explore these key forces that influence the Indian market.

Every price change is a reaction to something, whether it's economic data, investor sentiment, government policy, or global events. These forces don't act alone. They often overlap, reinforce, or cancel each other out, making the market dynamic and unpredictable. As a trader, your goal isn't to predict every move. It's to observe, understand, and respond. When you pay attention to what's driving the market, whether it's strong buying from institutions, a change in global interest rates, or sudden news, you begin to recognize patterns. Successful traders don't react emotionally. They stay alert to the signals, understand the forces at play, and prepare for different scenarios with discipline and clarity.

The Government's Hand: Fiscal Policy in Action

The stock market doesn't just react to company news; it also pays close attention to what the government is doing. When the government announces tax changes or new spending plans, the market takes it seriously. For example, a cut in corporate tax can improve profits and lift the mood in the market. Similarly, when large-scale infrastructure projects are announced, certain sectors like cement, steel, or logistics can benefit, and their stocks start moving. On the flip side, when taxes go up or there's a cut in spending, it can slow things down.

Traders who follow these updates closely often get early signals on where the market might be headed next. On 25th October 2017, Finance Minister Arun Jaitley announced a ₹2.11 lakh crore bank recapitalization plan for public sector banks. These banks were dealing with a large number of bad loans and were unable to meet international capital requirements. The government's support helped these banks recover, strengthen their financial position, and lend more actively again. This move aimed to increase credit flow, boost private investment, and support overall economic growth. As expected, banking stocks reacted positively, as this announcement came at a time when they needed support the most. SBI, one of the biggest public sector banks, surged nearly 27% in a single day following the recapitalization news, showing how powerful such policy decisions can be in moving the market, as seen in Figure 1.11.

Fig. 1.11: *SBI's sharp surge after the ₹2.11 lakh crore bank recapitalisation plan in October 2017 on the daily timeframe*

The RBI's Role: Steering Through Monetary Policy

The Reserve Bank of India (RBI) plays a vital role in managing monetary policy. By adjusting interest rates and controlling the money supply, the RBI aims to maintain price stability and promote economic growth. For instance, lowering interest rates can encourage borrowing and investment, stimulating economic activity. Conversely, raising interest rates can help curb inflation. These monetary policy decisions can significantly influence market sentiment and asset prices.

On 9th April 2025, the Reserve Bank of India (RBI) reduced the repo rate by 0.25% to 6.00%. The move was made to support economic growth. Lower repo rates usually mean cheaper loans, more business activity, and a positive push for the banking sector.

After the announcement, Bank Nifty rallied sharply, reflecting strong investor confidence in the banking sector. The index saw a strong upward move as traders anticipated increased lending activity and better earnings potential for banks. Fig. 1.12 captures this immediate reaction, where the price moved swiftly in response to the rate cut on the daily timeframe.

Fig. 1.12: *Bank Nifty response to RBI's rate cut in April 2025 on the daily timeframe*

The Global Pull on Indian Stocks

"When the U.S. sneezes, the world catches a cold."
– Klemens von Metternich

This old saying still holds true, especially when it comes to the Indian stock market. The U.S. is the world's largest economy, and its influence stretches far beyond its borders. For India, the impact is most visible in the IT sector. Companies like TCS, Infosys, HCLTech, and Wipro depend heavily on American clients for business. So, when the U.S. economy slows down or companies there cut back on technology spending, Indian IT firms are among the first to feel it.

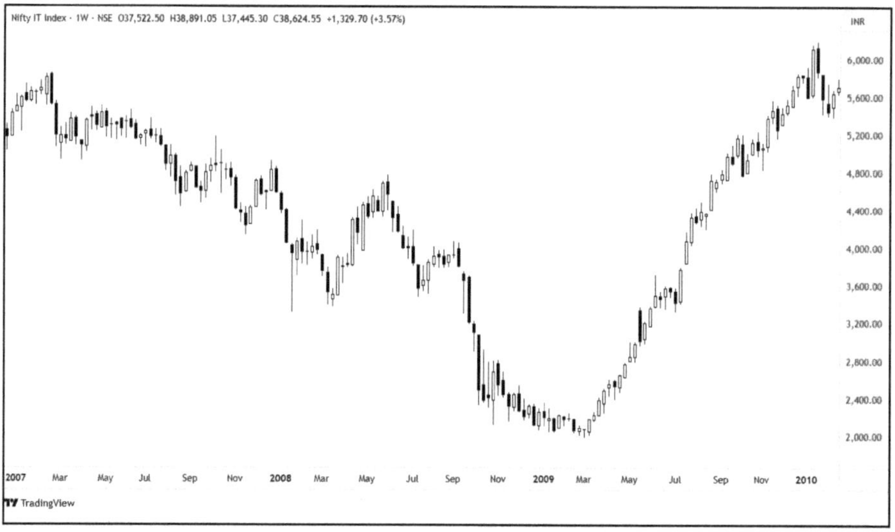

__Fig. 1.13:__ NIFTY IT drop during the 2008 global crisis on the weekly timeframe

We saw this clearly during the 2008 global financial crisis. As American companies slashed their IT budgets, Indian tech giants lost major contracts, and their stock prices dropped sharply. As shown in Fig. 1.13, the NIFTY IT index fell significantly during this time, reflecting the deep correlation between U.S. demand and the health of India's tech sector. On the flip side, when the U.S. economy is booming and companies are investing more in digital transformation, Indian IT firms benefit directly with stronger revenues and rising stock prices.

Institutional Activity: The Force Behind Big Moves

Big players like mutual funds, FIIs, and large portfolio managers have a strong grip on the Indian stock market. These institutions invest huge amounts of money, and their buying or selling can move stock prices significantly. When they buy heavily, markets often rise. But when they sell to manage risk or shift their portfolios, it can cause panic and sharp falls.

Fig. 1.14: *Daily timeframe showing the impact of FII selling on the Indian market*

For Indian traders, tracking these institutional moves is crucial, as it gives a clear picture of where the market might be heading. After the U.S. Federal Reserve hinted at raising interest rates, foreign investors began pulling money out of emerging markets like India. This shift in sentiment caused the rupee to weaken and led to sudden volatility across the Indian market. Between October 2024 and March 2025, this wave of FII selling triggered a sharp decline in stock prices, creating broad pressure across the market. Figure 1.14 highlights the impact during this period.

When you can connect what's happening with why it's happening, your trades become more meaningful and precise. Whether it's government policy, RBI decisions, global shifts, or institutional flows, these forces create the bigger waves in the market. But as traders, we don't just surf these waves blindly; we study how the price reacts.

Price Action: Decoding the Market's Movements

Price is where these forces leave their mark. It reflects everything the market knows, including news, earnings, sentiment, and expectations. Every movement on the chart is a response to these pressures. This is where price action comes in. It represents the purest form of market analysis, focusing solely on how price moves without relying on lagging indicators. Price action reveals the raw behavior of the market in real time. Traders who master it can interpret market sentiment, spot emerging trends, and anticipate key reversals. By understanding how price reflects trader behavior, you gain the clarity to trade with discipline and confidence.

To understand this better, imagine a roadside tea seller. For hours, no one stops at his stall. He wipes the counter, rearranges cups, and keeps an eye on the road. Then someone halts, orders a cup, and takes a sip. A passerby notices and stops. Within minutes, a small crowd forms. The tea seller didn't change anything; the crowd reacted to the behavior of the first buyer. That's what price action is. It's not about prediction. It's about watching what actually happens and understanding how people respond. Charts tell the same story. Not in words, but in candles.

Now that we've seen how price action reflects the underlying forces in the market, let's look at how traders actually use it in real time. Certain price behaviors appear again and again on the charts, such as support and resistance levels, trend lines, patterns, and candlestick signals. Once you learn to recognize these setups, you start seeing how the market communicates its next move.

Support and Resistance Levels

Ever noticed how prices often bounce from certain levels? That's not a coincidence; it's where demand kicks in. These areas are called support. On the other hand, when prices keep getting rejected near the same zone, it's resistance. These zones show where traders take action, and understanding them is your first step to mastering price action, as seen in Fig. 1.15. These behaviors don't happen randomly. The crowd gathers at specific places on the chart, just like the tea stall attracts people at a busy street corner. These are areas where price reacts again and again. Traders call them support and resistance levels.

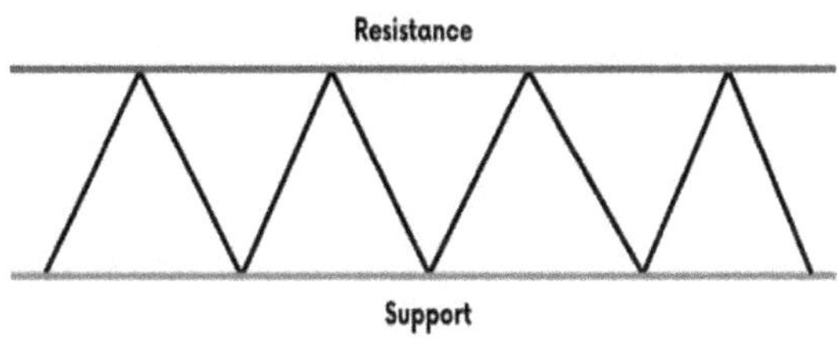

Fig. 1.15: *Range-Bound Structure with Support and Resistance*

Trendlines

Watch any chart for a while, and you'll notice the price follows paths. Sometimes it climbs steadily, sometimes it falls, and sometimes it drifts. Draw a line along that path, and suddenly, the story becomes clearer. That's what a trend line does; it shows you the road the market is taking. And here's the thing: the market respects these lines until it breaks them. It touches them, pulls away, comes back again, but when that line finally breaks, it's often the market's way of saying, "Something's changed." It helps you stay with the move as long as it lasts and alerts you when momentum begins to fade. This kind of directional clarity is shown in Fig. 1.16.

Fig. 1.16: *Identifying Market Direction with a Trendline*

Chart patterns

Once you start seeing how price respects levels and follows trend lines, you begin to notice something else. When you were a kid, you might have looked up at the sky and seen shapes in the clouds, like a rabbit, a bird, or maybe a car. It was your mind spotting patterns where others saw nothing.

That's how chart patterns work, too.

Price doesn't move without meaning. Sometimes it forms shapes like triangles, double tops, or cups. These are not random. They are clues. Some suggest the trend will continue. Others hint at a reversal. Once you learn to spot them, you begin to see the market with more clarity.

Triangle Patterns - Breakout Signals

Triangle patterns occur when the price begins to consolidate, creating a narrowing range between support and resistance levels. These patterns suggest that the market is in a temporary pause, where neither buyers nor sellers have full control. As the range tightens, pressure builds, and eventually, the price breaks out in one direction. There are three main types of triangle patterns:

When triangle patterns appear on the chart, they don't all look the same. Some lean upward, others downward, and a few tighten from both sides. Each type reveals a different kind of pressure building up in the market, and knowing how to read them can give you a valuable edge. You can spot these formations in Fig. 1.17, where the triangle patterns reflect different market pressures.

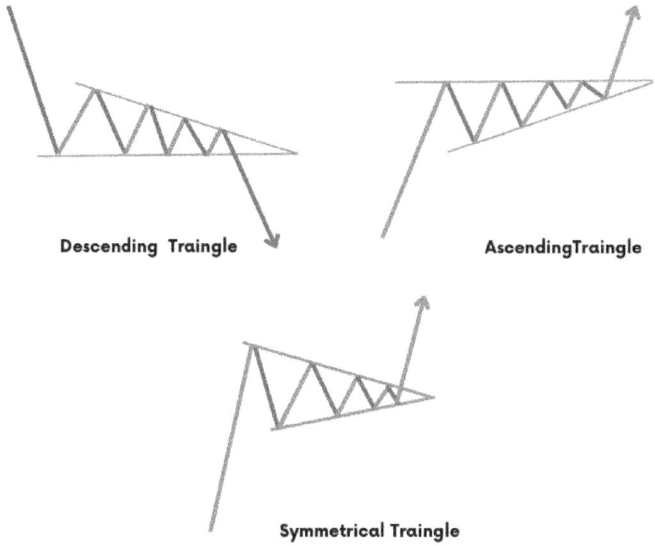

Fig. 1.17: *Triangle Chart Patterns – Continuation and Reversal Signals*

An ***ascending triangle*** forms when buyers keep pushing from below, creating higher lows, while sellers hold the line at a fixed resistance. It signals strength from the buyers. If price breaks above the resistance, it often triggers a sharp rally.

A ***descending triangle*** does the opposite. Sellers keep stepping in at lower levels, forming lower highs, while buyers defend a support zone. When that support finally gives way, it usually leads to a strong fall.

A ***symmetrical triangle*** shows hesitation from both sides. Buyers and sellers both pull back, and the range gets tighter. When the breakout finally happens, it often comes with momentum in whichever direction wins the tug of war.

Double Top & Double Bottom – Trend Reversal Signals

Sometimes, the market doesn't make a decision right away. It hesitates. It tests a level once, pulls back, and then returns, almost like it's reconsidering. This second attempt often reveals the truth: whether buyers have more fuel to push higher, or whether sellers are still holding strong. Imagine someone going for a job interview. The first round goes okay, but the company isn't fully convinced. They call the candidate again for a second round. If the performance still doesn't impress, they decide not to proceed. That's it. No offer. These classic reversal behaviors are captured in Fig. 1.18.

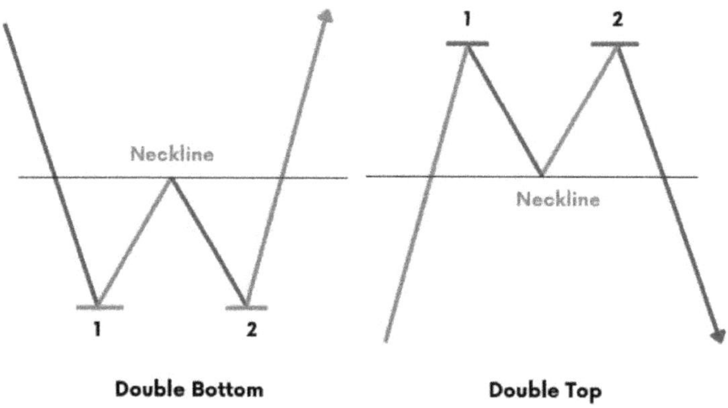

Fig. 1.18: *Double Bottom and Double Top Patterns – Reversal Setups*

That's a ***double top***.

The price tried once to break a resistance. It was rejected. Tried again. Rejected again. The decision is made; the market moves down. Now, imagine another person interviewed for a role. He was nervous the first time. Barely made it through. But the company saw potential and gave him a second shot. This time, he nailed it. Got the offer. Got the start. That's a ***double bottom***. The price tested support. Held. Came back again. Still didn't break down. Then it surged above resistance. Buyers took charge. A fresh rally begins.

Head & Shoulders – Trend Reversal

Think of this pattern like a warning sign. After a strong move, the market struggles to push higher. Not every trend ends in panic. Sometimes, it fades out quietly and gives you a clear warning if you know what to look for. One such signal is the ***Head and Shoulders*** pattern. It starts with a strong move up, followed by a pullback. Then the market pushes even higher, forming a new peak, but that high does not hold for long. The next attempt fails to beat it, and the price slips again. This sequence, peak, higher peak, lower peak, forms a structure that resembles a head between two shoulders. If price breaks the support line connecting the lows, known as the neckline, it usually confirms that buyers are exhausted, and a downtrend is beginning.

The Inverse Head and Shoulders work the same way, just in reverse. The market makes a low, rebounds, dips to a deeper low, then fails to go lower. When the price finally breaks above the neckline, it signals that sellers are weakening, and a bullish reversal may be underway. Both versions of the pattern are highlighted in Fig. 1.19.

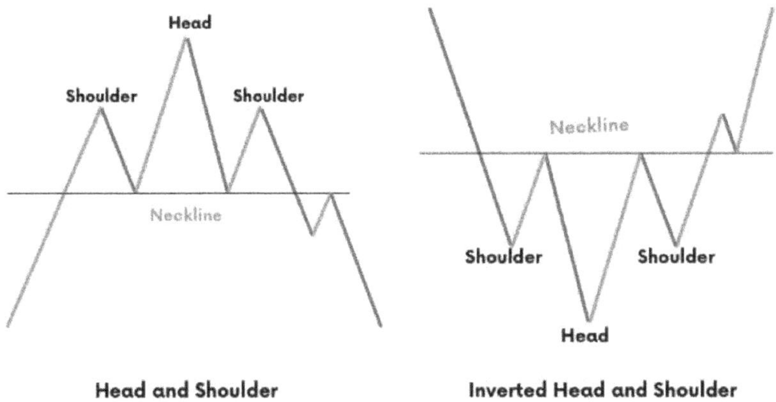

Fig. 1.19: *Head and Shoulder Patterns – Bearish and Bullish Reversals*

Cup & Handle – Bullish Continuation

This pattern starts with a smooth recovery. Price drops, stabilizes, and gradually climbs back to its earlier high, forming a rounded shape that looks like a cup. But instead of breaking out right away, the market pauses. It pulls back slightly, forming a small dip beside the cup. This is the handle. This typical structure is shown in Fig. 1.20. That handle isn't a weakness. It's a moment of rest. A pause that clears out hesitation before the real move begins. Once the price crosses above the resistance formed at the top of the cup, momentum often kicks in with strength. What follows is usually a decisive breakout, powered by fresh buying interest and confidence.

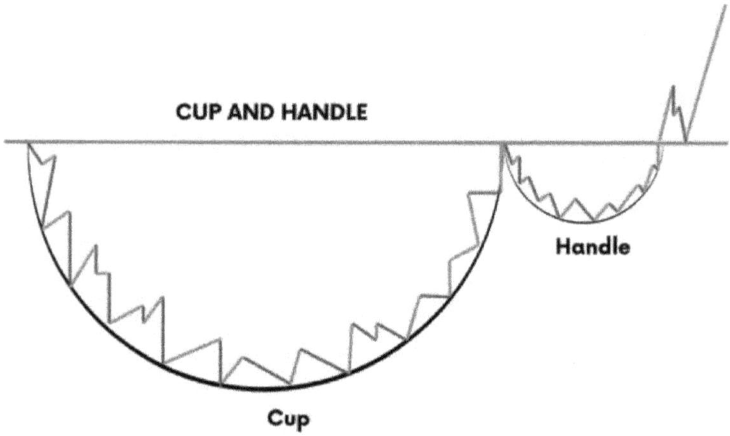

Fig. 1.20: *Cup and Handle Pattern – A Bullish Continuation Formation*

Candlestick Patterns

Before a big rain, there's always a change in the wind. A few drops fall, the air smells different, small signs that something is about to happen. In the market, candlestick patterns are like those early signs. They may look small, but they often appear just before a bigger move begins. These single or multi-bar formations quietly signal momentum shifts long before the trend becomes obvious. Fig. 1.21 illustrates key bullish formations that help traders identify early signs of strength, while Fig. 1.22 highlights the most common bearish candlestick patterns that warn of downside pressure

- ***Bullish Engulfing:*** A strong reversal pattern where a large green candle completely engulfs the previous red candle, signaling a bullish shift.
- ***Morning Star:*** A three-candle pattern with a small-bodied candle between a red and a green candle, indicating a potential trend reversal.
- ***Bullish Pin Bar:*** A candle with a long lower wick and a small body, suggesting rejection of lower prices and a bullish reversal.
- ***Bullish Harami:*** A two-candle pattern where a small green candle is contained within the previous red candle, signaling a potential uptrend.

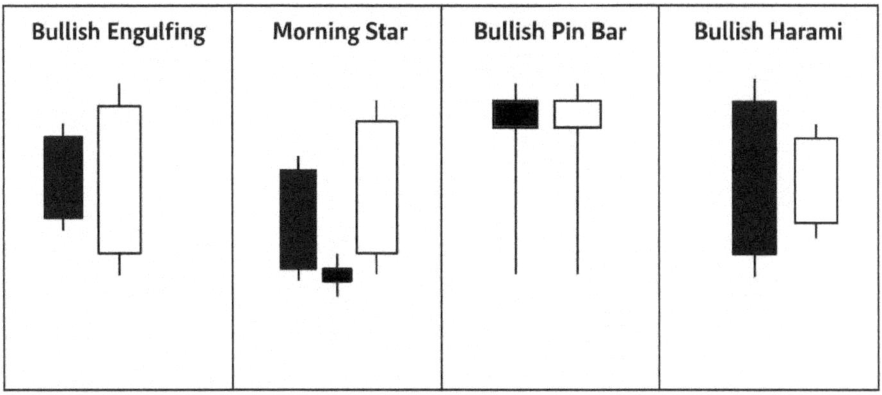

Fig. 1.21: Bullish Candlestick Patterns

- ***Bearish Engulfing:*** A strong reversal pattern where a large red candle completely engulfs the previous green candle, signaling bearish dominance.
- ***Evening Star:*** A three-candle pattern with a small-bodied candle between a green and a red candle, indicating a potential bearish reversal.
- ***Bearish Pin Bar***: A candle with a long upper wick and a small body, suggesting rejection of higher prices and a bearish reversal.
- ***Bearish Harami:*** A two-candle pattern where a small red candle is contained within the previous green candle, signaling a potential downtrend.

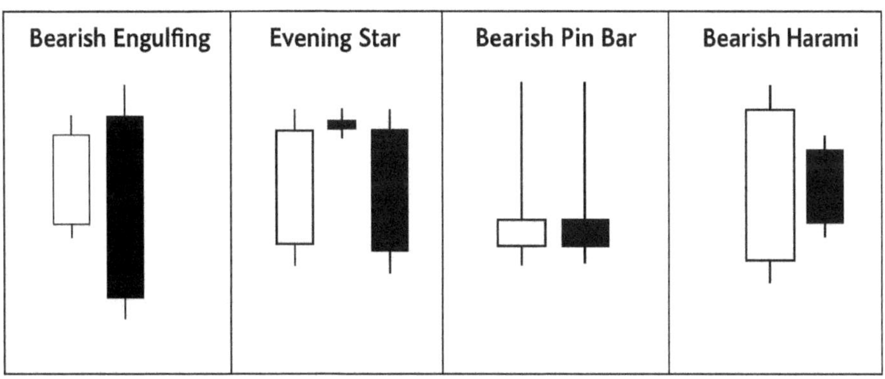

Fig. 1.22: Bearish Candlestick Patterns

Role of Critical Levels in Price Action

Think about visiting your hometown after a long time. Even if many things change, there are always a few familiar spots you never miss: the old tea shop, the temple corner, or your school gate. You pause there, out of habit. So does everyone else.

In the market, price also pauses at familiar places. These are levels where it has reversed, bounced, or broken out before. Traders remember them, even if not consciously. And when the price comes back to those zones, the same reaction often happens again. They're not magic levels. They're memory zones. And the more times the price reacts at a level, the stronger that memory becomes.

Historical Highs and Lows:

Among all the critical price zones, historical highs and lows stand out. These are the levels where the market once reached an extreme: the highest point buyers pushed, or the lowest point sellers drove it. They're not just technical markers. They carry memory, emotion, and significance. When price revisits a historical high, traders pause. Sellers may take profits, and buyers hesitate. It becomes a test: is the market ready to move higher, or will it get rejected again? If price breaks above that level with strength, it signals something new. There's no resistance above. The chart opens up. Momentum builds fast.

Similarly, when the price approaches a historical low, it raises concern. Traders watch closely. If price holds, the level gains more weight. But if it breaks, it triggers a message that weakness has taken over. With that support gone, the fall can intensify, simply because everyone remembers that this was the last known floor. These levels are not predictions. They're checkpoints. Places where the market previously paused or turned. And when price returns, those same reactions, fear, hesitation, and conviction, often return with it.

***Fig. 1.23:** Historical High Breakout in IRFC on the weekly timeframe*

This weekly chart of IRFC illustrates a historical high breakout above the resistance level. The stock had been consolidating below this level for an extended period before successfully breaking out with strong momentum. This kind of breakout setup is shown in Fig. 1.23, where IRFC pushes into new territory after a long consolidation. A historical high breakout signals strong bullish sentiment, as it indicates that the stock is moving into uncharted territory. Traders often look for such breakouts to ride the momentum, with the expectation of further upside if the breakout sustains with volume confirmation.

The chart represents the weekly price movement of BARBEQUE on the NSE. A significant Historical Low Breakout is highlighted, indicating that the stock has broken below a previously established support level. Such a breakout often signals strong bearish momentum, suggesting potential further downside unless a reversal pattern emerges. A move like this can shift long-term sentiment, just as seen in Fig. 1.24 with BARBEQUE breaking its historical low. Traders typically watch for confirmation through volume analysis and price action in the coming sessions.

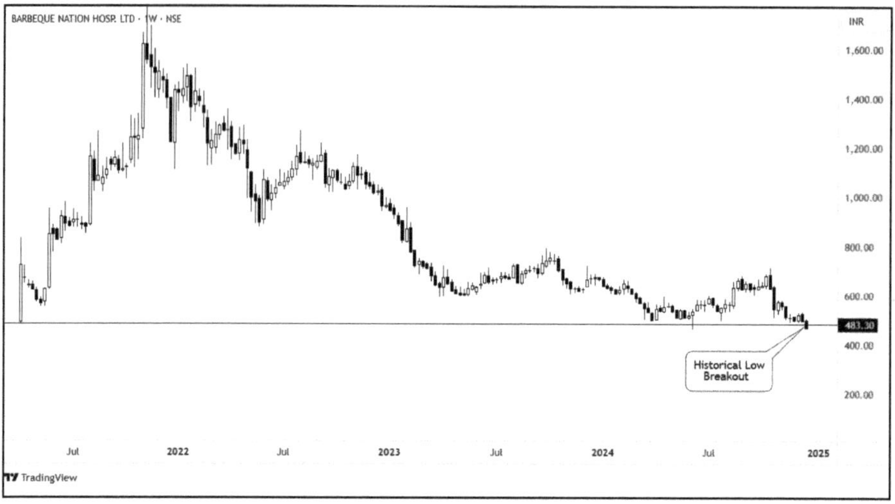

Fig. 1.24: *Historical low breakout in BARBEQUE seen on the weekly timeframe*

52-Week High and Low:

While historical levels reflect long-term memory, markets also react sharply to more recent milestones. The 52-week high marks the strongest point price has reached over the past year. As the price nears this level, many traders begin to book profits, anticipating resistance. But when price breaks through and holds above it, that signals strength and renewed optimism.

On the other hand, the 52-week low represents a critical support area. If it holds, it can spark a rebound. But if the price breaks below it, it suggests further weakness ahead, as the market moves into unfamiliar territory.

This price action can be seen clearly in Fig. 1.25, where Union Bank breaks past its 52-week high on the weekly chart. The breakout indicates strong bullish momentum, as the price has surpassed a key level where sellers previously dominated. Traders typically look for confirmation through sustained price action above 50, and a retest of this level could offer a buying opportunity. A clear example of this reversal is seen in Fig. 1.26, where AWL reacts sharply from its

52-week high of ₹411, where the price tested the resistance but failed to sustain upward momentum. This rejection indicates strong selling pressure, leading to a downward move.

***Fig. 1.25:** Weekly chart showing a strong 52-week high breakout in Union Bank*

***Fig. 1.26:** AWL reverses from the 52-week high on the weekly timeframe*

The breakdown is clearly shown in Fig. 1.27, where Astral slips below its 52- week low on the weekly chart. This breach of support signals strong selling pressure, and if the price remains below this level, the downward trend is likely to continue.

***Fig. 1.27:** Breakdown below the 52-week low in Astral seen on the weekly chart*

This shift is reflected in Fig. 1.28, a reversal from the 52-week low, indicating strong buying interest at a key support level. The stock previously tested this level but bounced back, confirming it as a significant demand zone. The recent reversal suggests a potential shift in trend, with buyers stepping in to defend the support. If the price sustains above this level, it could lead to a recovery, while a breakdown below may signal further weakness. Traders will watch for follow through price action to confirm the reversal.

However, these levels also play a crucial role in mean reversion trading. When the price approaches the 52-week high, it often experiences pullbacks as traders book profits, leading to a temporary reversal before continuing the trend. Similarly, when price nears the 52-week low, buying interest increases, causing a potential bounce back toward the mean. Institutional traders and long-term investors closely monitor these levels to gauge market strength and make strategic investment decisions. Recognizing these previous zones helps traders capitalize on both breakout opportunities and mean reversion setups, enhancing overall trading efficiency.

Fig. 1.28: *NIFTY shows a reversal from the 52-week low on the weekly timeframe*

Monthly High and Low:

Just like the 52-week levels show annual milestones, monthly highs and lows provide short-term pivot zones. They act as checkpoints for swing traders looking to ride trends or catch early signs of exhaustion.

This daily chart of Narayana Hrudayalaya Ltd (Fig. 1.29) highlights a monthly high breakout above the ₹1,417.35 resistance level. After a steady uptrend, the stock decisively broke past its previous monthly high, closing significantly higher with strong bullish momentum. This breakout is captured in Fig. 1.29. This breakdown is reflected in Fig. 1.30, where Infosys slips below its monthly low of ₹1,793.70 on the daily chart. It marks a clear breach of support and signals increasing weakness, with sellers driving the price lower and potentially setting up further downside movement.

Fig. 1.29: Monthly High Breakout in Narayana Hrudayalaya on the daily timeframe

Fig. 1.30: Monthly low breakout in Infosys on the daily timeframe

Weekly High and Low:

Weekly highs and lows show where the latest fights between buyers and sellers have taken place. When price crosses above a weekly high, it reflects growing buyer strength and confidence. A fall below the weekly low suggests sellers are gaining control in the short term.

The shift in momentum is visible in Fig. 1.31, where M&M breaks above a key resistance level on the 1-hour chart, triggering a weekly high breakout and setting the stage for a potential uptrend continuation.

This hourly chart of Tata Chemicals, shown in Fig. 1.32, highlights a weekly low breakout where the stock slips below a key support level. This suggests bearish momentum, signaling potential further downside.

Fig. 1.31: *Weekly high breakout in M&M on the 1-hour timeframe*

Fig. 1.32: *Weekly low breakout in Tata Chemicals on the 1-hour timeframe*

Daily High and Low

The daily high and low represent the highest and lowest prices of a single trading day. These levels are vital for intraday traders and scalpers focusing on short-term movements. A break above the daily high suggests strong buying interest, while a break below the daily low signals increased selling pressure. Traders use these levels to gauge market sentiment and set trade targets. Additionally, they often act as support and resistance for future sessions.

This 5-minute chart of TVS motor showcases a Previous Day High (PDH) Breakout, a strong bullish signal indicating momentum continuation.

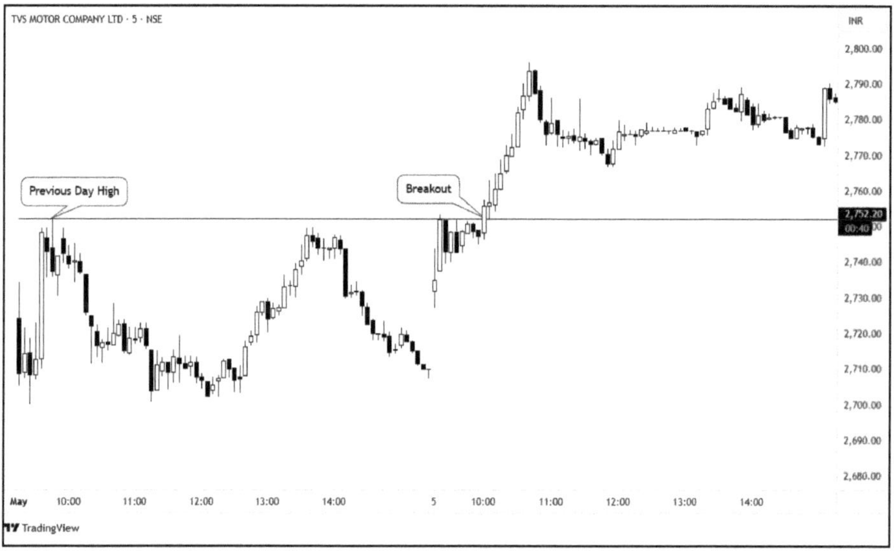

Fig. 1.33: Previous day high breakout in TVS Motor on the 5-minute timeframe

This 5-minute chart of Wipro showcases a Previous Day LOW (PDL) Breakout, a strong bearish signal indicating momentum continuation.

Fig. 1.34: Wipro breaks below the previous day low on the 5-minute chart

My Favourite Candlestick Pattern

Some candlestick patterns don't need a complex setup to make their point. A weekly hammer is one such pattern. It forms near-key lows, showing that sellers had the upper hand early in the week, but buyers came in strong and took control by the end. This shift in sentiment often hints at a potential reversal.

This weekly chart of Tata Steel Ltd highlights a hammer candlestick pattern, which typically signals a potential trend reversal from a downtrend to an uptrend

Fig. 1.35: *Hammer in Weekly timeframe of Tata Steel The Bahubali Candle: The Market's Knockout Punch*

A Bahubali Candle is one that takes control of the chart with full dominance. When a Bullish Bahubali Candle slams through resistance, it's like a knockout punch, signaling that the bulls are in full control. Conversely, a Bearish Bahubali Candle breaking through support suggests a fierce sell-off is underway. These powerful formations, especially when they occur at key price levels, can change the entire game.

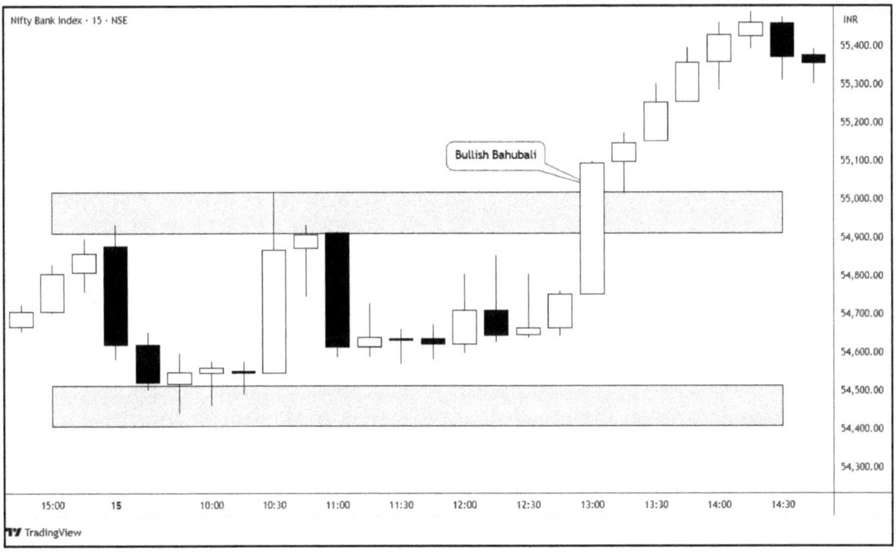

Fig. 1.36: Bullish Bahubali Candlestick Pattern

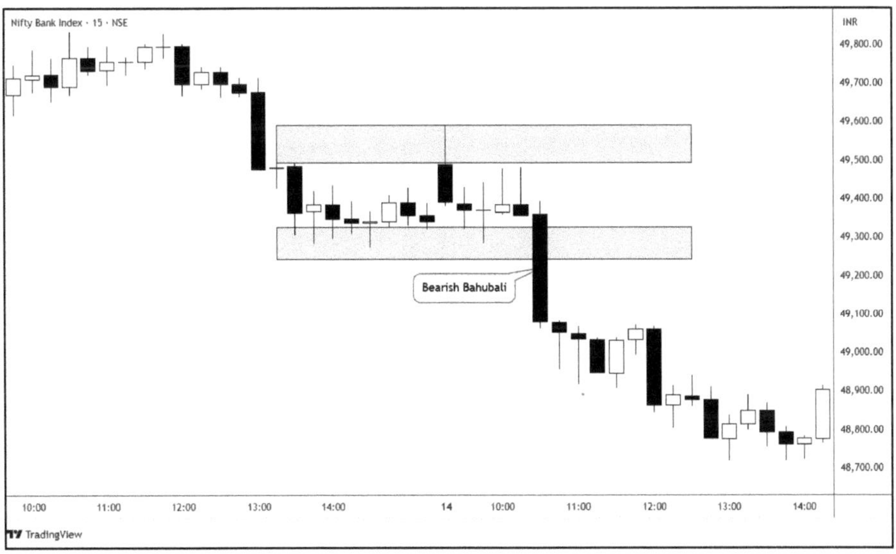

Fig. 1.37: Bearish Bahubali Candlestick Pattern

Structure Gave Me the Vision, CPR Gave Me the Trigger

This chapter isn't just about charts or setups. It's about the shift in mindset that every trader must go through. I wrote this based on lessons I learned the hard way, by jumping into trades too early, by ignoring the bigger picture, and by chasing moves without understanding the story behind them. If there's one thing I want you to take away from this chapter, it's that the market rewards those who observe before they act. Every move on the chart tells a story, and your job is to read that story with clarity, not emotion. From supply-demand dynamics to chart patterns and macroeconomic drivers, it all comes together when you start seeing structure, not chaos. That's when trading becomes a skill, not a gamble.

But here's the challenge I faced next, and one you might be facing too. Even after learning how to read structure, I still struggled with execution. I couldn't keep drawing zones for every stock, every day. In a fast-moving market, it simply wasn't practical.

That's when I found a better way.

Chapter 02

YOUR FIRST STEP INTO THE WORLD OF CPR INDICATOR

When I first started using CPR, it didn't feel like discovering a secret weapon. It felt more like finding a calm voice in the middle of market noise. No flashy alerts, no overcomplicated formulas, just clear zones that seemed to guide price like clockwork. Looking back now, I realize my best trades all had one thing in common. They respected CPR levels. And the worst trades? Almost every one of them ignored this range completely.

But the more I used it, the more one question kept coming back:

Where did this tool come from? And why does it work so consistently across different market conditions?

I had to trace its roots to find out.

Before Charts, There Was Math

Back in the days before electronic charts and algorithmic trades, floor traders scribbled numbers on chalkboards and notepads. With nothing more than yesterday's high, low, and close, they calculated a single number that helped them guess where the market might pause, bounce, or reverse. This simple tool was called the pivot point. It didn't promise magic, but for many, it offered structure in the madness. A way to walk into the day with a plan.

Simple, yes. But surprisingly effective.

For those traders, the pivot point became part of their daily ritual. Before the opening bell, they would mark that number on paper, ready to face the session with a clear roadmap. It was simple math, but it offered clues about where the price might hesitate, bounce, or break. Over time, this lone value began guiding everything from entries to stop losses.

As markets grew faster and more unpredictable, traders began looking for tools that could do more than just mark levels. They wanted something that could adapt with price, reflect momentum, and respond to changing volatility. The old pivot point was good, but it needed refinement. That's when new ideas began to emerge, turning a single number into a flexible range that could guide trades more effectively throughout the day.

This was the turning point when pivot-based tools began to evolve. Mark Fisher brought structure and clarity to the method. Then came Frank Ochoa, who refined it even further, shaping it into what we now know as the Central Pivot Range. This chapter is about that evolution. How a simple average turned into a pivot range. And how CPR, built on real-world trading needs, became a reliable lens through which thousands of traders now view the market.

Here's how that classic pivot point was calculated using just three numbers from the previous session.

Table 2.1: *Classic Pivot Point Calculation*

Pivot Levels	Formula
Pivot Point (PP)	(High + Low + Close) / 3
Resistance	(2 × PP) – Low
Support	(2 × PP) – High

From a Single Number to a Pivot Range

What started as a single reference point was no longer enough. Traders needed something that moved with the market, not something stuck in the past. That's when the idea of a range came into play, not just one level, but a zone that reflected the market's heartbeat.

And that shift didn't happen by accident. It came from the real-world experiences of traders who were deep in the action. One of the first to push this evolution forward was Mark Fisher, a young trading prodigy who began on the floor of the COMEX. He didn't just follow the old methods. He questioned them. So, Fisher gave the pivot point a makeover. He built something more flexible, a pivot range. Instead of watching a single price, he focused on zones where buyers and sellers were most likely to clash. Areas where liquidity pooled. Places where the market paused before its next move.

This wasn't about adding complexity. It was about creating clarity. His book *"The Logical Trader"* took this real-world experience and turned it into a structured method. A range that helped traders read the flow, not chase it.

> ***"The pivot range is where the market is likely to find support or meet resistance. If it manages to break through the pivot range, the market would likely make a significant move in that direction."***
>
> ***– Mark Fisher***

Fisher didn't just adjust a few numbers. He changed the way traders think about support and resistance. Instead of relying on fixed levels, he introduced the idea of ranges that adapt with time and volatility. It was built on experience. In those pages, Fisher explained how to map out key pivot zones. He showed how liquidity and momentum shape price behavior, and why understanding those shifts is more valuable than memorizing setups. Over time, his work became a go-to resource for traders looking to bring structure into fast-moving markets. But Fisher's work was just the beginning.

Traders use these ranges to spot potential breakout and reversal zones. When the price holds above the range, it often signals a bullish breakout. If the price gets rejected from the range, it points to selling pressure.

Table 2.2: *Fisher's Pivot Range*

Component	Formula
Daily Pivot Price	(High + Low + Close) ÷ 3
Second Number	(High + Low) ÷ 2
Difference	Daily Pivot Price – Second Number
Pivot Range 1	Daily Pivot Price – Difference
Pivot Range 2	Daily Pivot Price + Difference

Observing how price behaves around these pivot ranges helps traders plan better entries, exits, and manage short-term trades with more clarity.

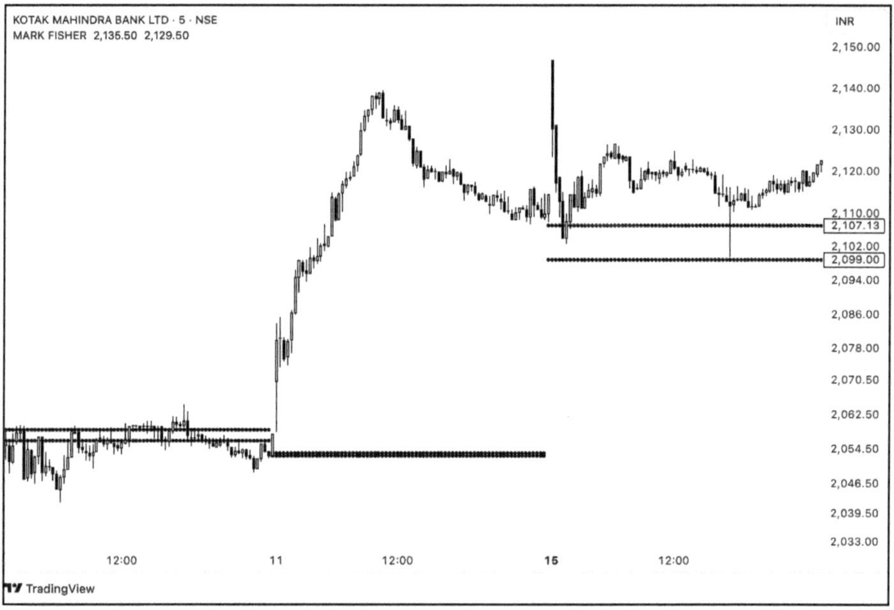

Fig. 2.1: *Mark Fisher Pivot Range Representation in Kotak Mahindra Bank (5-Minute Timeframe)*

On the first day, the distance between Mark Fisher Pivot Range 1 and Range 2 was small for Kotak Mahindra on a 5-minute time frame as seen on Fig. 2.1, which typically suggests that the stock should trend well or show high volatility. However, despite this, the stock did not trend as anticipated and remained relatively sideways, not showing the expected volatility or movement. This lack of movement on the first day suggests that there is a high possibility for the stock to trend well the next day. As expected, the next day, the Kotak opened above the Fisher range with a strong Bahubali candle, signaling a powerful breakout. The trend then moved very well, capturing the anticipated volatility and strong directional movement that was expected after the consolidation.

After the rally, Range 1 and Range 2 became wider. As we know, these ranges are calculated from the previous day's high, low, and close, and when the market moves strongly, such as in this rally, the range expands. This wider range indicates increased volatility, and traders can now reassess potential support and resistance levels as the market adjusts to the new momentum.

Let's look at the chart Fig. 2.2 of Grasim Industries Ltd. on a 15-minute timeframe. On the first day, the stock was trading in a sideways direction, staying within the Mark Fisher Pivot Range. This kind of movement indicates that the market was in consolidation, with neither the bulls nor the bears taking control. The price was trapped within a narrow range, showing indecision in the market.

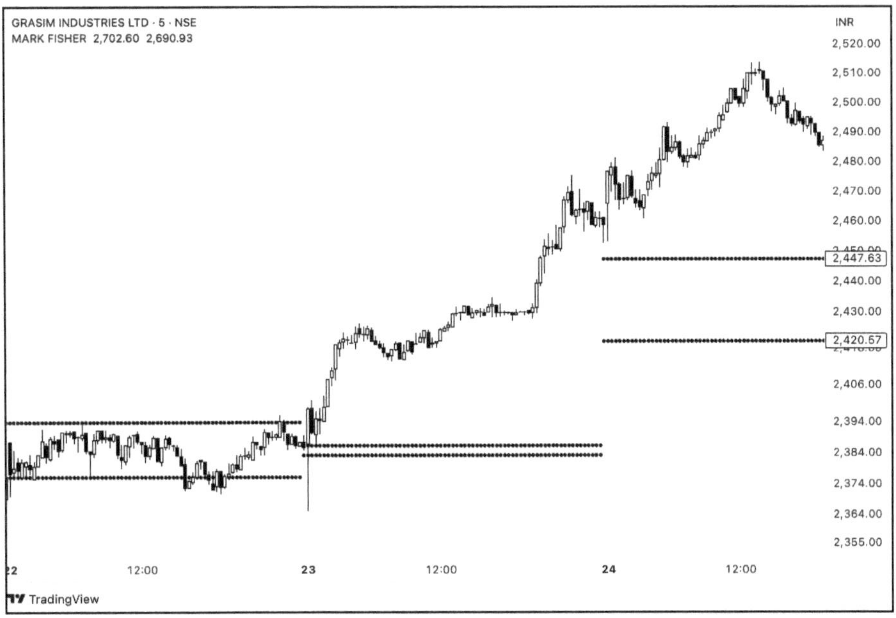

Fig. 2.2: Mark Fisher Pivot Range Representation in Grasim Industries Ltd (15-Minute Timeframe)

The next day, the pivot range became less wide, which indicated a potential trending day. As expected, the first 15-minute candle of the next day closed above the pivot range, signaling a breakout and a potential upward trend. The price then rallied strongly, confirming that the market was indeed trending as anticipated.

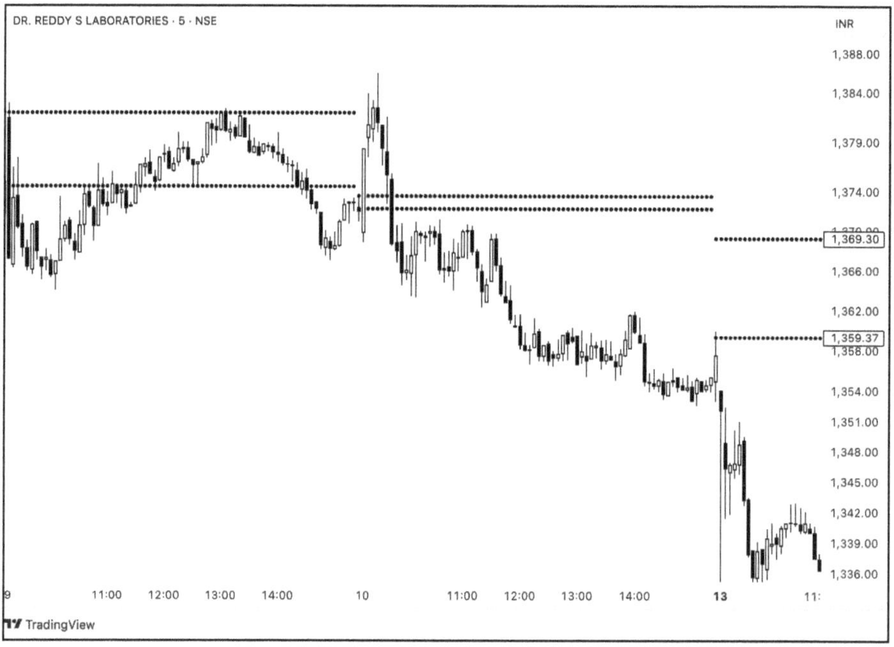

Fig. 2.3: *Mark Fisher Pivot Range Representation in Dr. Reddy's Laboratories Ltd (15-Minute Timeframe)*

Looking at the chart of Dr. Reddy's Laboratories Ltd. on a 15-minute timeframe, on the first day, the stock initially consolidated near the pivot range, with the price moving sideways within a narrow range. During this period, traders were waiting for a breakout in either direction. Eventually, the price moved downward, signaling the continuation of the bearish trend and indicating that the market was likely to trend lower after the consolidation. On the second day, the stock gave a fake bullish breakout, briefly moving above the pivot range, which led some traders to believe that the market was turning bullish. However, this breakout turned out to be a false signal, as the price quickly reversed and started moving downward again. This "bull trap" or "fake breakout" likely hunted the stop losses of traders who went long after the breakout. As the price reversed and continued downward, traders should have re-entered the short trade, capitalizing on the continuation of the bearish trend. The fake breakout served as a clear signal that the stock was not ready to go higher, and the downward move presented a strong opportunity for traders to profit from the market's rejection of higher prices. Using the pivot range as a key reference point for entry and stop loss levels would have helped manage the trade effectively.

Frank Ochoa: Innovating and Modernizing Pivot Trading

Just when traders started getting comfortable with pivot ranges, the market introduced a new challenge. The rise of intraday volatility, faster execution demanded something sharper. More adaptive. That is where Frank Ochoa stepped in. Frank Ochoa was not just another analyst. He was a trader in the trenches, someone who knew that in fast-moving markets, even small delays could cost big. He looked at what Fisher built and asked, "How can we make this faster? Smarter? More in sync with today's market rhythm?"

That's where CPR came in.

Ochoa didn't reinvent the wheel, but he reshaped it. By transforming a static concept into a dynamic range, he created a tool that worked across timeframes, asset classes, and trading styles. Whether it was an index opening with a gap or a stock consolidating before a breakout, CPR offered clarity when the screen was filled with noise. His book, "*Secrets of a Pivot Boss*", brought this method to the trading world. It wasn't just a technical manual. It was a strategy guide rooted in real market experience.

Definition and overview of CPR

Think of CPR as the market's balance point. Not just a single price, but a zone where the tug of war between buyers and sellers often plays out. It is calculated from the previous day's high, low, and close, but what it reveals is deeper. When price dances around this central range, it is not just indecision. It is a buildup. Compression. A sign that the market is gathering energy. And when price breaks away from it, that energy is released, often in strong, directional moves. More than just levels on a chart, CPR gives traders a map of pressure zones. It shows where big players might step in. Where breakouts could form.

And where reversals might catch the unprepared. Here's how the CPR Levels are calculated using three key values from the previous trading session:

Table 2.3: *Central Pivot Range (CPR) Calculation Structure and Formula Breakdown*

Level	Formula
Resistance 3 (R3)	R1 + (PDH – PDL)
Resistance 2 (R2)	CP + (PDH – PDL)
Resistance 1 (R1)	(2 × CP) – PDL
Top Central Pivot (TC)	(CP – BC) + CP
Central Pivot Point (CP)	(High + Low + Close) / 3
Bottom Central Pivot (BC)	(PDH + PDL) / 2
Support 1 (S1)	(2 × CP) – PDH
Support 2 (S2)	CP – (PDH – PDL)
Support 3 (S3)	S1 – (PDH – PDL)

For experienced traders, CPR isn't just a bunch of lines on a chart. It's more like a lens that brings the market's intentions into focus. It helps cut through the noise and shows where the real action might happen. When price stays close to the CPR, it's often a sign that the market is gearing up for something, either a strong upward push from the bulls or a sharp move down if the bears take charge. That central zone holds quiet clues about who's gaining control. For traders who know what to look for, CPR can be the early warning signal before the market really starts to move. Another advantage of CPR is its versatility across different trading styles.

Day traders use CPR to determine intraday trend direction and breakout levels. ***Swing traders*** rely on it for identifying key support and resistance zones. ***Institutional traders*** incorporate CPR into their strategies for better trade execution and market positioning. Whether the market is trending or consolidating, CPR helps traders make well-informed decisions with greater accuracy.

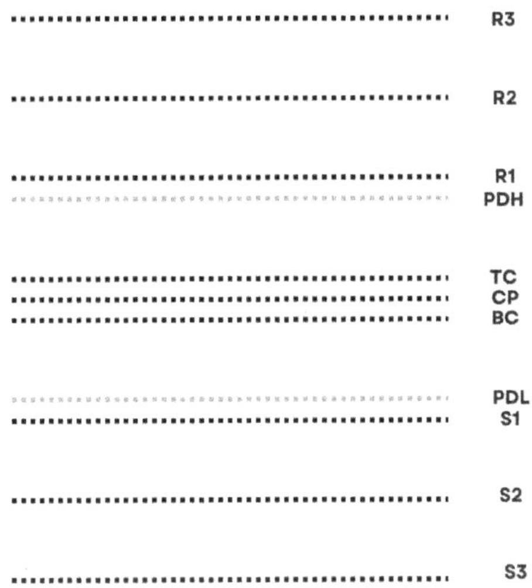

Fig. 2.4: *Central Pivot Range (CPR) Key Levels*

Key CPR-Based Trading Levels

1. **Central Pivot Point (CP):** The core equilibrium level, representing the average price of the previous day.
2. **Top Central Pivot (TC):** An extension of the pivot level that helps filter out false bullish breakouts and provides clarity on the prevailing market trend.
3. **Bottom Central Pivot (BC):** An extension of the pivot level that helps avoid false bearish breakdowns and provides clarity on the prevailing market trend.

PDH – Previous Day High. It shows the highest price the stock reached yesterday. If today's price goes above this level, it shows strength.
PDL – Previous Day Low. It shows the lowest price the stock reached yesterday. If today's price falls below this level, it shows weakness.
Note: These two lines are usually shown in a lighter color to separate them from CPR levels. They act as a reference points for breakout or reversal setups.

What Are R1, R2, and R3? A Basic Look at Resistance Levels

In technical analysis, resistance levels are crucial for identifying potential price obstacles in market movement. These levels, derived from the Central Pivot Range (CPR), allow traders to anticipate where the price might face selling pressure and potentially reverse or consolidate.

Table 2.4: *Central Pivot Range (CPR) Resistance Levels Pivot Range*

Level	Label	What It Tells You
R1	First Resistance	Often acts as the first price barrier above CPR. A breakout above R1 suggests bullish strength.
R2	Second Resistance	If the price sustains above R1, R2 is the next target, often indicating a strong bullish trend.
R3	Third Resistance	The final resistance level where prices tend to face strong selling pressure.

Table 2.4 outlines the three primary resistance levels: R1, R2, and R3. Each provides insight into the strength of an ongoing bullish move. As the price climbs above each level, it reflects increasing market confidence and trend momentum. Understanding how these levels function gives traders an edge in planning entries, exits, and managing risk during bullish setups.

Positioning After a Break Above R1

A break above the first resistance level (R1) signals that buyers are taking control, indicating a shift in market sentiment. This isn't just a rise in price; it's a moment of confidence, often confirmed by a strong green candle closing above R1 and supported by a spike in volume. This kind of price action reflects decisive buying and gives the breakout validity. Once this confirmation is clear, it's time to act with conviction by entering a position.

For example, consider a stock trading at ₹198, with R1 at ₹200. After a confirmed close above ₹200, you enter at ₹201. This disciplined entry sets the stage for capitalizing on the upward momentum, provided the price holds above R1.

Taking Partial Profits at R2

As the price approaches the second resistance level (R2), the upward move may start to lose steam, making it a critical zone to secure gains. Booking partial profits here allows you to protect capital while staying in the trade for potential further upside. A balanced approach is to exit half of your position.

Continuing the example, suppose the price reaches ₹205 (R2). You sell half of your quantities. This move not only banks profits but also reduces risk, keeping you positioned for the next phase of the trend.

Assessing Market Strength at R2

Reaching R2 doesn't guarantee the trend will persist, so careful observation is key. Traders must evaluate price action. Do fresh bull candles form? Is there sustained buying pressure? These signals determine whether holding the remaining position is warranted.

For instance, a strong bullish candle closing near or above ₹205 indicates continued buyer enthusiasm. This confirmation of strength justifies holding your remaining quantities, as it suggests the market may push toward the next resistance level with conviction.

Final Exit Near R3

If momentum carries the price to the third resistance level (R3), it often signals a powerful, though potentially overstretched, trend. Exiting here is a disciplined way to capture the remaining gains before a possible reversal.

In our example, suppose the price hits ₹212 (R3). You exit your remaining quantities. So, you entered at ₹201/- exited partially at ₹205/- then exited the remaining quantities at ₹212/-. This structured approach, entering at R1, scaling out at R2, and exiting at R3, maximizes gains while managing risk effectively.

Understanding Support: S1, S2, S3 in Market Analysis

Support levels are essential markers in technical trading that indicate where a price may pause or decline due to increased selling interest. These levels, particularly in the context of the CPR (Central Pivot Range), help traders identify potential zones of demand during a downtrend.

The following table 2.5 explains the three key support levels: S1, S2, and S3. Each offers unique insights into bearish momentum and potential price reversals. Knowing how to interpret these levels enables traders to make more informed decisions, manage risk effectively, and recognize opportunities during falling markets.

Spotting the Breakdown Below S1

A breakdown below the first support level (S1) signals that sellers are gaining the upper hand, driving bearish momentum. This move is more than a price drop; it's the market's first hint of a shift toward deeper declines, often confirmed by strong red candles or elevated volume. Once the price sustains below S1, it's time to consider a short position to capitalize on the emerging downtrend.

Table 2.5: *Central Pivot Range (CPR) Support Levels*

Level	Label	What It Tells You
S1	First Support	Acts as the first price floor below CPR. A break below S1 suggests bearish control.
S2	Second Support	Further decline indicates a strong downtrend, with S2 being the next target.
S3	Third Support	The last support level where prices may experience a reversal or heavy buying interest.

For example, imagine a stock trading at ₹205, with S1 at ₹202. After a confirmed close below ₹202, you initiate a short position. This early entry positions you to ride the bearish wave as it develops.

Partial Booking at S2: Lock in While Riding the Trend

As the price approaches the second support level (S2), the downward momentum may slow, signaling a potential pause or bounce. This is a strategic moment to lock in partial profits, securing gains while keeping exposure to further downside. Covering half of your position strikes a balance between risk management and opportunity.

Continuing the example, suppose the price reaches ₹196 (S2). You exit half of your quantities. This step not only banks gains but also sets the stage for assessing whether the downtrend will persist.

Watch for Price Behavior Near S2

Support levels in a downtrend reveal critical insights about market dynamics. Near S2, observe the price action closely: Does a strong green candle form, suggesting a bounce, or do red candles dominate, indicating continued selling pressure? These cues guide your decision to hold or adjust your position. For instance, if a red candle forms or the price closes below ₹196, it confirms sustained bearish momentum. This signal gives you confidence to maintain your remaining quantities, targeting the next support level with a clear focus on the unfolding trend.

Targeting S3: Completing the Move

The third support level (S3) often marks the culmination of a downtrend, where exhaustion or a potential reversal may occur. Exiting here is a disciplined way to capture the remaining profits before the market shifts.

In our example, assume the price drops to ₹190 (S3). You cover your remaining quantities. So, you entered at ₹201, exited partially at ₹196, then exited the remaining quantities at ₹190. This structured approach, entering at S1, scaling out at S2, and exiting at S3, maximizes returns while navigating the risks of a bearish market.

Comparative Analysis: Pivot Points vs. Central Pivot Range (CPR)

The table below compares Pivot Points and CPR across six trading strategies. CPR's versatility shines in dynamic, fast-paced environments like intraday scalping and gap setups, outperforming traditional pivot points.

Table 2.6: *The Pivot Points vs. CPR comparison*

Criteria	Pivot Points	CPR
Intraday Scalping	✗	✔
Trend Following	✗	✔
Range Trading	✔	✔
Breakout Trading	✔	✔
Gap Up/Down Setups	✗	✔
Pre-market Planing	✗	✔

This comparison underscores the broad applicability and responsive nature of the Central Pivot Range (CPR) across diverse trading strategies, showcasing its greater utility compared to traditional pivot points. While both tools offer value, CPR distinguishes itself as a more robust and insightful framework for navigating evolving market conditions.

Decoding CPR

The journey from basic pivot points to the Central Pivot Range marks more than just a shift in tools. It reflects how traders have adapted to faster and more complex markets. What began as a single reference point is now a dynamic system that adjusts with price, momentum, and volatility. CPR does not just react to the market; it helps you stay a step ahead of it. In the next chapter, we will discover how the width of the CPR acts like a silent signal hinting at breakout days, sideways markets, and potential reversals. Let's decode the core trading styles around CPR and learn how to read the language of the market effectively.

Chapter

03

A DEEP DIVE INTO CPR STRUCTURES

A missile doesn't fly in a straight line. It constantly adjusts its course, reading new data, correcting its angle, and inching toward the target. It doesn't drift or change its target. It simply realigns until it hits. That's the mindset a trader needs. Because the market never moves in a straight line either. Every trader dreams of catching the perfect move, that clean breakout, that early entry, that trend that just keeps going. But the market rarely plays out that smoothly. What looks like a proper setup one moment can fall apart the next. Price moves fast, and the pressure to react faster often leads to mistakes.

This is where CPR comes into play, not as a magic formula, but as a structured way of reading the market. And it doesn't tell you what will happen. It shows you what's possible. It tells you whether the market is building pressure, cooling down, or preparing for a breakout. It shifts your mindset from reacting to preparing.

In the previous chapter, we explored how CPR emerged through years of real world trading experience. But once the market opens, history takes a back seat. Setups appear and disappear within minutes, and confidence must be backed by clarity. This is where CPR becomes more than just calculated lines.

In this chapter, we don't discuss timeframes. The focus is purely on structure, understanding each CPR type, and knowing how to spot it. That's the foundation for everything that follows.

And it all begins with two subtle clues formed before the market opens: the width and the position of the CPR. These are not just technical details. They are quiet signals that tell you whether the market is getting ready to move, stay quiet, or trap you in between. **This is your starting point: Is there energy? And where is it focused?** Let's break this down further and see how CPR width, when combined with CPR position, forms the basis for all setups.

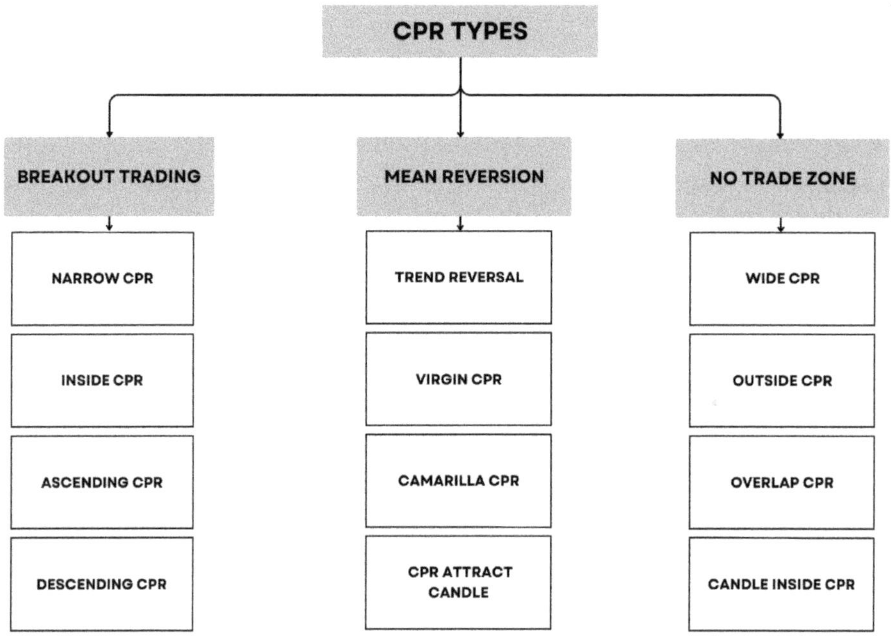

Fig. 3.1: *Classification of CPR Types Based on Trading Scenarios*

Let's begin with the setup that can be most rewarding when it works well: Breakout Trading

Breakout Trading

The biggest profits in trading don't come from complicated strategies. They come from spotting the moment a trend is about to begin, and getting in before the rest of the world catches on. That's the power of breakout trading. The edge lies in timing. Not in reacting, but in anticipating. Experienced traders don't chase trends. They prepare for them.

And that's where CPR earns its place.

Even when the chart appears calm, CPR is at work. It quietly lays the foundation, marking zones where pressure builds, where energy compresses. And if you know what to look for, you'll start to see the signs. Narrow CPRs, Inside CPRs, Ascending CPRs, and Descending CPRs aren't just technical patterns. They are structural footprints. Quiet clues left behind by the price that hint at what's coming next.

Narrow CPR

Narrow CPR is a lot like a traffic signal at a busy intersection. For a while, everything is still. Vehicles line up. Engines running, but no movement. Then the light turns green. In seconds, motion returns. Everyone moves at once, not randomly, but with direction and force. A narrow CPR works the same way. When the signal comes, whether it's a breakout candle, a volume spike, or a clean move beyond CPR, the market releases that energy in one powerful burst.

A narrow CPR forms when the previous session's high, low, and close are clustered tightly together, causing the Central Pivot Range for the current session to contract into a tight band. One key characteristic of a narrow CPR is how closely the TC, Pivot, and BC levels are packed together. The range is tight, and the distance from the CPR to R1 or from the previous session's high to R1 is also much smaller than usual. When such compression appears, it often leads to a breakout, as the price doesn't stay contained for long. For traders, this setup signals that the market is preparing for a potential directional move. As shown below, the tighter the CPR band, the more aggressive the breakout potential. A narrow CPR often leads to trending moves, while an extremely narrow CPR can signal strong, one-sided momentum.

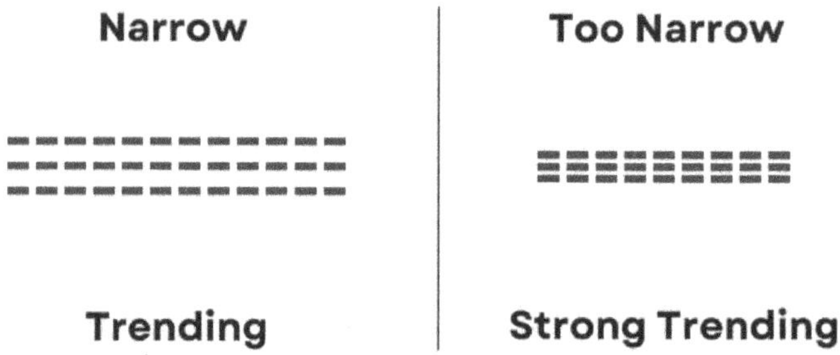

Fig. 3.2: *Narrow vs. Too Narrow CPR – Strength of Expected Trend*

The charts below showcase how narrow CPR setups play out across different stocks. In each case, the Central Pivot Range is visibly compressed, reflecting a phase of low volatility in the previous session. Once price breaks out of the tight CPR zone, whether to the upside or downside, the move tends to be clean, directional, and often sustained. Notice how price remains stable and range bound before the breakout, then quickly expands with strength once the structure breaks. These examples reinforce a core principle of CPR-based trading in that when the range contracts energy builds and when that energy is released it often creates high-probability trending opportunities for prepared traders.

Fig. 3.3 and Fig. 3.4 highlight bullish breakouts from narrow CPR zones, while Fig. 3.5 and Fig. 3.6 demonstrate bearish breakouts, showcasing how this setup works effectively in both directions.

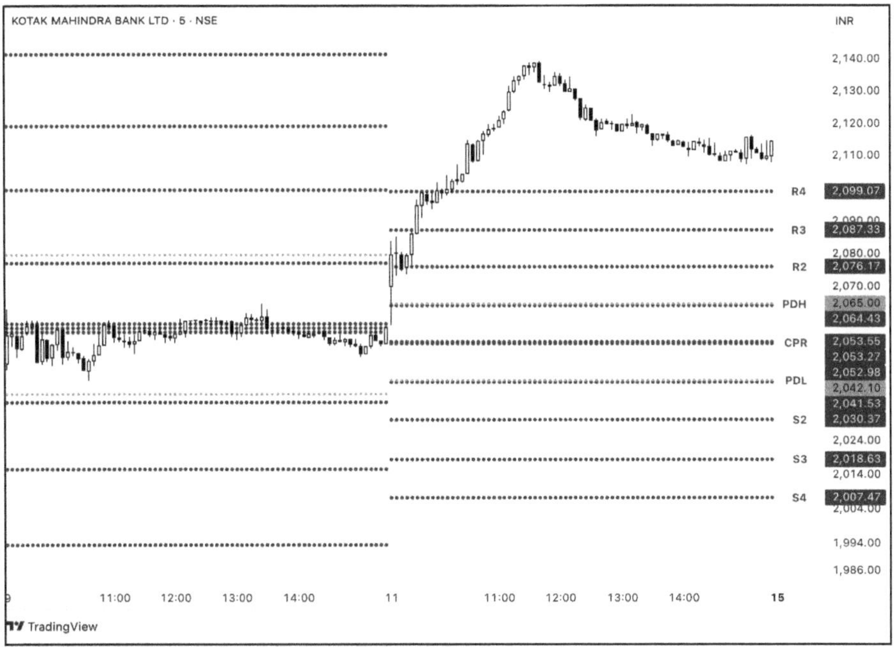

Fig. 3.3: *Narrow CPR in kotak Mahindra Bank Ltd*

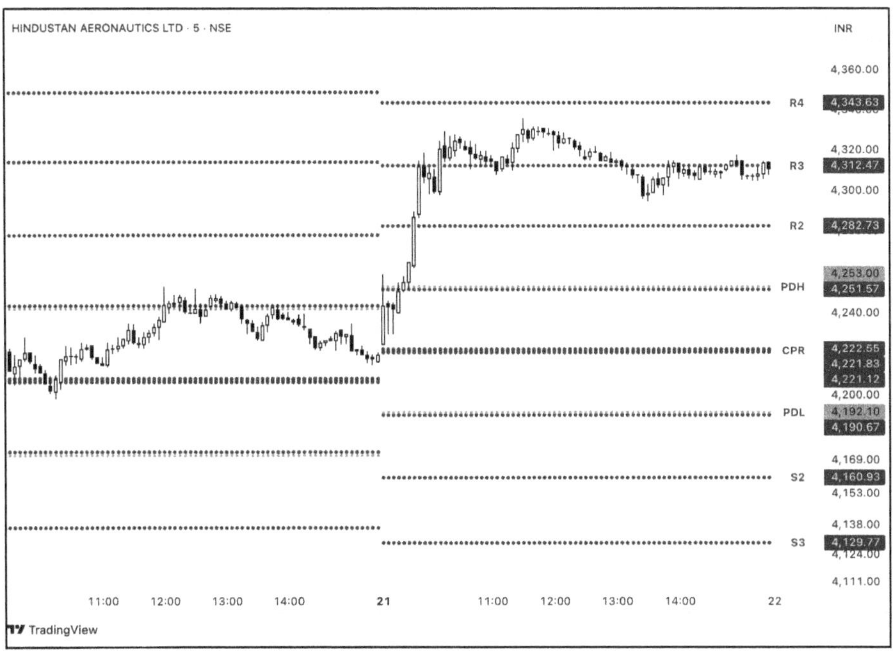

Fig. 3.4: *Narrow CPR in Hindustan Aeronautics Ltd*

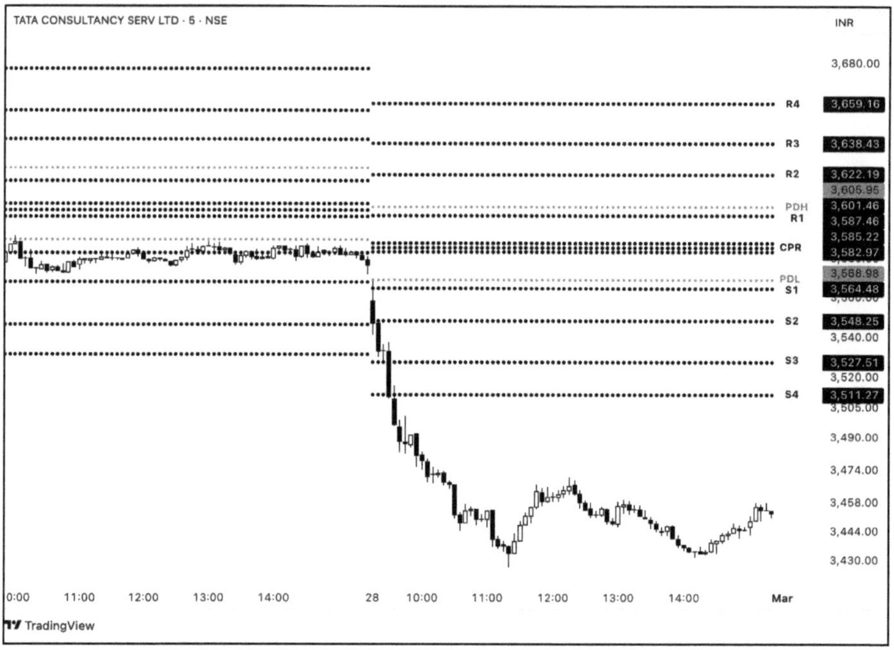

Fig. 3.5: *Narrow CPR in Tata Consultancy Service Ltd*

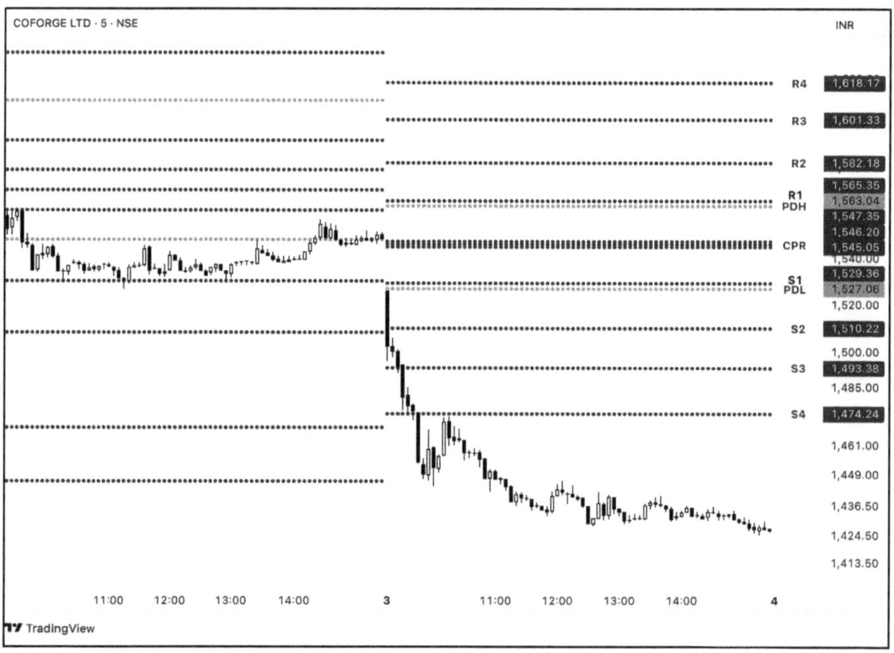

Fig. 3.6: *Narrow CPR in Coforge Ltd*

Inside CPR

Inside CPR is like the talented guy in the room who holds back within the limits. He doesn't show off, doesn't chase attention, and doesn't reveal what he's truly capable of until the time is right. Most overlook him because he stays within the structure, saying little, doing less. But when the moment comes, he delivers without hesitation. The market behaves the same way.

An Inside CPR forms when the Current Session's CPR is completely trapped within the Previous Session's CPR range. It signals quiet compression, not a lack of movement, but energy being stored. Once price breaks out of this zone, the move is often sharp and directional. While a narrow CPR focuses on the band's tightness, an Inside CPR is more about location. Even if the CPR isn't extremely narrow, this setup should be treated like a breakout structure with strong potential.

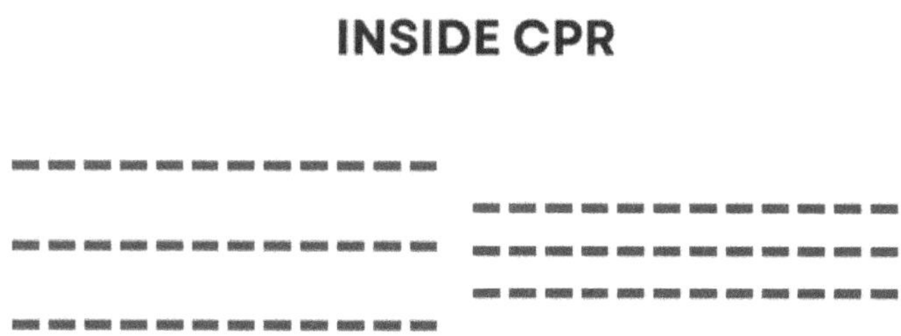

Fig. 3.7: *Inside CPR structure*

The charts below capture how Inside CPR setups transition from balance to breakout. Before the move, the price stays quiet and controlled, offering no clear bias. But once structure breaks, direction emerges clearly with strong follow through. Fig. 3.7 and Fig. 3.8 show bullish breakouts, while Fig. 3.9 and Fig. 3.10 show clean bearish moves, highlighting how this setup performs effectively in both directions.

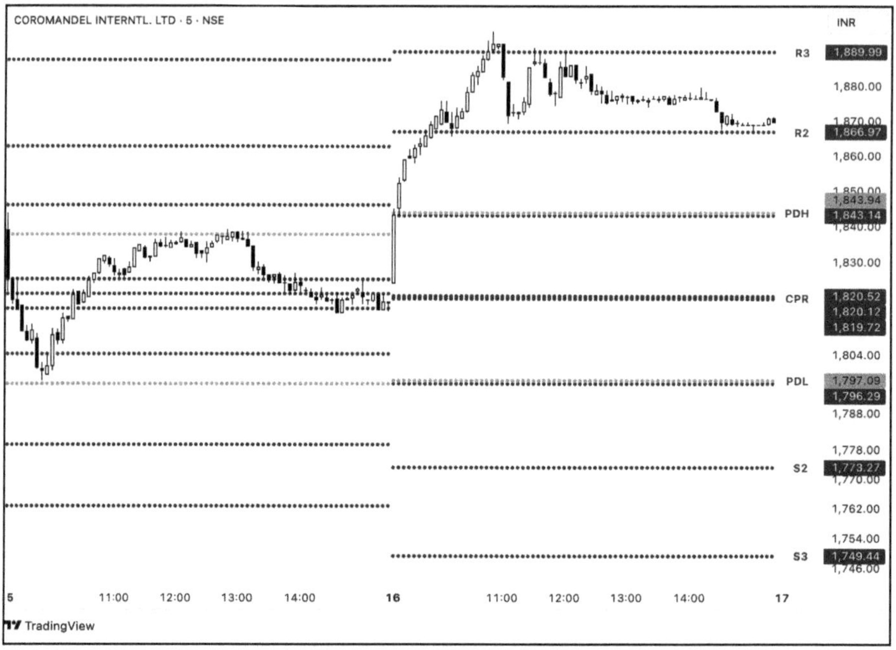

Fig. 3.8: Inside CPR in Coromandel International Ltd

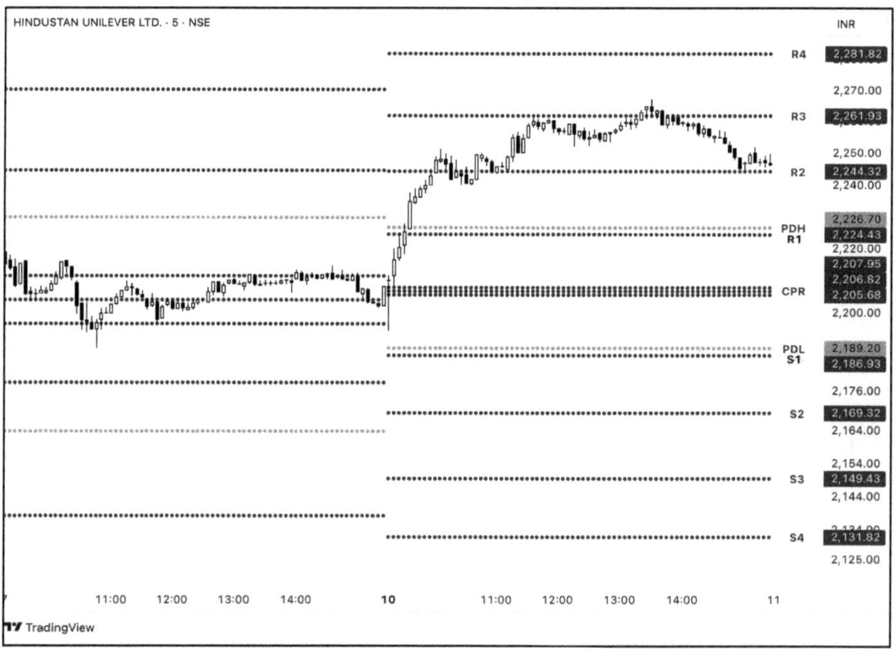

Fig. 3.9: Inside CPR in Hindustan Unilever Ltd

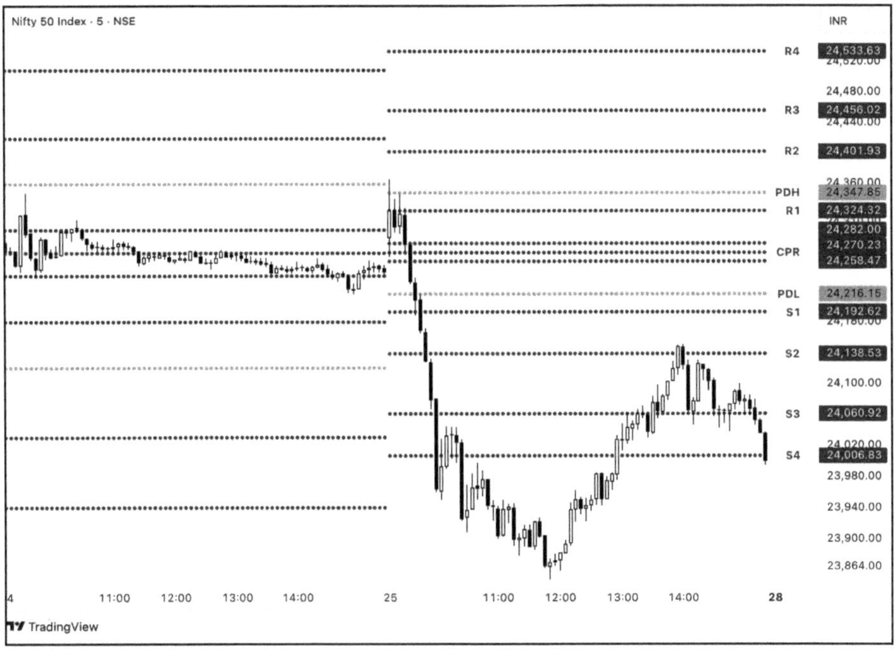

Fig. 3.10: *Inside CPR in Nifty 50*

Fig. 3.11: *Inside CPR in Adani Enterprises Ltd*

Ascending CPR

A rising CPR structure is like stepping onto an upward escalator. Even if you just stand still, the structure lifts you higher. Each session, the CPR forms higher than the previous session. This steady climb indicates that the market isn't just moving up temporarily. It is being revalued. Buyers are confident, and the support zone itself is shifting higher. Even minor pullbacks tend to attract fresh buying because the underlying structure favors continued strength. As long as this upward escalator keeps moving, momentum remains in favor of the bulls. Traders aligned with the structure are not fighting the market. They're going with the trend, letting the structure do the heavy lifting.

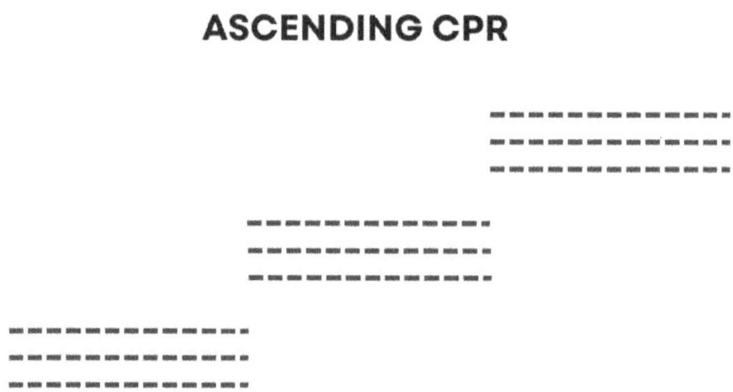

Fig. 3.12: *Ascending CPR Structure*

Look at these charts. You will notice how the CPR keeps shifting higher with each session. That's your first clue. The market isn't just bouncing, it's building. Each session opens with a new CPR level, a little higher than the last, and price keeps respecting it. See how price takes support at the CPR, pauses briefly, and then pushes higher? The CPR acts like a base, guiding the trend session after session.

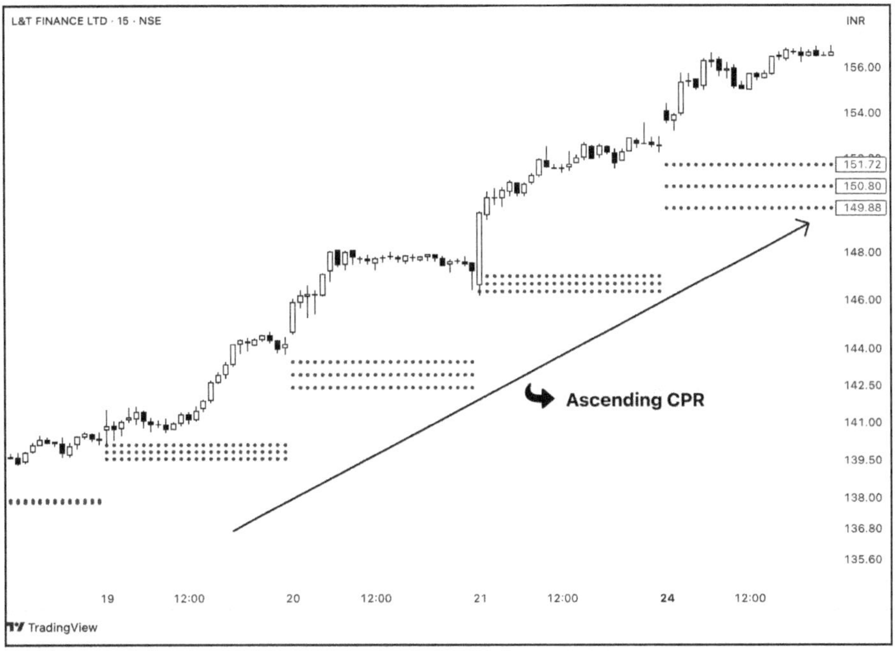

Fig. 3.13: Ascending CPR in L&T Finance Ltd

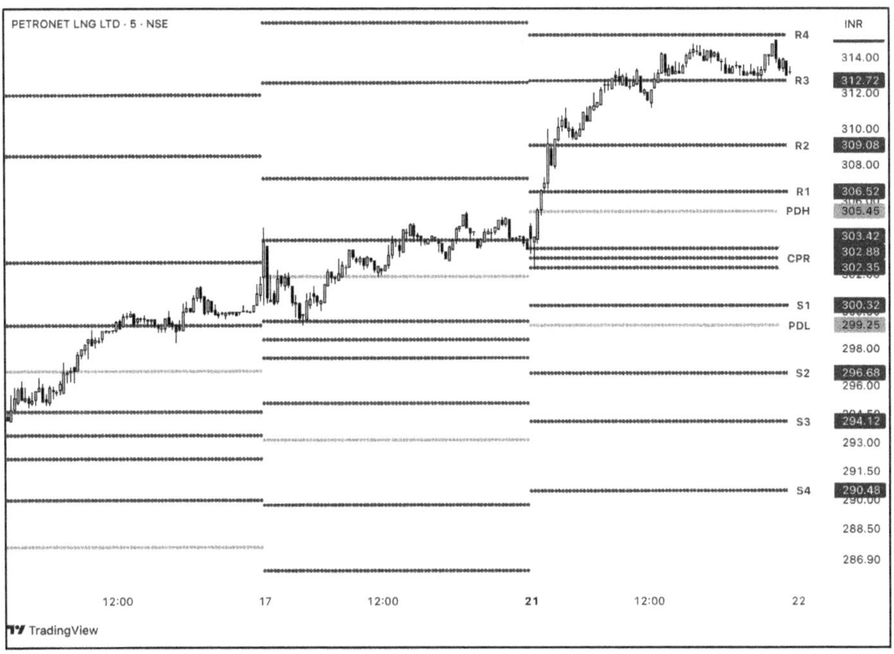

Fig. 3.14: Ascending CPR in Petronet LNG Ltd

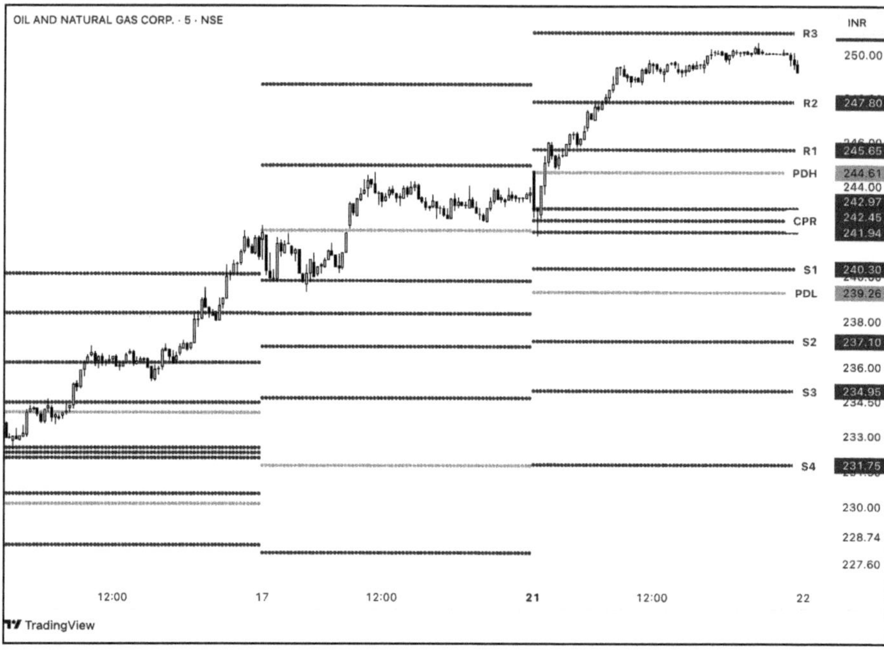

Fig. 3.15: Ascending CPR in ONGC

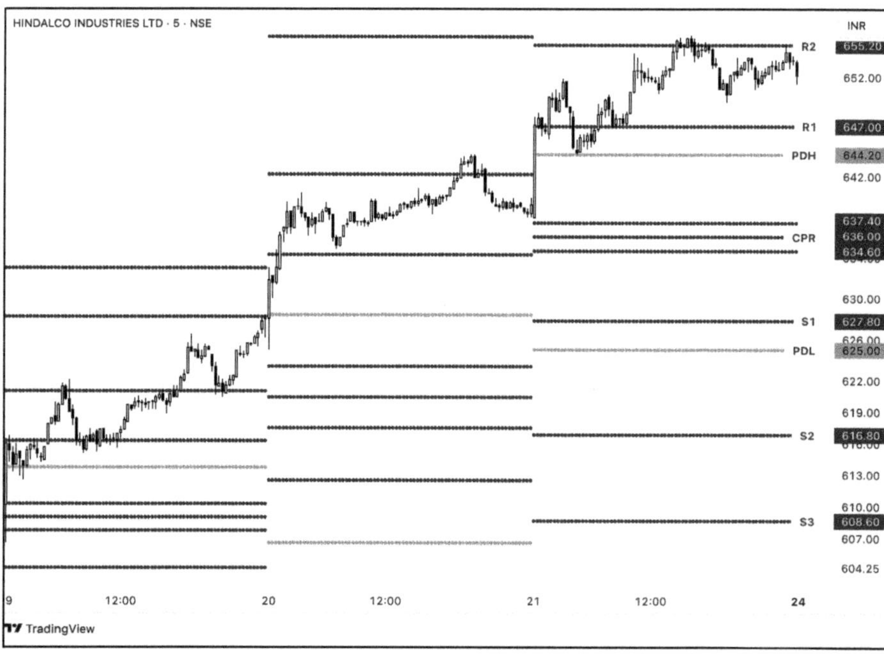

Fig. 3.16: Ascending CPR in Hindalco Industries Ltd

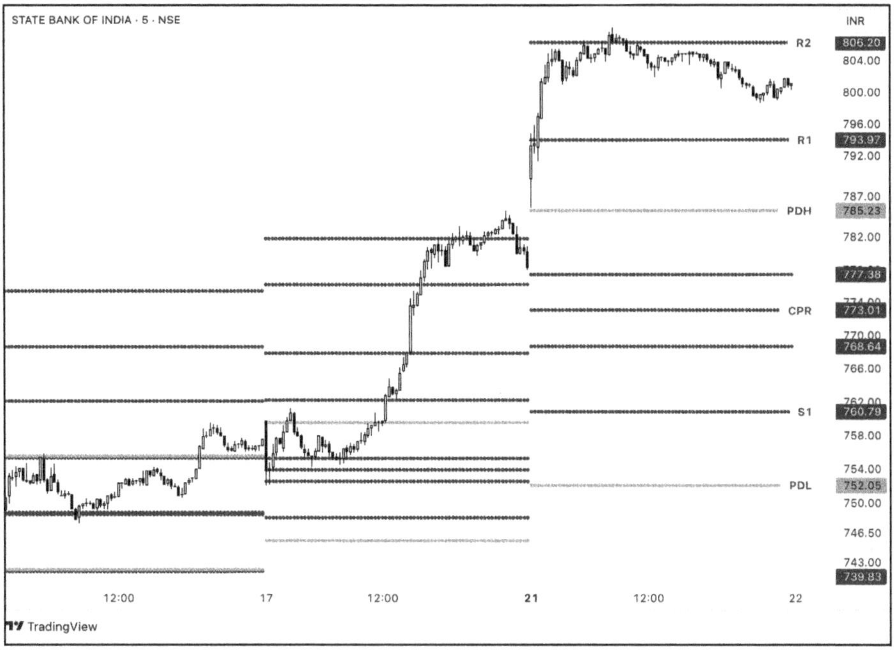

Fig. 3.17: *Ascending CPR in State Bank of India*

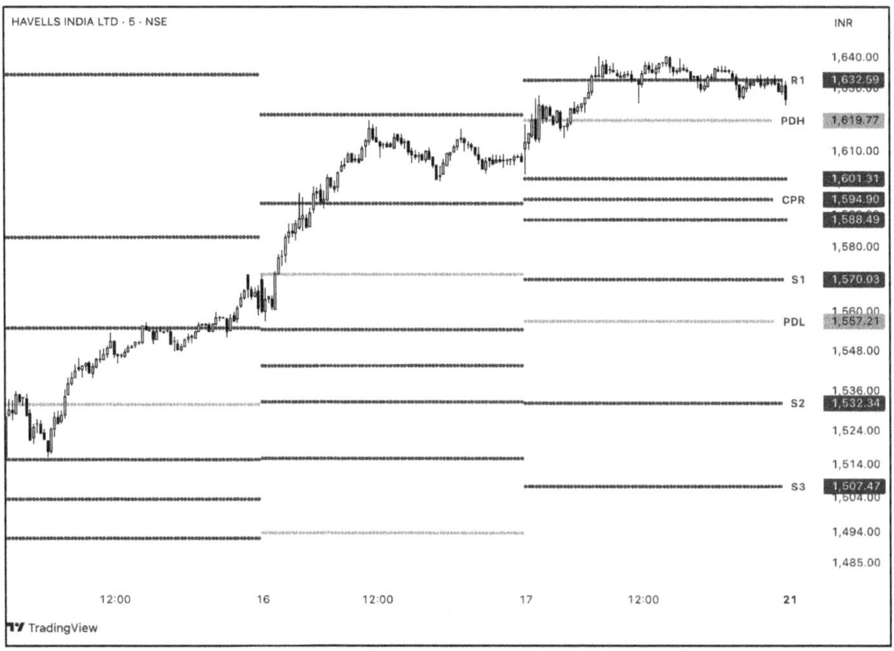

Fig. 3.18: *Ascending CPR in Havells India Ltd*

Descending CPR

Similar to ascending CPR, but in the opposite direction. It's a falling structure like stepping onto an escalator that's going down. You might try to walk up, but each step pulls you lower. The structure itself is working against you. Even though the price tries to rise, it keeps getting pulled back down because the structure is built for decline.

That's exactly what a descending CPR shows. Each session levels are set lower than the previous session. Until that escalator stops descending, every upward move is just a temporary push against a stronger trend.

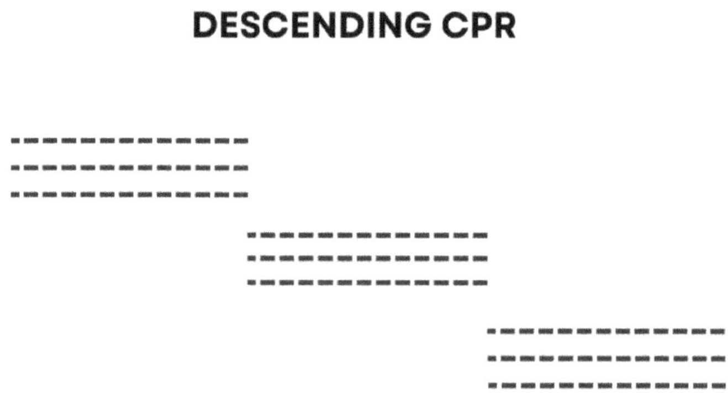

Fig. 3.19: Descending CPR Structure

Observe the chart below and notice how the CPR moves down session by session. Each session, the market opens with a structure that's lower than the last. This isn't just a dip, it's the anatomy of a developing downtrend. Sellers are staying in control, and this is the signature of a Descending CPR. Every time the price touches the CPR and fades, the message is clear. It's not time for the bulls. Until price breaks that pattern, every bounce is just another opportunity for bears to step in.

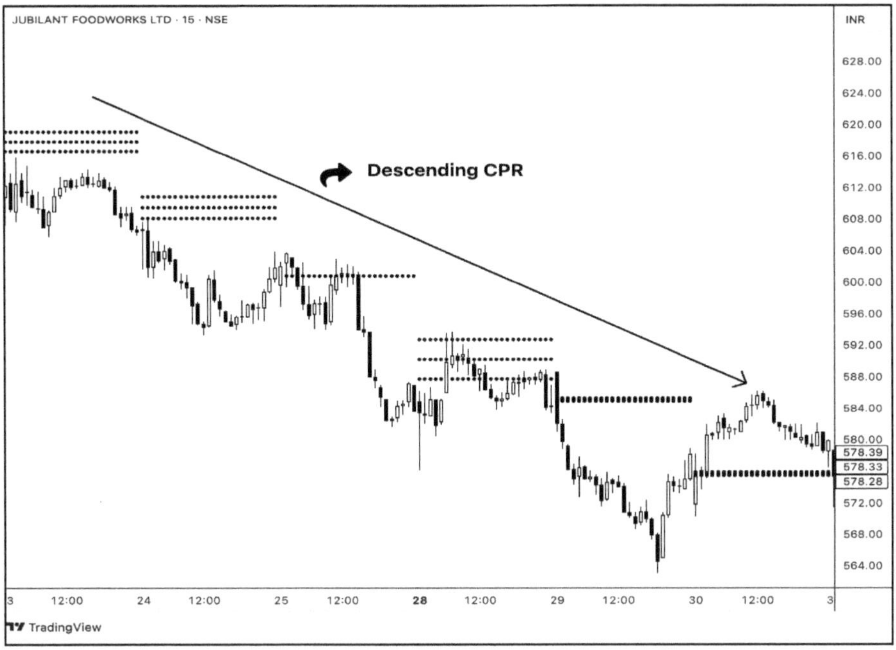

Fig. 3.20: Descending CPR in Jubilant foodworks

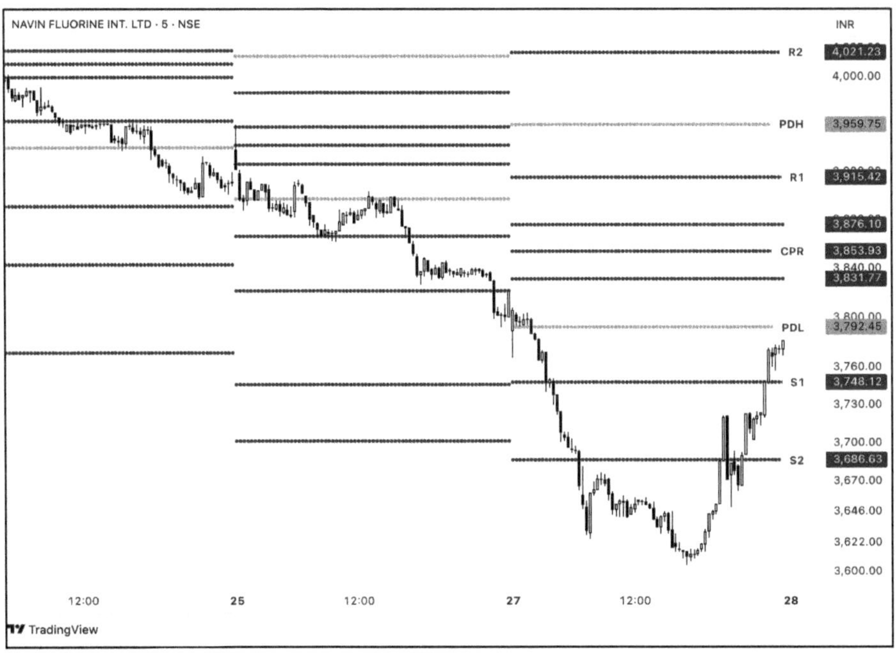

Fig. 3.21: Descending CPR in Navin fluorine

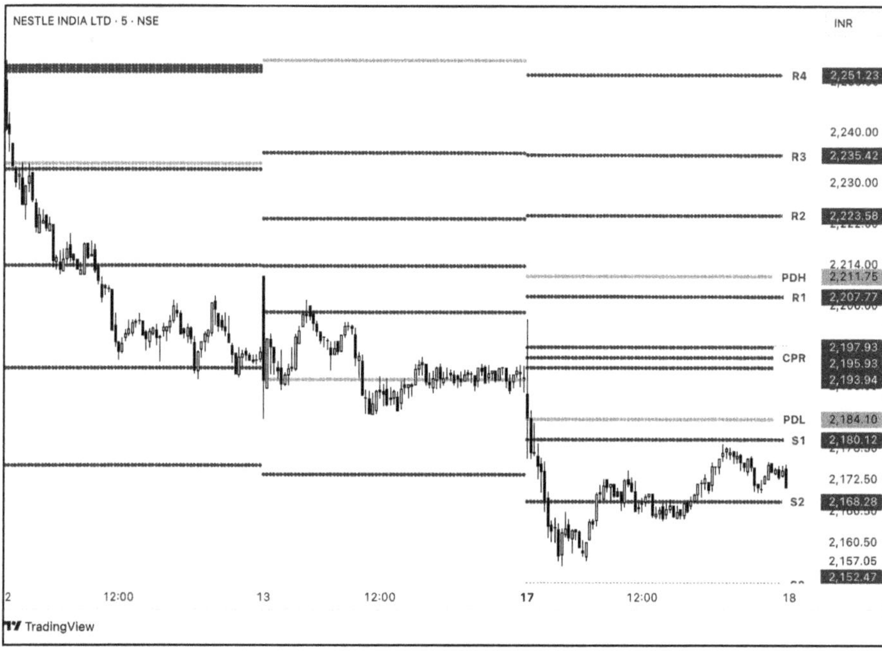

Fig. 3.22: *Descending CPR in Nestle India Ltd*

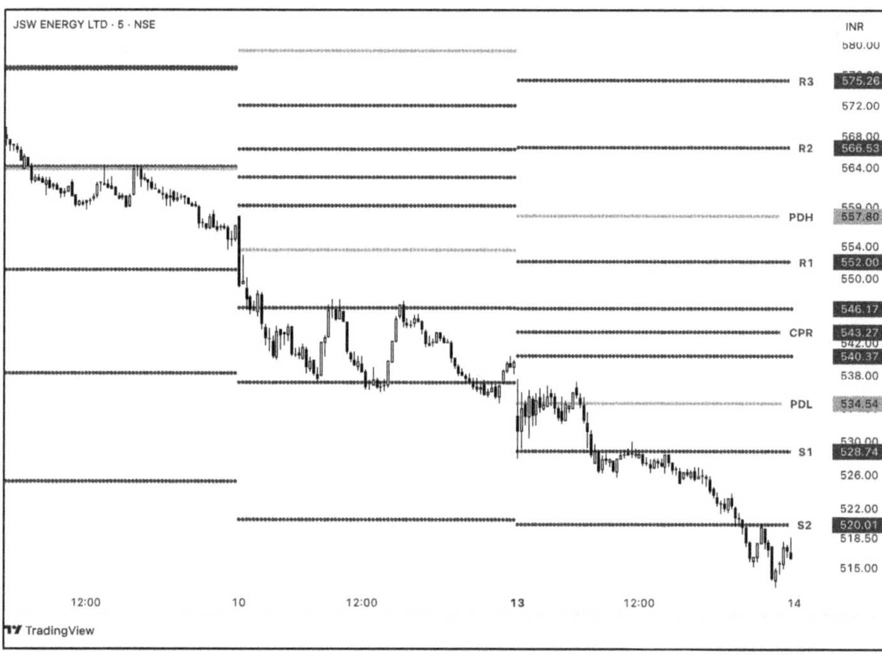

Fig. 3.23: *Descending CPR in JSW Energy*

Reversal Setups

If there's one thing that can make a huge difference to your trading results, it's spotting reversals before everyone else does. And that's where CPR comes in. Understanding how to spot these moments of exhaustion, when the market is ready to flip, is a game-changer. Reversals don't happen without warning. Ascending trend reversals, descending trend reversals, Virgin CPRs, Camarilla levels, and CPR candle attraction all reveal hidden shifts in structure and intent.

Ascending CPR Trend Reversal

At first glance, an ascending CPR suggests strength. Price is trending upward, CPR is rising, and buyers seem in control. But sometimes, that strength is misleading. Watch what happens when the price fails to stay above the CPR. That's your first clue. The market is no longer respecting the structure. Higher CPRs are not attracting higher price acceptance. Momentum fades, and the structure that once supported the uptrend begins to break down.

Fig. 3.24: *Ascending CPR Trend Reversal Structure*

An ascending trend reversal doesn't announce itself loudly. It starts with subtle rejection, hesitation at higher levels, and fading bullish candles. See the charts below. The CPR is still rising, but the price is no longer following it with strength. Instead of bouncing, the price starts slipping below. That's the first hint that the bulls are losing control, and the market is getting ready to turn.

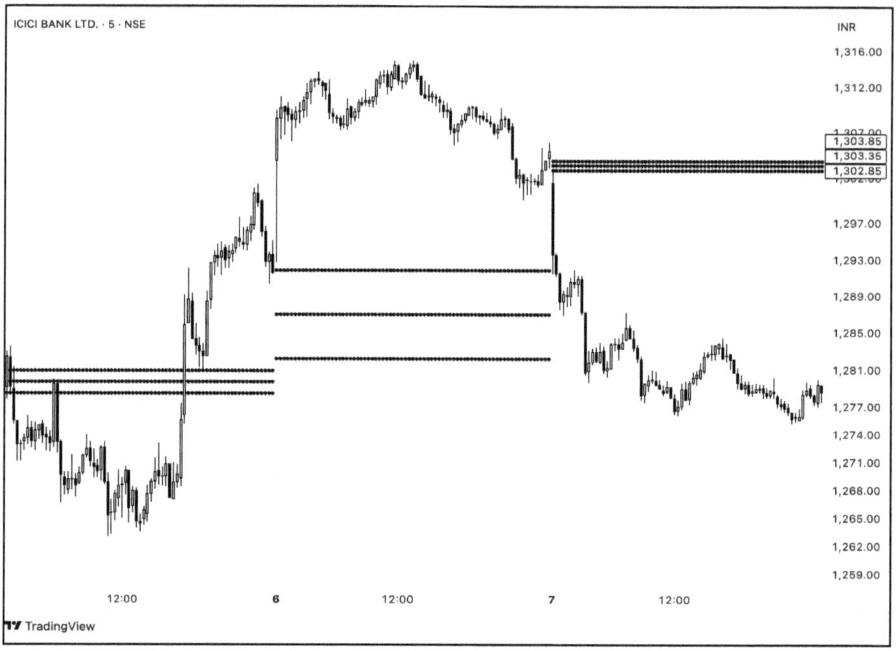

Fig. 3.25: Ascending CPR Trend Reversal in ICICI Bank Ltd

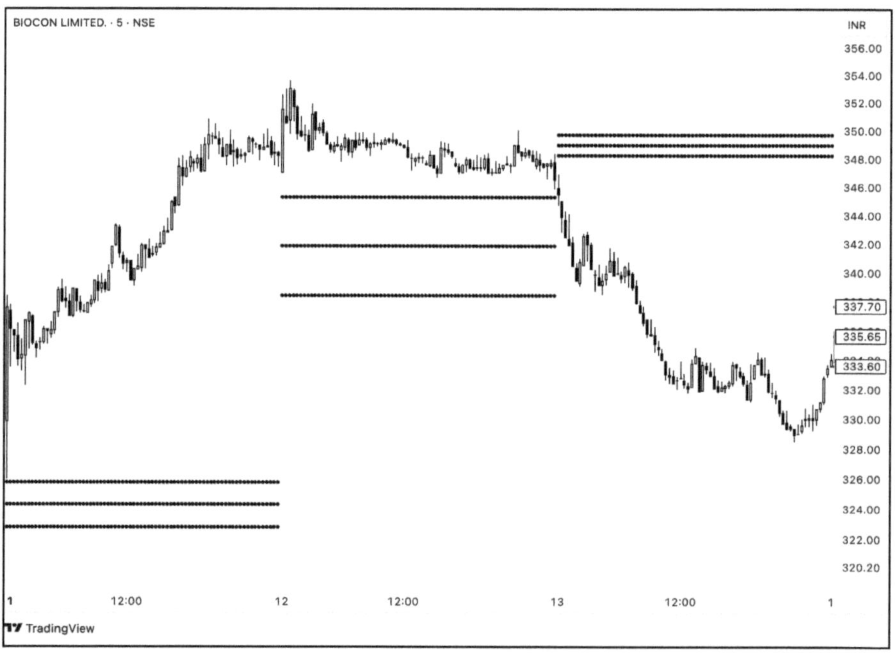

Fig. 3.26: Ascending CPR Trend Reversal in Biocon

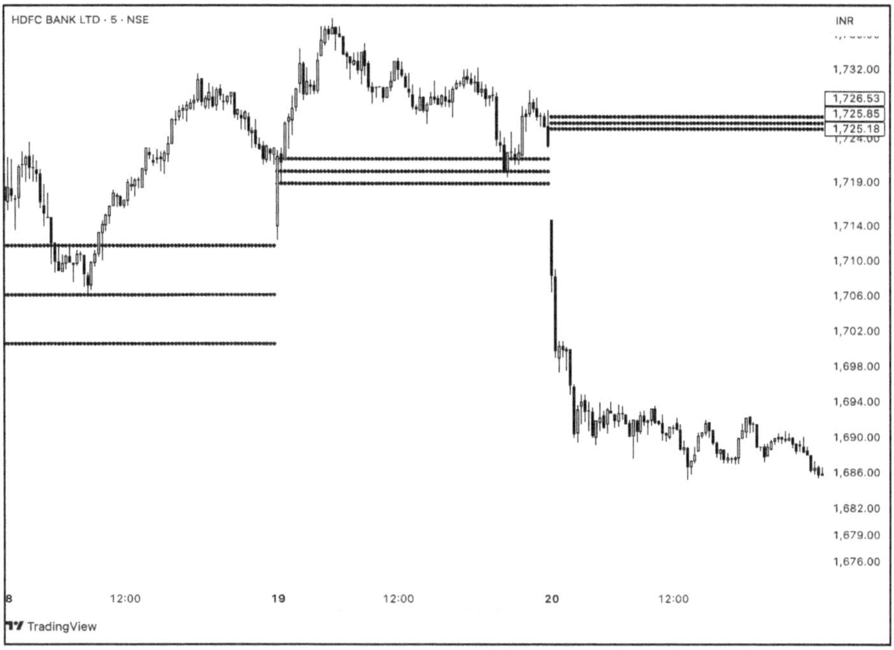

Fig. 3.27: *Ascending Trend Reversal in HDFC Bank Ltd*

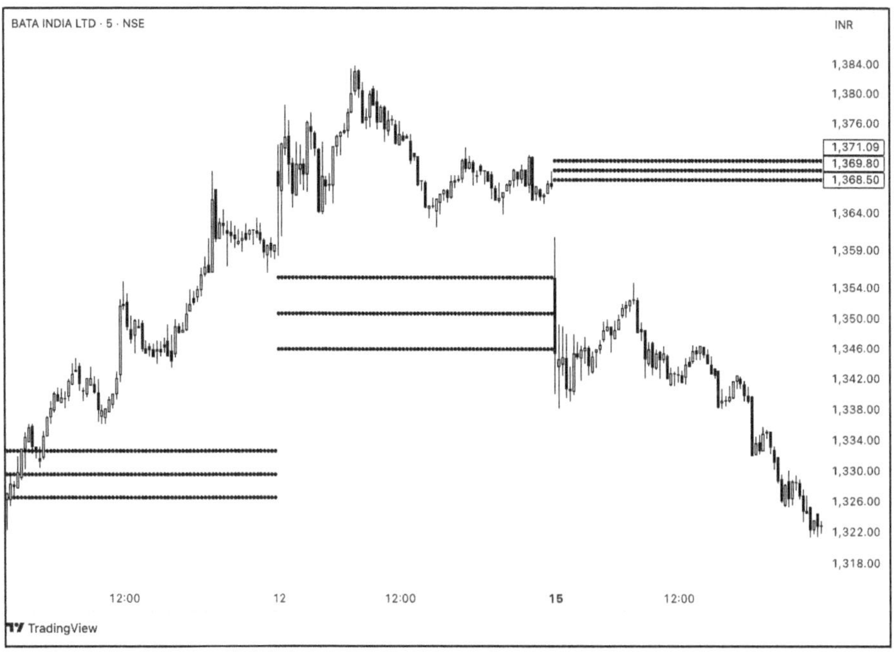

Fig. 3.28: *Ascending Trend Reversal in Bata India*

Descending Trend reversal

Like the ascending reversal, where strength begins to fade, here it's the weakness that begins to lose grip. That's when a reversal is often near. In this setup, the CPR continues to descend, but the price no longer follows. Instead of staying below the range, the price opens strong. Sometimes even above the CPR. Attempts to push it down fail. The selling pressure that once dominated is no longer effective.

Descending CPR trend reversals often surprise traders who are still expecting the trend to continue. But for those watching the structure, it's not a surprise. It's a signal. A market that stops respecting falling CPR levels is quietly signaling a change in trend.

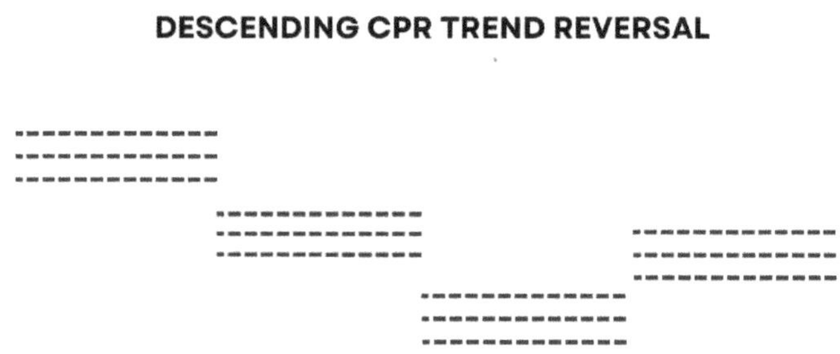

Fig. 3.29: *Descending CPR Trend Reversal structure*

On the charts below, CPR drops session after session, but price now sits above it instead of sliding further. That mismatch signals the downtrend is weakening and the control is starting to pass to the buyers, and the first leg of a recovery often begins from that point.

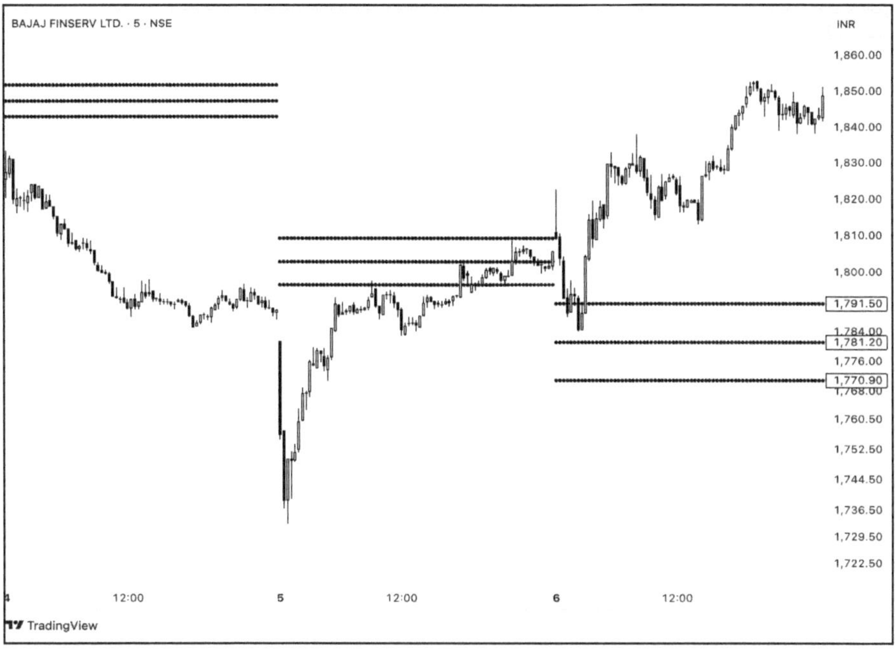

Fig. 3.30: *Descending Trend Reversal in Bajaj Finserv*

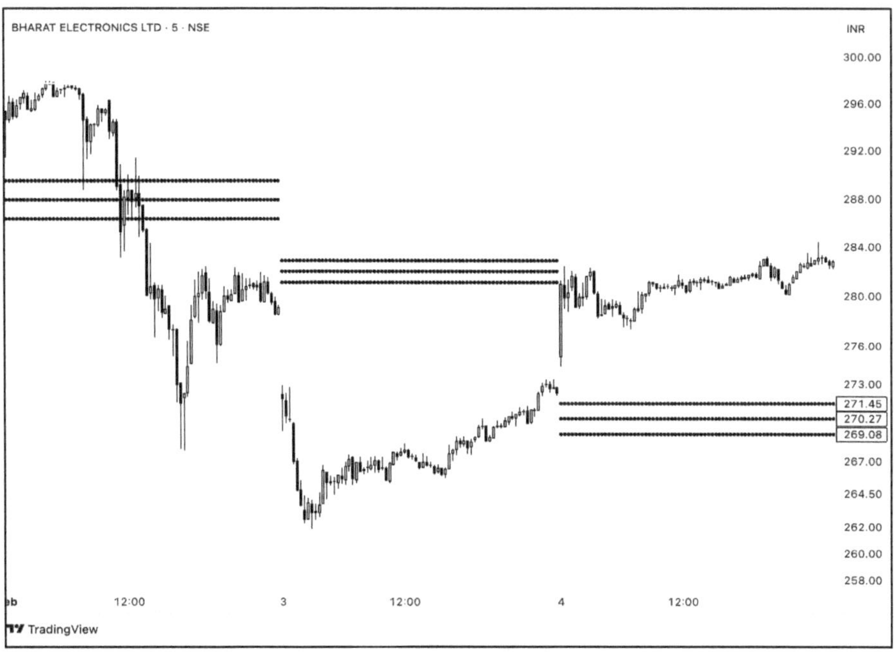

Fig. 3.31: *Descending Trend Reversal in Bharat Electronics*

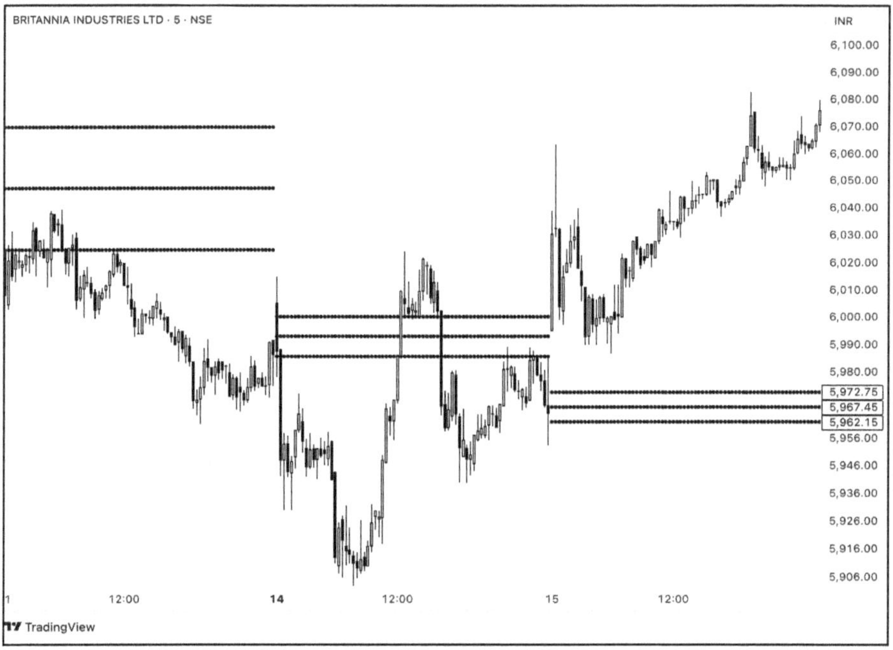

Fig. 3.32: *Descending Trend Reversal in Britannia Industries*

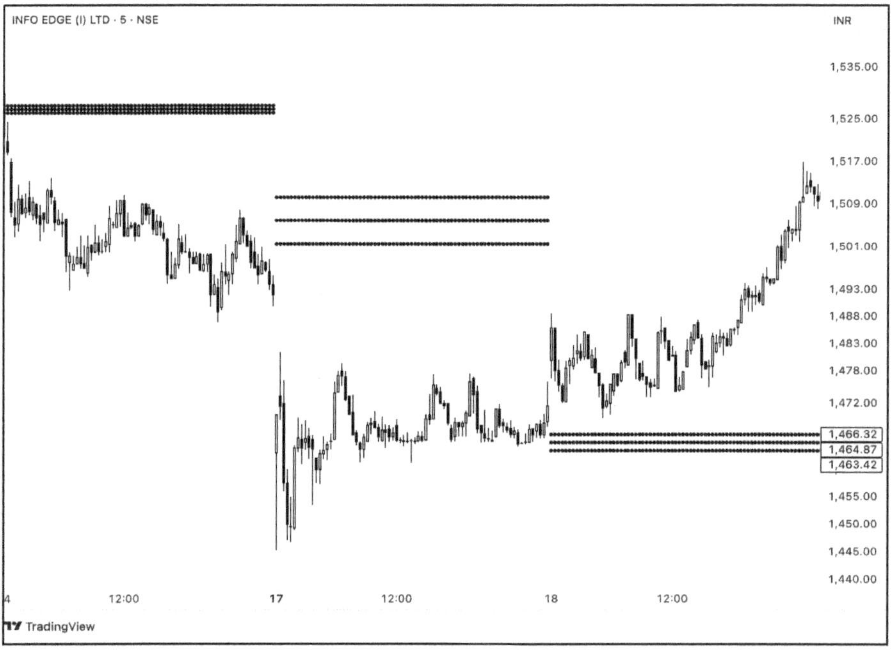

Fig. 3.33: *Descending Trend Reversal in Info Edge*

Virgin CPR

A Virgin CPR is formed when the price does not touch the CPR zone throughout a trading session. If the CPR remains untouched, it is considered a Virgin CPR for the next trading session until it gets tested. This zone often acts as a strong support or resistance level. When the price eventually revisits it, it may lead to sharp reversals or reactions. However, if the price breaks through this area decisively, it may indicate the start of a new trend backed by strong momentum. As traders, timing matters, and so does relevance. A Virgin CPR is not a forever zone. It is a window. And windows do not stay open forever. After a few sessions, its power starts to fade and the market begins to shift its focus elsewhere.

Notice the charts. Throughout the session, price never touches the Central Pivot Range. This untouched zone is called a Virgin CPR. It shows that the market skipped its usual balance point. Price may not return to this level right away, but traders keep it marked. When price revisits the zone in a later session, the reaction is often sharp enough to stop the move and even reverse the trend.

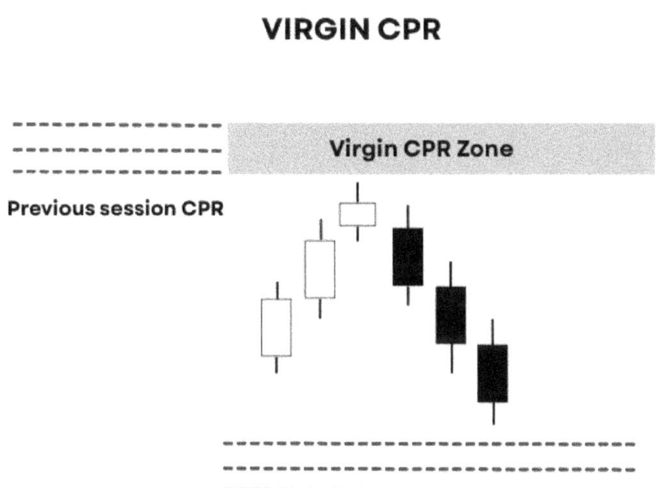

Fig. 3.34: Virgin CPR Setup

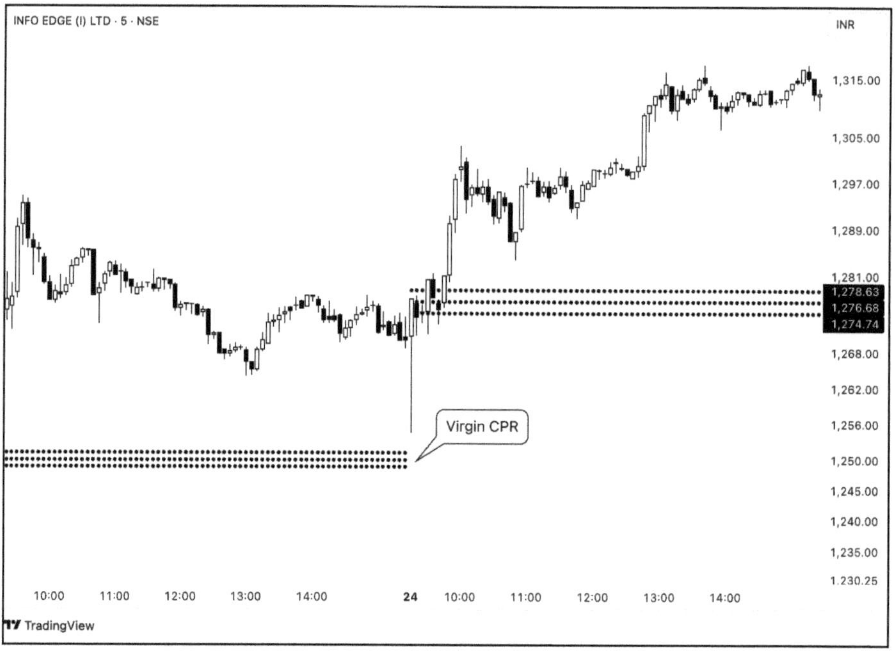

***Fig. 3.35:** Info Edge Ltd. shows a rally from the Previous Session's Virgin CPR zone.*

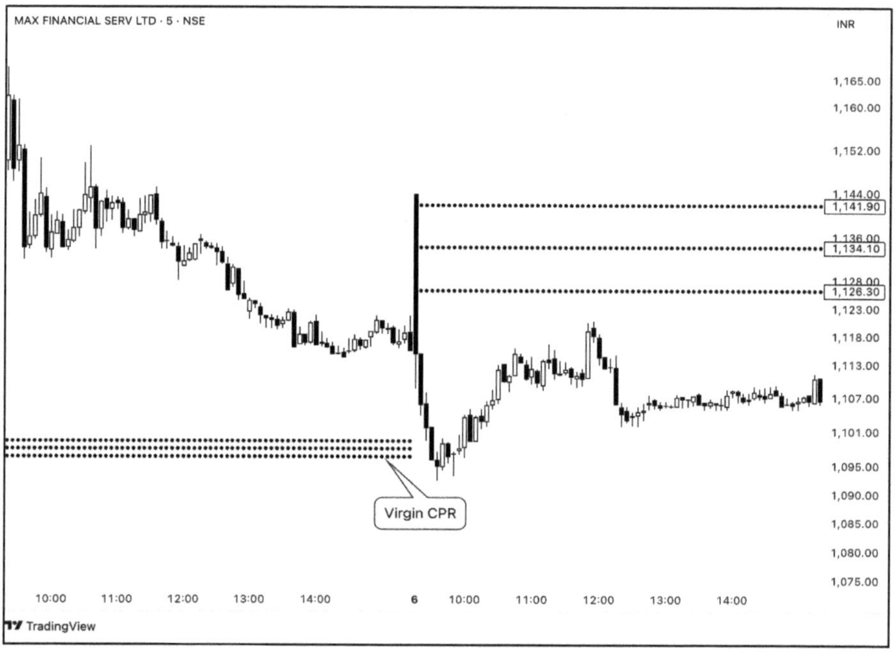

***Fig. 3.36:** Max Financial Services Ltd. shows a rejection from the Previous Session's Virgin CPR zone.*

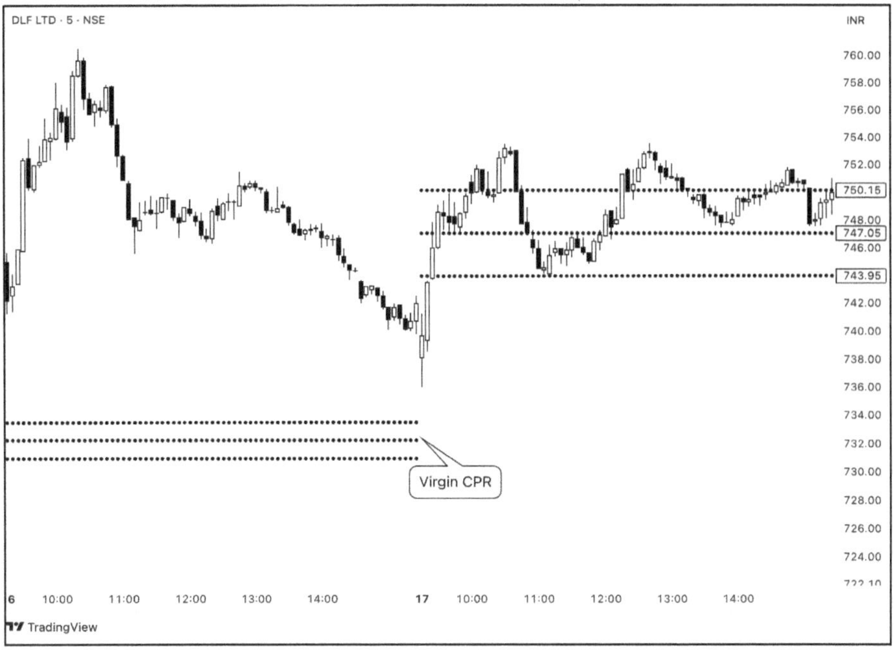

Fig. 3.37: *DLF Ltd. shows a rally from the Previous Session's Virgin CPR zone.*

Fig. 3.38: *GAIL(India) Ltd shows a rejection from the Previous Session's Virgin CPR zone.*

Camarilla Inside CPR

Some of the best trades don't come from chasing momentum. They come from patience. From watching the market quietly unfold and letting price come to you.

When Camarilla levels, especially Camarilla S3 and R3, fall inside the Central Pivot Range (CPR), the market is not gearing up for a breakout. It's pausing. This rare alignment signals a moment of indecision, where neither buyers nor sellers have a clear upper hand. But in that very pause lies opportunity. When both sides hesitate, price often reverses. This is not a breakout zone. It's a reversal zone. In such moments, breakout trades often fail to follow through, and trends lose their steam before they even begin. What takes shape instead is a mean-reversion environment, where price tends to reverse.

Here's how to approach it.

- If price moves toward Camarilla R3, now sitting inside the CPR, treat it as a potential resistance zone. This isn't just a number on your chart. It's where price might hesitate. If price reaches this level and starts to show signs of rejection, it could mark the start of a reversal move. A short entry here would target the lower part of the range, often aiming toward Camarilla S3.
- On the other side, if price drifts down toward Camarilla S3, which is also within the CPR, it becomes a potential support zone. If the market fails to break below and begins to show bullish signals, it may offer a clean long opportunity, with Camarilla R3 as a target.

While some traders may assume that targeting Camarilla S3 or R3 is too far, that's not the case. Camarilla S3 or R3 sits very close to CPR S1 or R1, making it a practical and well-aligned target. This setup isn't about catching explosive trends. It's about recognizing when the market is reversing. This setup isn't for chasing trends, it's for catching the turn before it's obvious. However, if Camarilla S3 and R3 do not fall inside the CPR, simply turn off the Camarilla levels and stick to the CPR-based structure. Let CPR alone guide your setup and decision-making.

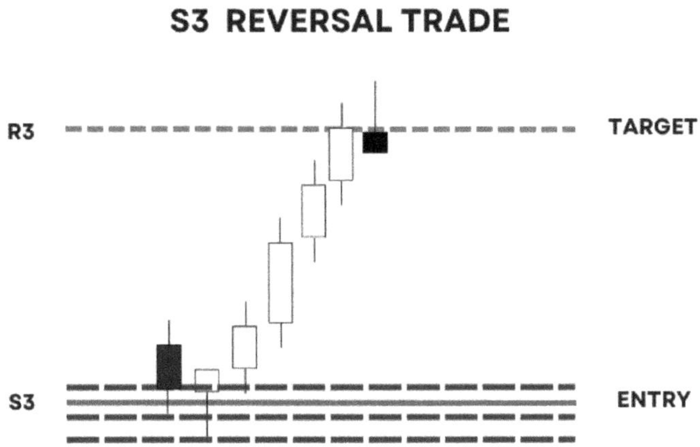

Fig. 3.39: *Camarilla S3 within CPR Setup*

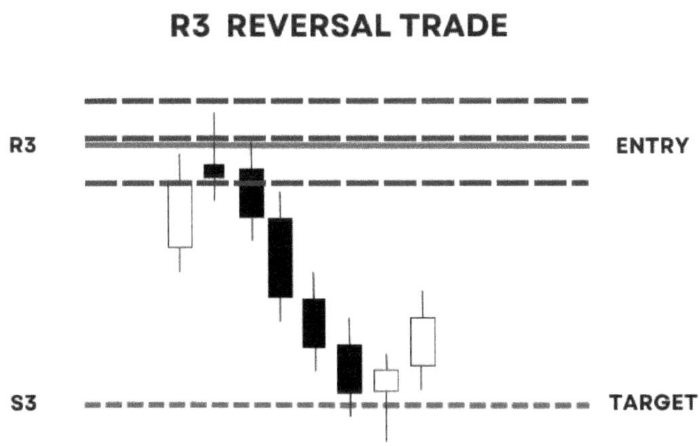

Fig. 3.40: *Camarilla R3 within CPR Setup*

In the charts that follow, you'll notice Camarilla S3 and R3 levels sitting inside the CPR. Watch what happens when price moves toward the zone. It may seem like a quiet approach at first, but the reaction is often quick and sharp. Price touches the level and immediately pulls back. That kind of movement tells you the market is not ready to move forward. These sudden turns often mark the beginning of a reversal.

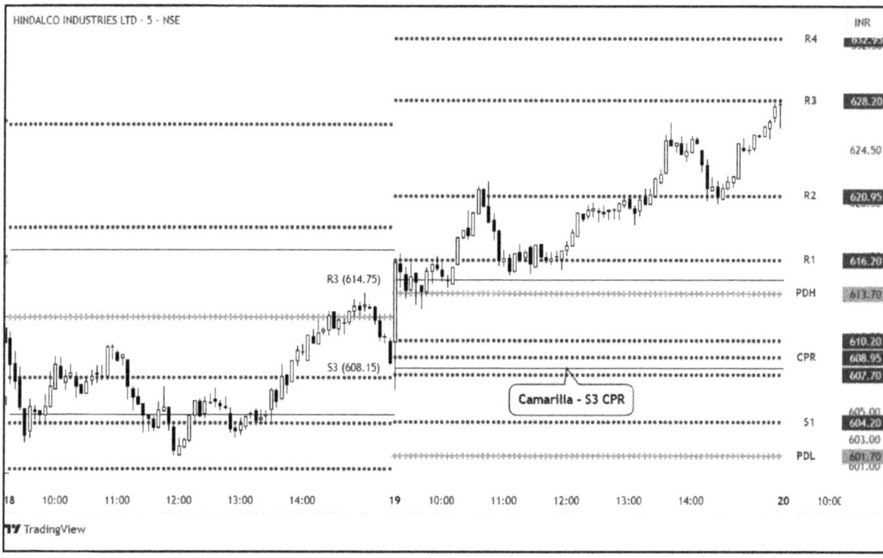

Fig. 3.41: *Hindalco Industries Ltd shows a Camarilla S3 reversal inside CPR*

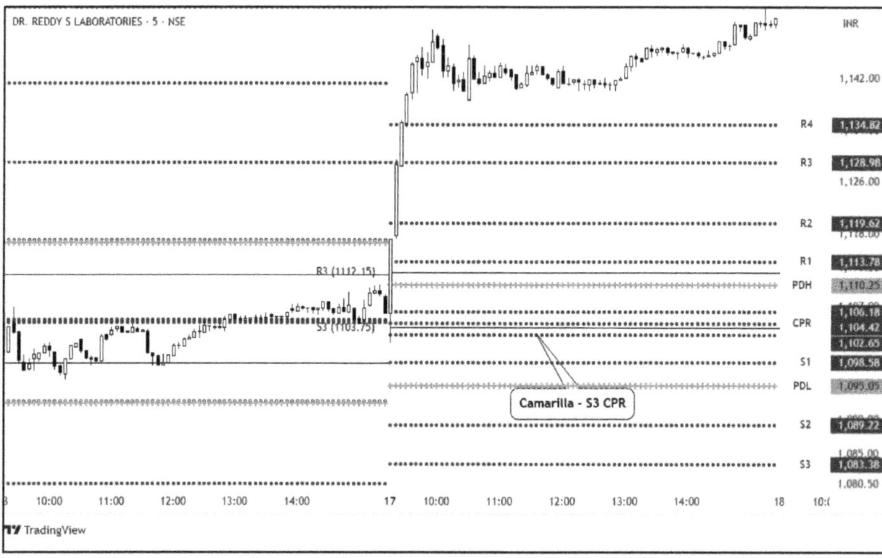

Fig. 3.42: *Dr. Reddy's Laboratories shows a Camarilla S3 reversal inside CPR*

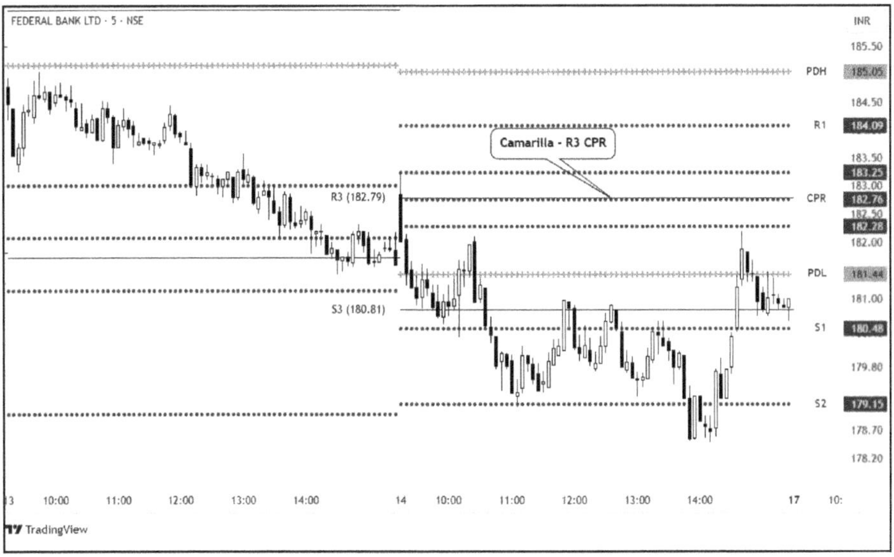

Fig. 3.43: *Federal Bank Ltd shows a Camarilla R3 rejection inside CPR*

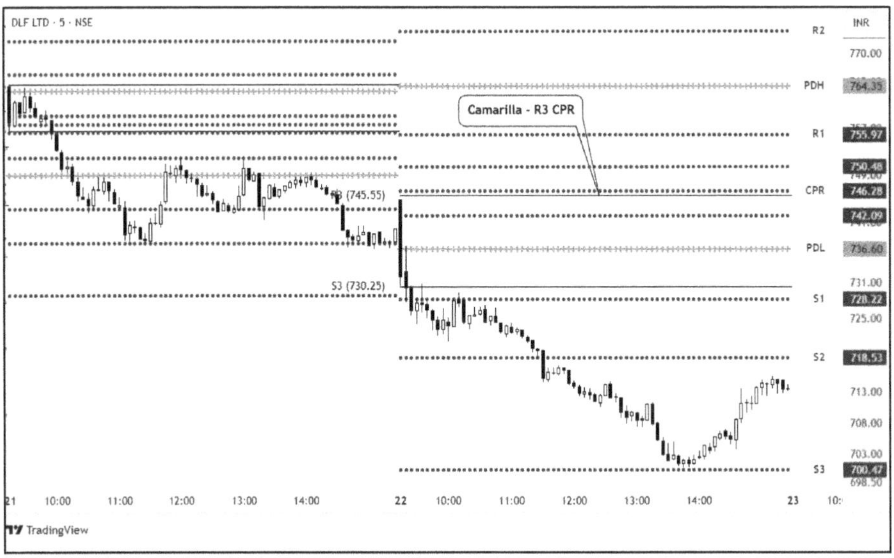

Fig. 3.44: *DLF Ltd shows a Camarilla R3 rejection inside CPR*

CPR Attract Candles

In trading, certain levels act like gravity. No matter how far the price stays, it seems to snap back, as if pulled by an invisible force. One of the strongest magnets on an intraday chart is the Central Pivot Range (CPR).

This setup is built around a simple principle: CPR attracts candles.

When price opens far from the CPR, either due to an overnight gap or early volatility, but fails to build on that momentum, it often starts drifting back toward the CPR. Why? Because CPR represents equilibrium. Fair value. A zone where buyers and sellers last found balance. And markets always remember where balance was last found.

Think of it like this: when price is stretched too far from the CPR without strength to keep it moving, it doesn't just stop, it returns. CPR attracts candles. And if you can spot this early, you're not reacting to price, you're anticipating the reversion before it happens.

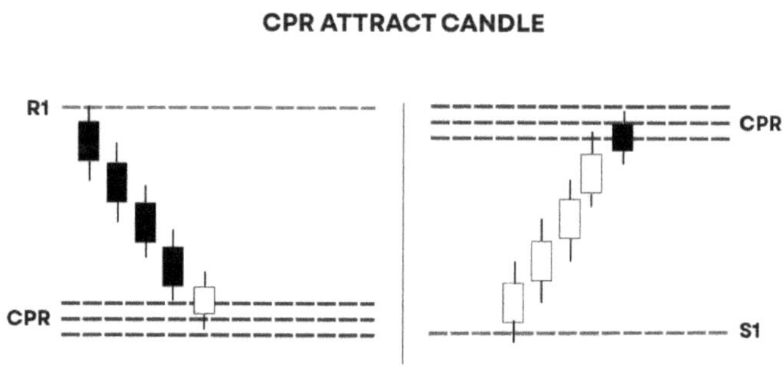

Fig. 3.45: CPR Attract Candle reversal setup

Look at the charts carefully. The session starts with price far from the CPR, giving the impression of a strong directional move. But as the session unfolds, there's no follow-through. You can see how the market naturally returns to that zone, giving traders a clean opportunity to anticipate a reversion move when the initial push begins to fade.

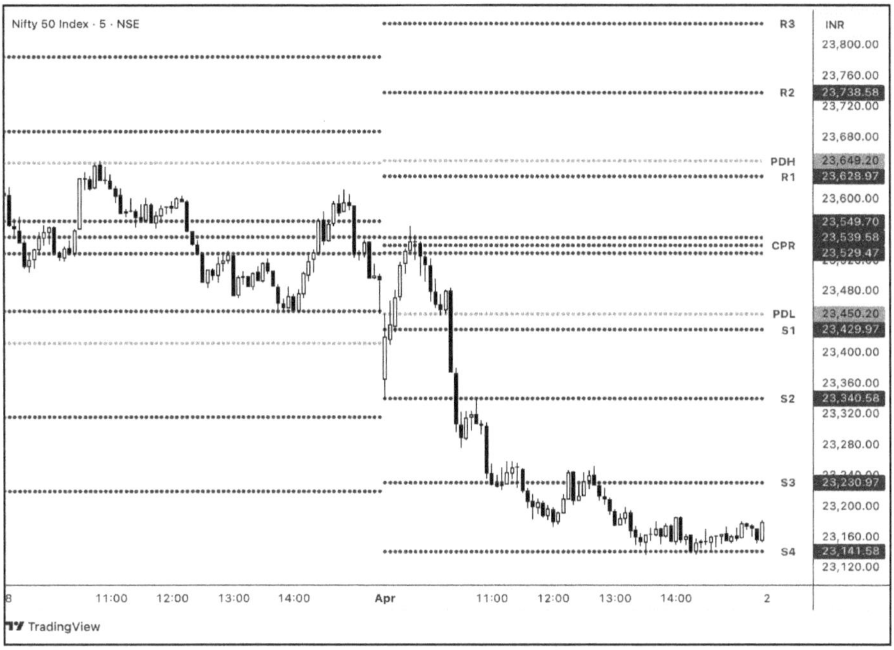

Fig. 3.46: NIFTY 50 INDEX chart showing a CPR attract candle

Fig. 3.47: Bharat Electronics chart showing a CPR attract candle

Fig. 3.48: SBIN chart showing a CPR attract candle

Fig. 3.49: INFOSYS chart showing a CPR attract candle

No Trade Zones

You don't always have to enter to win. Some of your best trades are the ones you didn't take. The days you watched the CPR, saw no clean structure, and simply stepped back. There's strength in knowing when not to act. Some days, not trading is the most profitable decision

How do you know when to stay out of a trade?

When the CPR is wide, overlapping across sessions, completely outside the previous range, or when candles remain stuck inside the band, that's the market telling you to wait..

Wide CPR

A wide CPR signals that the market has already spent its energy. The big move, whether up or down, has likely happened in the previous session. Now, the structure suggests a shift from momentum to balance. When CPR levels are widely spaced, it suggests that the market has already experienced high volatility, and the likelihood of a clean directional move has reduced. More often, what follows is a period of sideways action or choppy, indecisive price behavior.

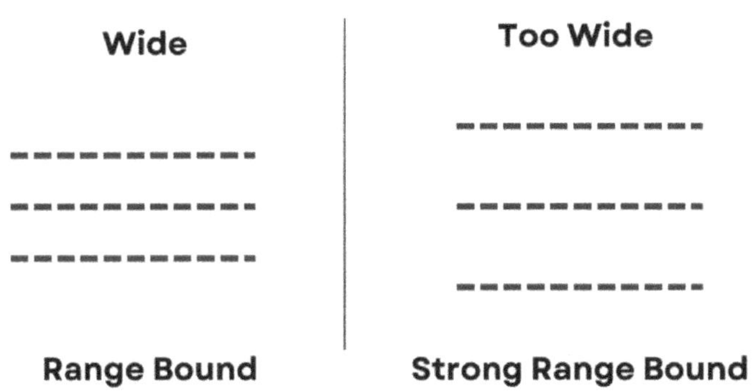

Fig. 3.50: *Wide Vs Too Wide*

One key characteristic of a wide CPR is not just the distance between TC, Pivot, and BC, but also how stretched the levels appear overall. The distance from the CPR to R1 or previous session's high to R1 tends to be larger than usual. This creates a broader zone where price can stay trapped, making it harder for traders to find clean breakout entries.

The best move with a wide CPR is often to stay out. Recognizing that a session may not offer quality opportunities allows you to step back, wait for structure to tighten again, and avoid low-probability trades. Discipline is a strategy in itself, and knowing when not to trade is just as important as knowing when to enter.

See the charts below. There's no real momentum here. The CPR is wide, and price is just moving around without direction. It's not breaking out, not trending, just stuck. When the CPR looks like this, it usually means the big move already happened in the previous session. Now the market's just settling down. This is where traders often jump in, thinking something is about to start. But most of the time, nothing happens. It's better to wait.

***Fig. 3.51:** Wide CPR in Syngene International Ltd*

Fig. 3.52: *Wide CPR in Hero Motocorp Ltd*

Fig. 3.53: *Wide CPR in Nestle India Ltd*

Outside CPR

An outside CPR forms when the Current Session's CPR is completely outside the Previous Session's CPR. This setup suggests that the market has experienced a strong directional or volatile move in the prior session, potentially leading to exhaustion.

An Inside CPR often signals preparation before the move. In contrast, an Outside CPR suggests potential exhaustion after the move. Understanding this helps traders know when to stay patient and when to step in with conviction.

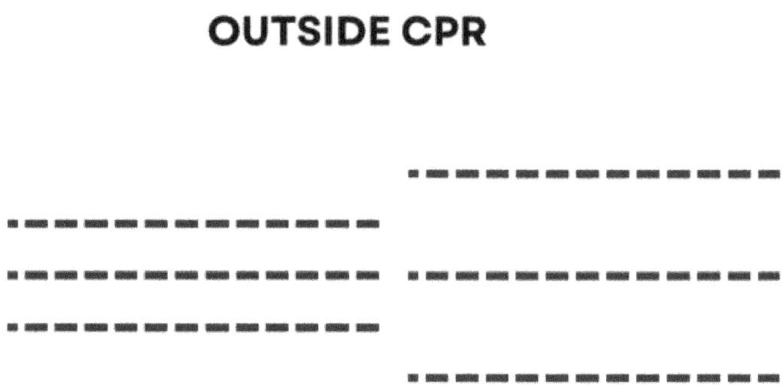

Fig. 3.54: Outside CPR pattern.

Take a look at the chart below. The CPR for the current session is placed completely outside the previous day's CPR. This usually happens after a strong volatile move in the market. When you see this kind of shift, it's often better to stay out and let the market settle before looking for a setup.

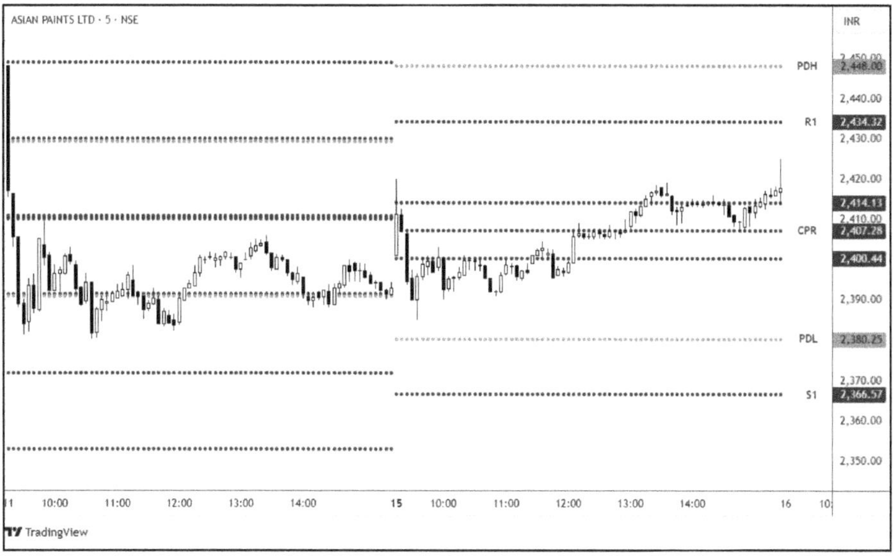

***Fig. 3.55:** Outside CPR in Asian Paints Ltd*

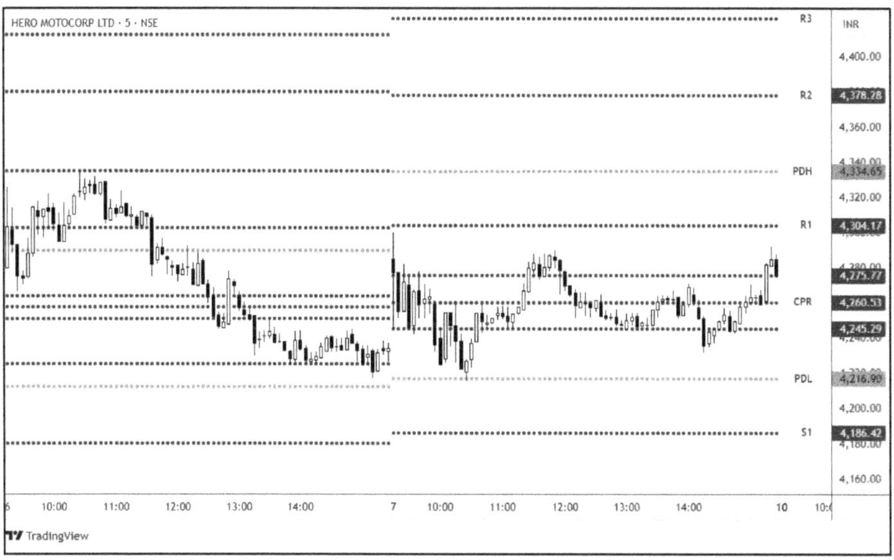

***Fig. 3.56:** Outside CPR in Hero Motocorp Ltd*

Fig. 3.57: Outside CPR in Divis Laboratories Ltd

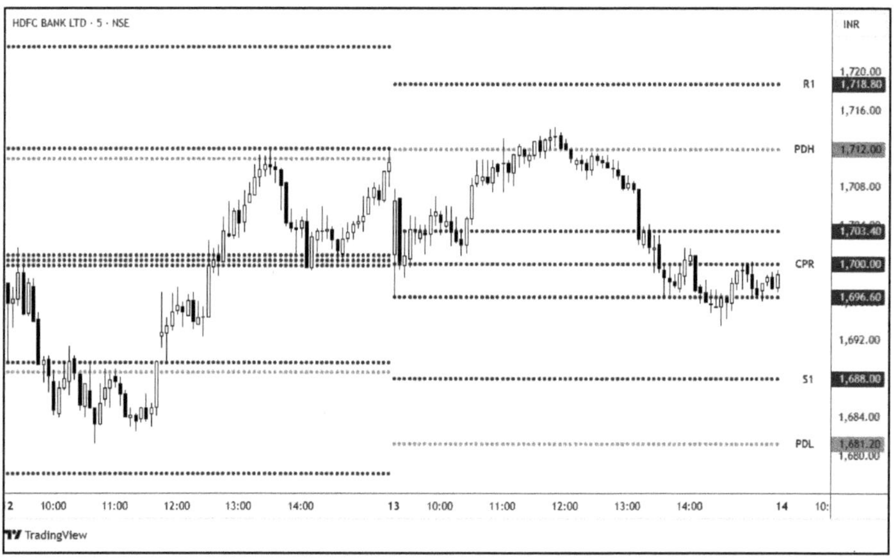

Fig. 3.58: Outside CPR in HDFC Bank Ltd

Overlapping CPR

An Overlapping CPR occurs when multiple consecutive sessions have CPR levels that are closely aligned or slightly overlapping. This structure reflects a market that is lacking direction. Price continues to rotate around the same levels without building momentum or showing intent. It is a phase where the market appears busy, but nothing meaningful is happening. Traders often find themselves entering trades that go nowhere or get caught in quick reversals. Signals are weak, follow-through is limited, and the overall tone is uncertain.

During such periods, it is better to avoid trading. The market is not ready to trend, and setups often fail to reach targets. Patience during these times is not just a good habit, it's a form of protection. Let the structure shift. Let price break away from the cluster. Only then does the market offer clean opportunities worth taking.

After seeing the charts below, you can tell how hard it is to trade when the CPR stays in the same zone for multiple sessions. There's no clear push from either side, and price keeps bouncing around with no real direction. It looks like something might happen, but nothing follows through. This is where most traders get trapped, taking entries too soon and getting stopped out. When CPR keeps sticking to the same area, it's a sign to step back and let the market show real intent before making a move.

OVERLAPPING CPR

Fig. 3.59: *Overlapping CPR pattern observed in the chart.*

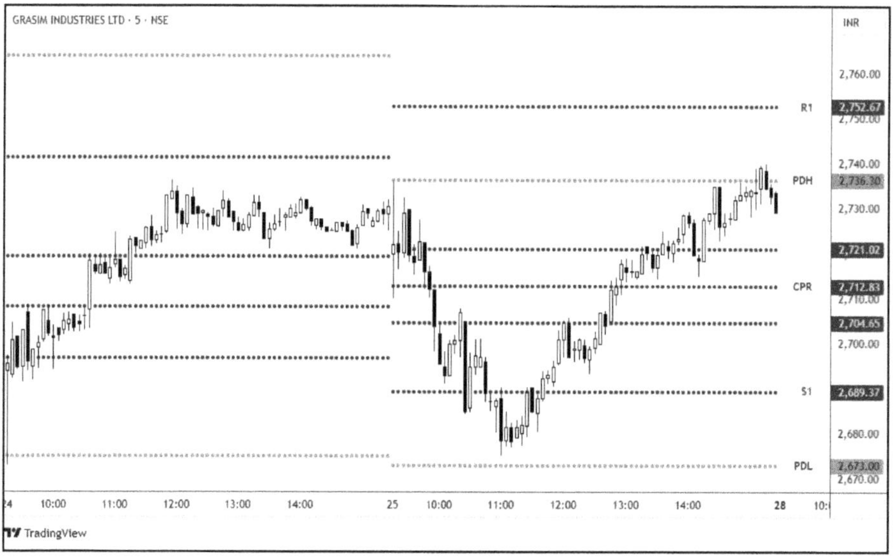

***Fig. 3.60:** Overlapping CPR in Grasim Industries Ltd*

***Fig. 3.61:** Overlapping CPR in ONGC*

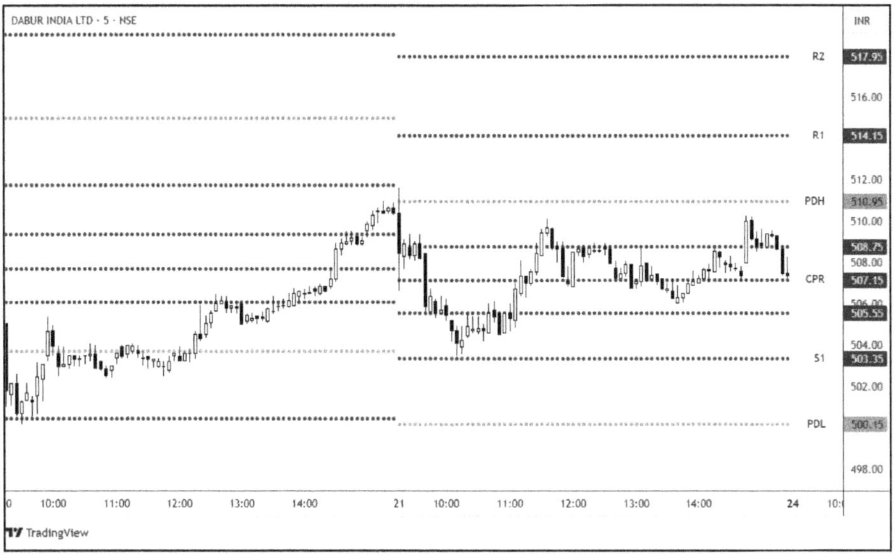

Fig. 3.62: Overlapping CPR in Dabur

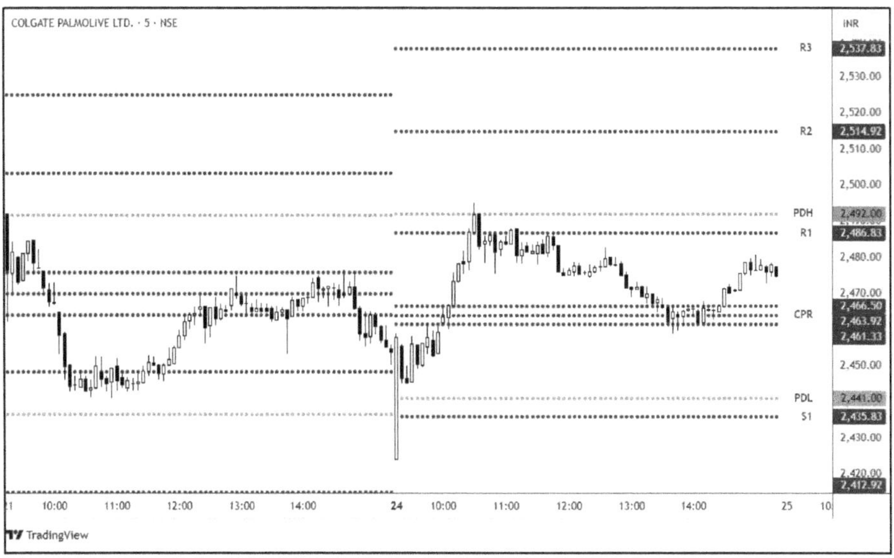

Fig. 3.63: Overlapping CPR in Colgate

Candle Inside CPR

In CPR-based trading, the area between the Bottom Central (BC) and Top Central (TC) levels often reflects a state of market balance, where neither buyers nor sellers are clearly in control. When price moves within this range, it usually indicates consolidation and hesitation. Directional trades during this phase can be risky, as price may fluctuate within the structure without commitment, leading to false breakouts or quick reversals.

This zone acts like a quiet waiting room. The market pauses, watches, and holds back. No decisions are made until a clear signal appears. Until price breaks above the TC or below the BC with strength and structure, it is better to stay patient. Avoiding trades here helps protect capital and keeps you ready for the real move when it begins.

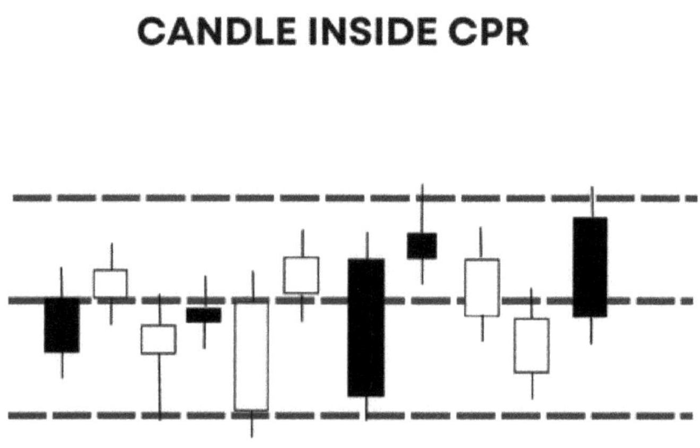

Fig. 3.64: *Candle inside CPR*

See the charts below. Price is stuck within the CPR, not showing any real strength in either direction. It moves a little up, then back down, without giving a clear signal. This kind of price action makes it difficult to trust any setup. Entries taken here often get reversed quickly. When you notice price staying inside the CPR for too long, it's better to wait. Let the market break out with intent before looking for a trade.

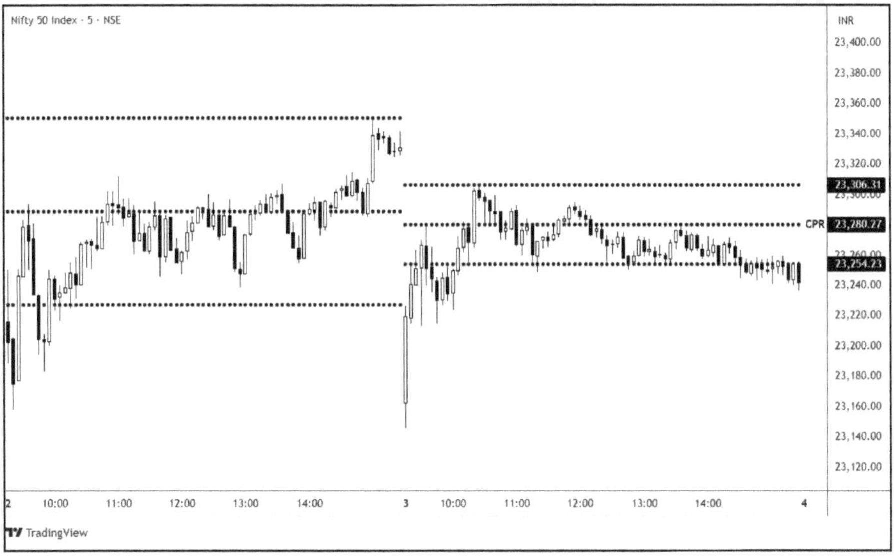

Fig. 3.65: *Nifty 50 inside CPR*

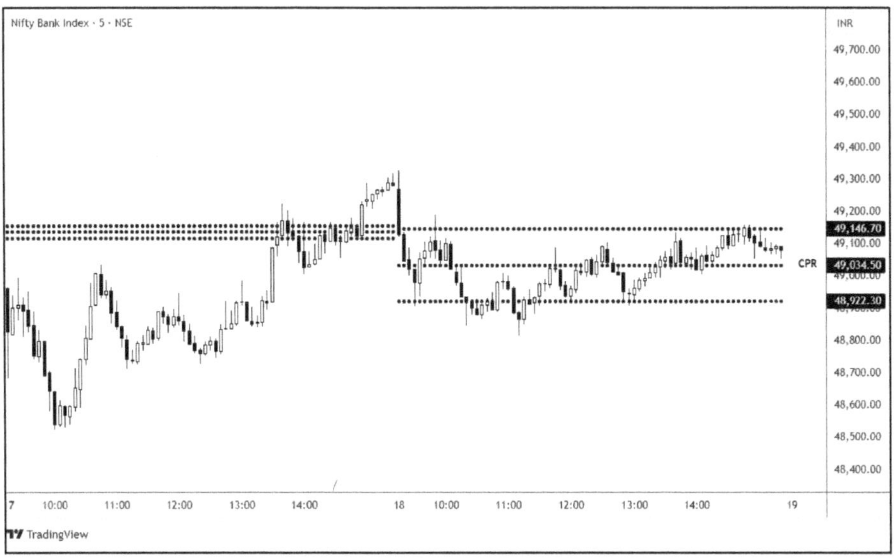

Fig. 3.66: *Nifty Bank Inside CPR.*

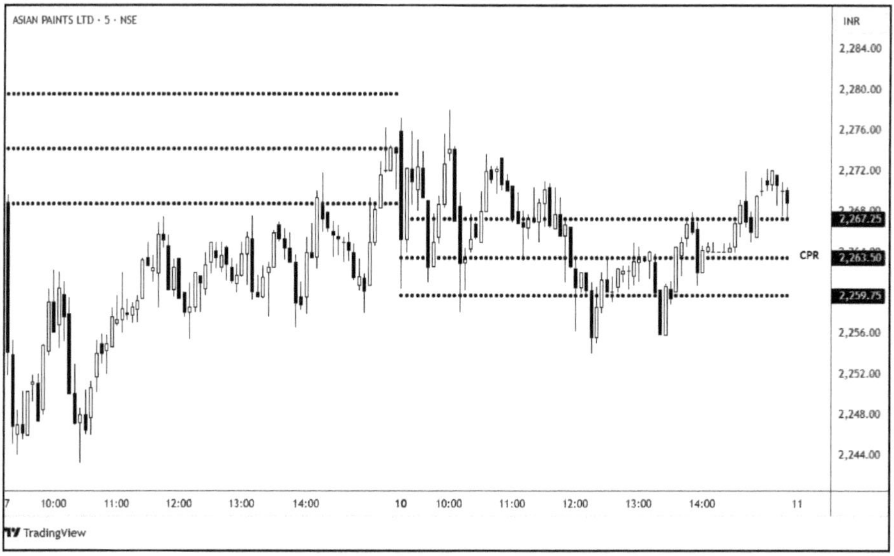

Fig. 3.67: *Asian Paints inside CPR*

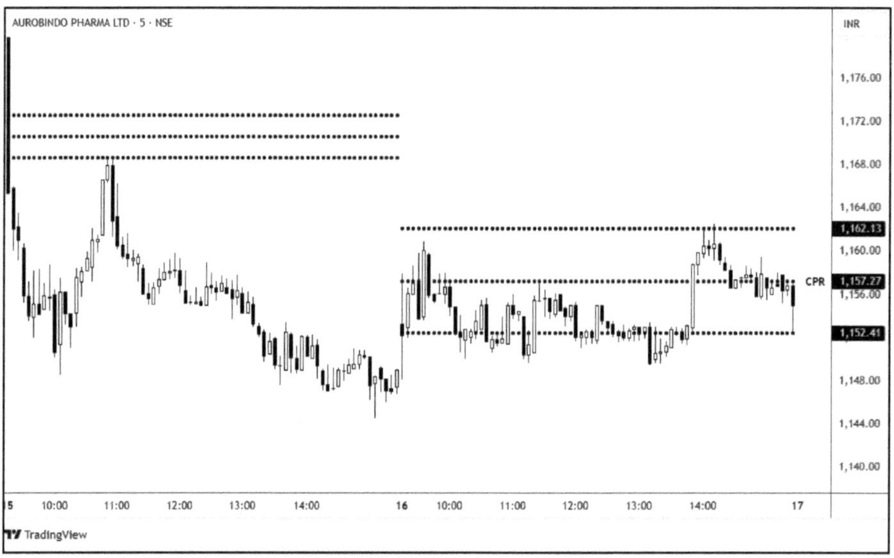

Fig. 3.68: *Aurobindo Pharma Ltd inside CPR*

The Developing Central Pivot Range (DPR)

The Developing Pivot Range (DPR) adjusts in real time with every new price bar that comes in, so you're essentially getting a constantly updated read on where the market's main "fair value" zone is each day. By the time trading wraps up, the final DPR reading becomes tomorrow's central pivot range, which means you already know the key levels that could act as support or resistance for the upcoming session.

It's almost like getting a sneak peek at what might happen next: you can compare how today's DPR lines up with tomorrow's levels to get a sense of the market's direction, momentum, or possible turning points. Being able to anticipate these zones gives you a solid edge when planning your trades for the day ahead.

Think of the chart as a simple roadmap, where the Central Pivot Range (CPR) lines in the middle serve as your main landmarks. When you see the price holding steady above the CPR, it signals that bullish momentum is firmly in control.

The first step is to wait until the price stays firmly above those CPR lines. That's your green light to enter a buy trade. Next, place your stop loss just beneath the CPR, like a safety net, so you can limit any losses if the market drops again. From there, watch the higher pivot points (often labeled R1 or R2) because they're clues for where the price might pause or turn around. You can use these levels to decide when to take some profit or tighten your stop loss if the price keeps rallying. This strategy helps you stay aligned with the market's direction while keeping your risk in check.

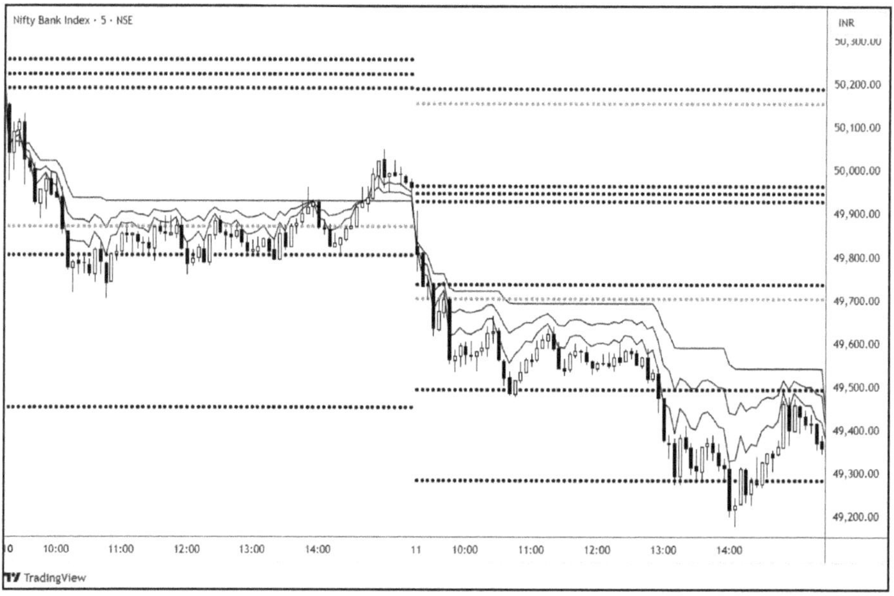

Fig. 3.69: BANK NIFTY five minute chart with daily CPR

On the first day, the Nifty Bank Index (5-minute timeframe) was trading sideways, and the developing CPR followed the price throughout the day. As the price moved, the developing CPR adjusted in real time, reflecting the market's ongoing behavior. By the end of the day, the developing CPR became narrow, indicating that the CPR for the next day would also be narrow, signaling a period of consolidation and potential for a breakout in the near future.

The next day, Nifty Bank opened just below the CPR, signaling a potential shorting opportunity. With the price failing to hold above the CPR, it looked like the bearish momentum was ready to take over. Traders could enter the short position, setting the stop loss at the CPR since it now acted as resistance. If the price broke back above it, the short trade would be invalidated.

The targets for this trade were S1 and S2, as these support levels were likely to be the next stopping points for the price. With the market showing weakness, the expectation was that the price would move down toward these levels. As the price headed lower, traders could lock in profits or trail their stop loss to secure gains while riding the downward trend. This was a simple setup: short the stock, keep the stop loss tight at the CPR, and aim for the next support levels.

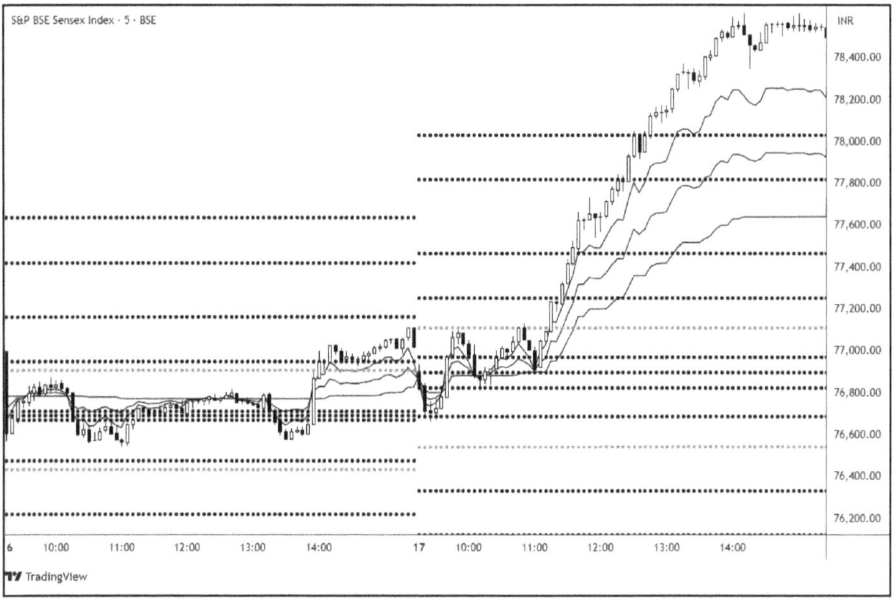

Fig. 3.70: *Sensex five minute chart with daily CPR*

On the 5-minute chart of the Sensex Index, the CPR for the day was unusually narrow. As per CPR principles, a narrow CPR generally indicates compression, the market is building pressure for a potential breakout. Under normal circumstances, such a setup suggests either a strong trending move or heightened volatility during the session. However, on this particular day, the index failed to trend. Instead of expanding into trending, the market remained largely sideways. When a narrow CPR day does not result in expansion, it often implies that the energy is being stored for the following session. Importantly, prices closed above the developing CPR by the end of the day. This closing behavior signaled bullish undertones and suggested that the probability of an upward move on the next day was high.

Contrary to expectations, the following day opened below both the current day CPR and the developing CPR. This initially created confusion and a bearish bias among many traders. However, price action revealed something critical, The market found strong support near S1 and the previous day's low. Multiple candles tested the S1 region, but it was never convincingly broken. Selling pressure failed to sustain below these support zones. This failure to break S1 was the first signal that bears were losing control. Soon after, the candles began to climb. Price moved back above the current day CPR and also reclaimed the developing CPR. This transition confirmed that bulls had regained control.

A long position could have been initiated once price sustained above the CPR, with Targets R1, R2, and higher resistance levels. Stop Loss Below the CPR. The key here was not to carry forward positions blindly from the first day. The objective was not positional speculation, it was preparation. The real edge lies in reading tomorrow's move from today's close. A trader can enter the next day with clarity and confidence. Understand today's close. Prepare for tomorrow's opportunity.

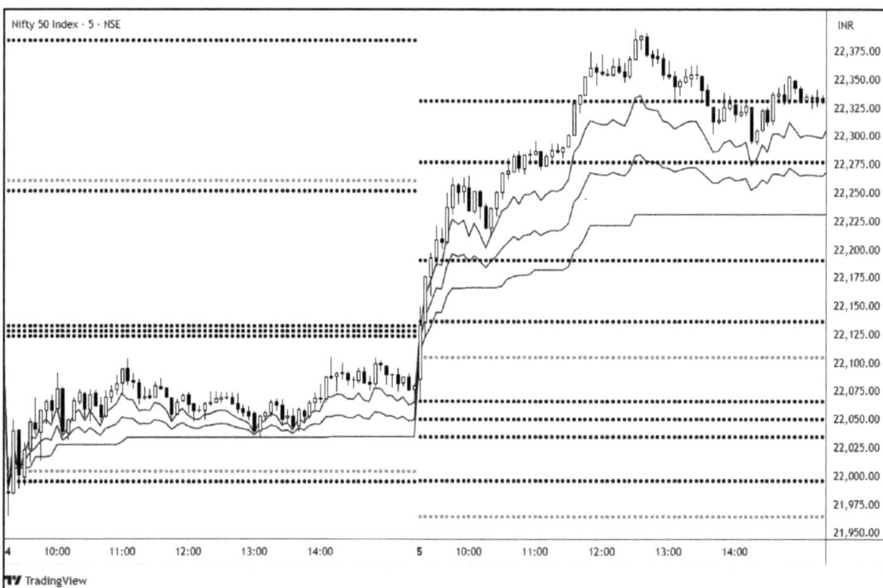

Fig. 3.71: NIFTY five minute chart with daily CPR

On the first day with the too narrow CPR, the Nifty 50 Index on a 5-minute timeframe was expected to either trend well or show high volatility, as narrow CPR usually signals the market is building up pressure for a breakout. However, on this particular day, the index did not trend as expected and remained relatively sideways, not showing the anticipated volatility. This means that the market is likely to trend the next day.

As expected, the next day, Nifty opened above the CPR and closed above the previous day's high level on the first 5-minute candle, indicating the start of the anticipated trend and creating a good long opportunity for traders.

Same Setup, Different Game

So far, we've looked at the key CPR setups: narrow, wide, inside, ascending, and descending. These structures reveal a lot about momentum, reversals, and everything in between. This chapter is all about the setups, how to read them, how to recognise them, and how to build clarity around structure without bringing timeframes into the picture.

This is where many traders go wrong. They use a swing mindset in a scalping setup, or they try to apply 3-minute logic to a monthly chart. That's when good setups fail, not because the structure was wrong, but because the timing didn't match the style.

The next chapter is not about finding new patterns. It's about refining your approach, learning how to switch gears without losing control, and knowing how to apply the same CPR types across different trading styles and timeframes.

Chapter 04

BUILDING AN EDGE WITH CPR ACROSS TIMEFRAMES

Anyone can enter a trade. Just like anyone can pick up a bat and face a bowler. But only a few know when to strike. Only a few know how to stay calm when everything speeds up. Sachin Tendulkar mastered it on the cricket field. Master traders master it in the markets.

The skill that separates them? Timing. And execution.

Think of it like this. You are standing at the crease at a packed Wankhede Stadium. The crowd is buzzing with energy. Shoaib Akhtar, the fastest bowler in the world, is charging toward you at full speed. At that moment, most batsmen either freeze into a defensive shot or swing desperately, trying to seize control of the situation. It is a split-second decision where instincts clash with judgment, and the right call makes all the difference. Get it wrong, and you are either bowled or caught. Get it right, and you send the ball racing to the boundary.

Now think about Sachin Tendulkar for a moment. Sachin did not swing wildly. He simply leaned into the ball with effortless grace. A sweet, crisp sound echoed across the stadium. Before anyone could even register what had happened, the ball had already raced to the boundary, untouched and unstoppable. His straight drive was not remembered for force and aggression, but for perfect timing and flawless execution. It was not just a shot. It was a statement of calmness under pressure.

Trading mirrors this in so many ways. Opportunities appear every day on the charts. Spotting a setup is just the start. The real game begins with how you execute it. Acting at the right time with precision is what separates good traders from great ones. If you hesitate, the trade is gone. If you rush, you risk acting on noise instead of confirmation. But even the best timing depends on what chart you're reading. To stay in sync with the market, you need to work with the right time frames and CPR levels that fit your trading style.

Before we get into that, let's ground ourselves in something more fundamental. These core principles apply no matter what kind of trader you are, whether you're holding a position for minutes or managing it over weeks.

Core Principles Before Every Trade

Mastering the habit of checking these factors before every trade is like a skilled batsman surveying the field carefully before playing his shot. It prepares you for success with focus, preparation, and clarity.

First, take a moment to check the overall trend. If the market is making higher highs and higher lows, it is likely in an uptrend. If it is forming lower highs and lower lows, it is probably in a downtrend. Trading with the trend is not just a rule. It is a survival tactic.

Next, mark your important levels. Weekly and monthly highs, 52-week extremes, and major swing zones. These are the spots where price usually reacts. They are not just numbers. They are pressure points where buyers and sellers fight for control.

Then, pay attention to the strength of candles near those levels. One solid move, like a Bahubali candle, tells you more than most indicators. When that candle forms at the right location and is backed by a clear reversal or continuation pattern, it becomes a moment worth noticing.

Finally, glance at the **CPR structure**.

- A narrow or inside CPR often means a breakout is around the corner.
- A wide or overlapping CPR might suggest the market is taking a breather.
- If the CPR keeps rising over the weeks or months, that's a sign of strength.
- When it keeps dropping, it hints at weakness

These aren't separate tools. They're layers of the same picture. When they line up, your conviction builds. When they conflict, it is better to wait than to act without clarity. Once you've done this basic prep, you're ready to adjust the CPR and timeframe to match your pace. Whether you prefer holding positions for several days like a swing trader or reacting quickly to price moves like a scalper, your approach must reflect your style.

Adjusting CPR and Timeframes for Different Trading Styles

Trading is not a one size fits all game. Some traders thrive on the speed of intraday moves, where quick decisions and fast execution are critical. Others prefer the patience of swing trading, holding positions for days or weeks to capture broader trends. Different timeframes require different mindsets, and your style must adapt accordingly. The table 4.1 below connects each trading style with its ideal timeframe and the corresponding CPR level used for analysis and execution. Each of these combinations sets the tone for how you approach the market. The longer the timeframe and the broader the CPR level, the more patient your style needs to be. The shorter the chart, the more aggressive and reactive your trading becomes.

Table 4.1: *Adjusting Time frames and CPR*

Time Frame	CPR	Style	Observation
Daily	Monthly CPR	Conservative Swing Trading	Hold up to 30 days
75 min	Weekly CPR	Aggressive Swing Trading	Hold up to 5 days
5 min	Daily CPR	Day Trading	Hold till EOD
3 min	Hourly CPR	Scalping	Hold for few minutes

Daily time frame with Monthly CPR - Conservative Swing trading

When trading on the daily chart using monthly CPR levels, trading feels like a Test match. It is not about how quickly you profit. It is about aligning yourself with the broader market trend, trusting the CPR structure, and staying calm through temporary noise. Just like a batsman builds his innings session by session, a trader must build his position carefully over days or weeks, focusing on survival and steady growth.

It is especially suitable for beginners who want to practice trading in a conservative, low noise environment. At the same time, experienced traders use it to stay aligned with the major market trends and avoid getting caught in short term fluctuations. Before entering any trade at this level, it is crucial to apply the core principles we have learned so far to stay on the right side of the market:

The table 4.2 below outlines how to use Monthly CPR on the daily chart to plan trades with clarity, discipline, and proper position sizing.

Table 4.2: *Planning Conservative Swing Trades Using Monthly CPR (Daily Timeframe)*

Monthly CPR	Setup	Suggested Position Size
Above	Strong Bullish	Full Position (75-100%)
Below	Stong Bearish	Full Position (75-100%)
Inside	No Clear Signal	Avoid Trade

Each chart below captures a different mood of the market. Observe how price reacts when it's above, inside, or below the Monthly CPR. Study the behavior. Ask yourself: would you enter here? Would you stay out? Let's walk through them one by one.

MONTHLY CPR ⬆

If the price is above the CPR, it usually signals bullish intent. Look at the CPR for September. It's narrow, and the price opens just above it. That's the first clue: a buildup of energy with bullish intent. Soon after, price breaks out and crosses above the Monthly CPR. The move continues with strength, eventually reaching all the way up to the R4 level, a clear sign of momentum and trend alignment. This is the kind of setup a conservative swing trader waits for: narrow Monthly CPR, price breaking above it, and a clean upside extension. One can go with full position size here, especially when entries are taken near the CPR with strong bullish candles.

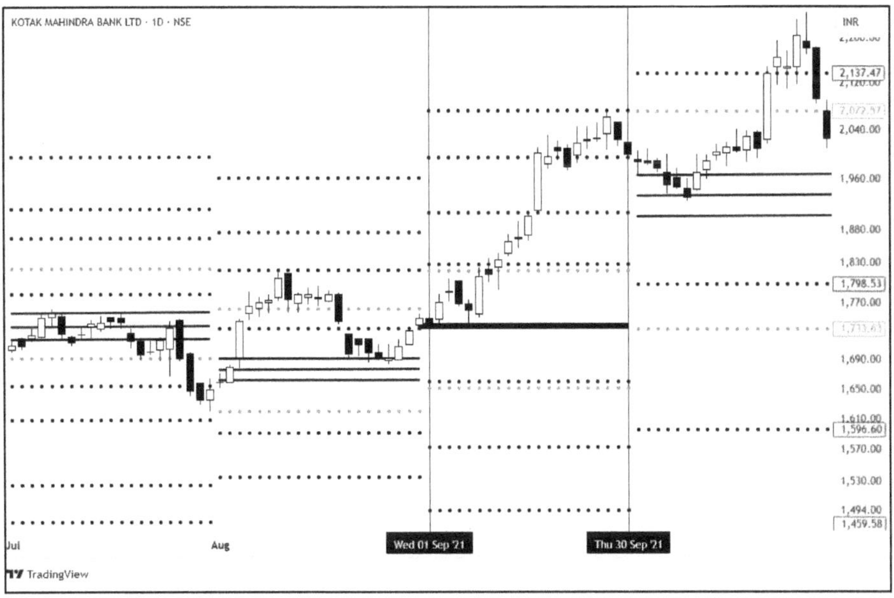

***Fig. 4.1:** Daily chart of KOTAK MAHINDRA BANK with Monthly CPR levels*

MONTHLY CPR

In this chart, price opens the month below the Monthly CPR and immediately shows weakness. There's no hesitation; the market starts off bearish and continues to drift lower. For a Conservative swing trader, this is a straightforward short setup. The structure is clean, and there's no confusion in direction. When price opens below a flat or descending CPR and continues to fall, one can go with full position size on short trades, especially if early candles confirm the momentum.

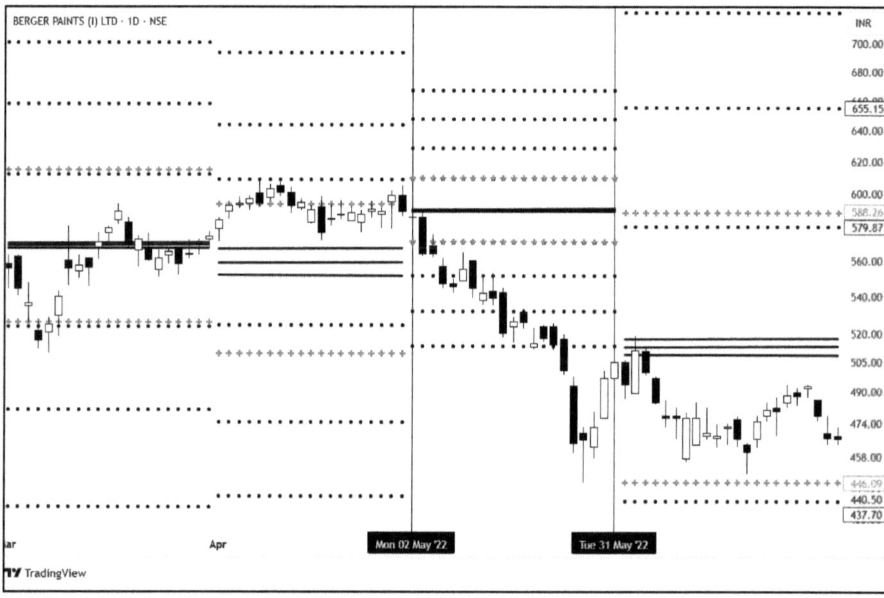

Fig. 4.2: Daily chart of BERGER PAINTS LTD with monthly CPR levels

MONTHLY CPR

Fig. 4.3: *Daily chart of POLYCAB INDIA LTD with monthly CPR levels*

In this chart, price opens the month right inside the Monthly CPR and stays trapped within it for several sessions. There's no clear breakout, no directional follow-through. Just choppy, indecisive movement. This is not a structure that rewards participation. Momentum is missing. The market is in balance. For a conservative swing trader, this is a clear no-trade zone. The best move here is to stay patient and avoid getting chopped in a sideways mess.

75 minutes Time Frame with weekly CPR - Aggressive swing trading

For aggressive swing trading, slightly faster timeframes like 75 minutes with weekly CPR offer a perfect balance between capturing strong and quick moves without getting caught in unnecessary market noise. The reason 75 minutes works so well is that the Indian market runs for 375 minutes. This divides evenly into five full 75-minute candles, providing clean and complete data without partial candles. It helps maintain a structured and reliable view of price action. If you are comfortable with the 1-hour chart and it fits your method, you may continue using it. The key is to remain consistent and align your trades with CPR levels for clarity.

Here, trading mirrors a One Day International. You balance patience with calculated aggression, rotating between waiting and acting.

Before we step into faster timeframes like 75 minutes, it is important to understand the natural learning curve in trading. Once you have practiced and gained consistency by trading conservatively with monthly CPR on the daily timeframe, you build a solid foundation. This disciplined start helps you transition smoothly into more active trading styles. Over time, you move from a cautious beginner to a confident and adaptable trader who can handle faster setups without losing structure. At this stage, combining the weekly CPR with a monthly CPR check gives you a structured way to trade with clarity. Table 4.3 below shows how to align your setups using both weekly and monthly CPR for stronger trades.

Table 4.3: *Aggressive Swing Trading Using Weekly CPR with Monthly Check*

Monthly CPR	Weekly CPR	Setup	Suggested Position Size
ABOVE	ABOVE	STRONG BULLISH	FULL POSITION (75-100%)
BELOW	BELOW	STRONG BEARISH	FULL POSITION (75-100%)
BELOW	ABOVE	BULLISH	MEDIUM POSITION (50-75%)
ABOVE	BELOW	BEARISH	MEDIUM POSITION (50-75%)
INSIDE	ABOVE/ BELOW	WEAK BULLISH/ BEARISH	LESS POSITION (25-50%)
INSIDE	INSIDE	NO CLEAR SIGNAL	AVOID TRADE

We'll begin with the most powerful scenario. Price is trading above both the Monthly and Weekly CPR, confirming strong bullish intent. Look at this chart.

MONTHLY CPR ↑ | WEEKLY CPR ↑

Price starts trading above the Monthly CPR at the beginning of the month, signaling a bullish higher timeframe structure. This confirms that the broader trend supports long trades. We can now shift to the 75-minute chart to look for execution opportunities in the same direction. On this 75-minute chart, price is also trading above the Weekly CPR. With both timeframes supporting the direction, one can go with full position sizing. This is a high-probability setup where structure, momentum, and timing all line up.

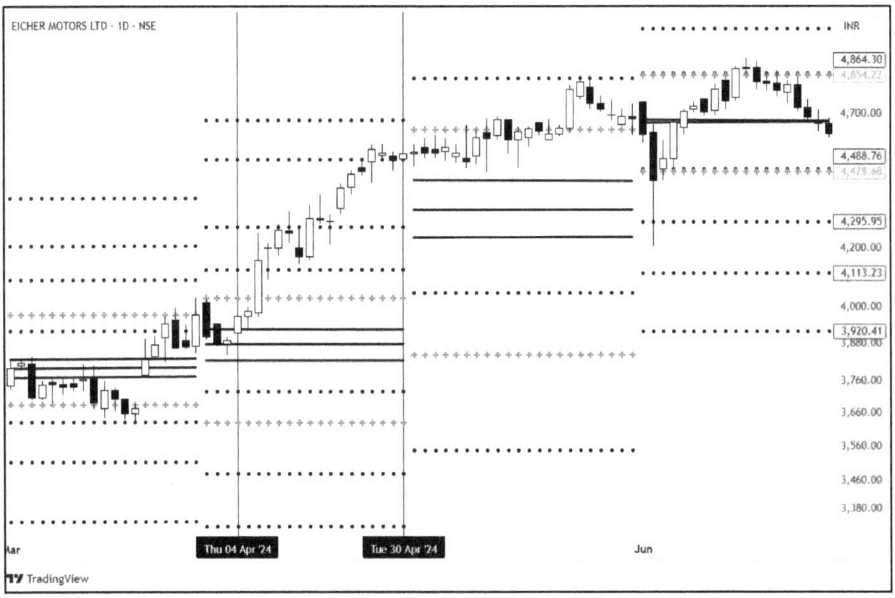

Fig. 4.4: *Daily chart of EICHER MOTORS LTD with monthly CPR levels*

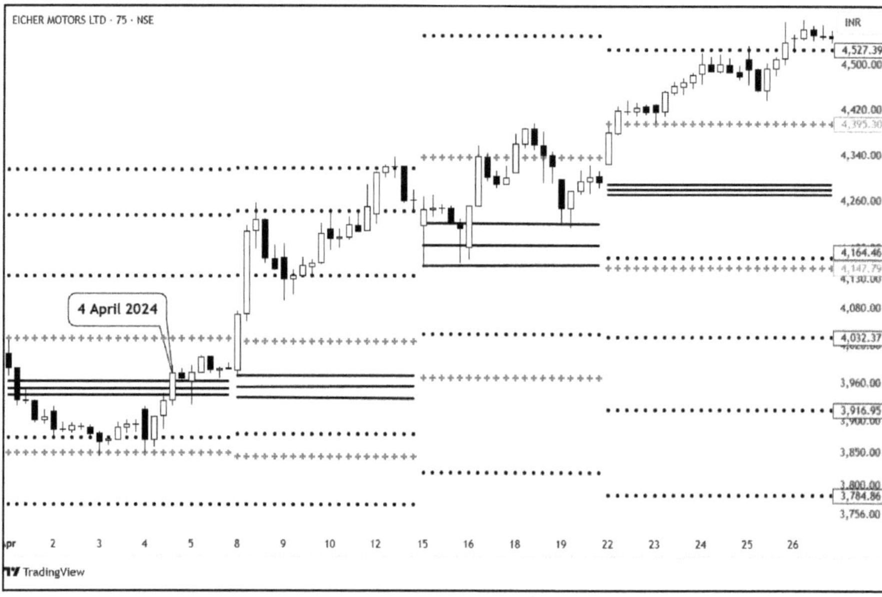

Fig. 4.5: 75-minute chart of EICHER MOTORS LTD with Weekly CPR levels

MONTHLY CPR ⬇ | WEEKLY CPR ⬇

The astral chart shows that the candle closed below the Monthly CPR on February 6, 2025. Price stayed under this level for the rest of the month. This pattern points to continued bearish pressure in the market. Momentum was on the side of sellers, limiting upward moves. Traders focused on short positions in line with the overall trend.

Observe the Weekly CPR chart closed below CPR, This reflects a bearish trend throughout that period, indicating sustained selling pressure. Price action during these days supports the continuation of the downtrend in the market. In both scenarios, the daily and weekly CPR charts show candles closing below their respective CPR levels, forming a clear downtrend.

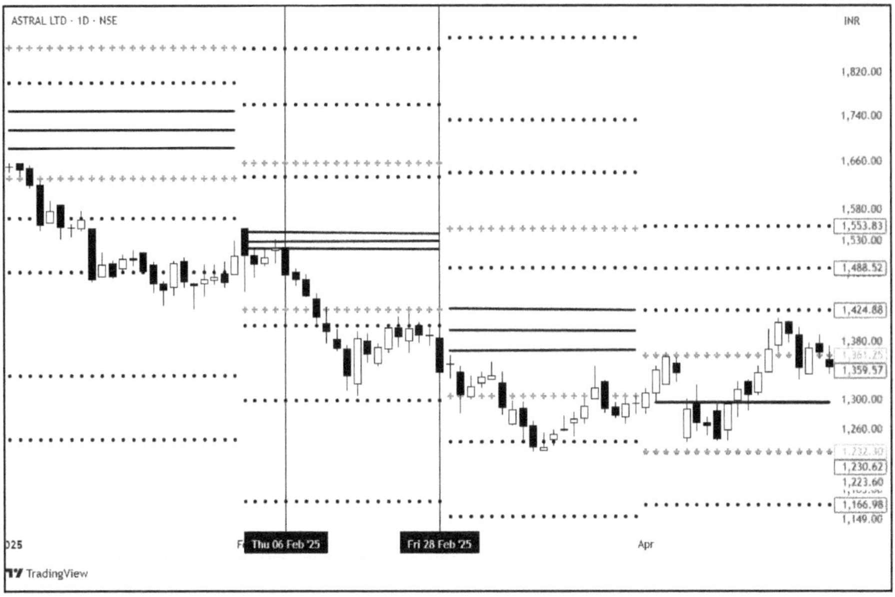

***Fig. 4.6:** Daily chart of ASTRAL LTD with monthly CPR levels*

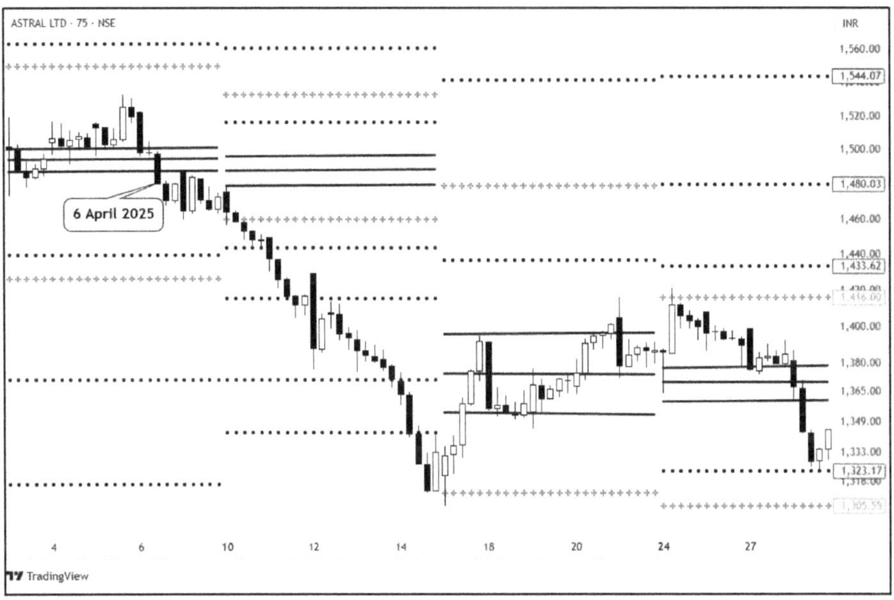

***Fig. 4.7:** 75-minute chart of ASTRAL LTD with Weekly CPR levels*

MONTHLY CPR ↓ | WEEKLY CPR ↑

However, if the two structures don't align, for example, the monthly is bullish but the weekly shows signs of weakness, then give more weight to the weekly CPR. It captures the near-term momentum and often sets the tone for the next few sessions. Weekly CPR reflects the short to medium term direction. In such situations, reduce your position size and trade cautiously, or wait patiently until both trends align for a higher conviction setup. You may start a one day match with an aggressive mindset, but if the pitch turns tricky, playing rash shots can bring an early end. A smart player adapts and waits. Similarly, when CPR signals clash, adjusting your approach protects your capital and keeps you in the game for better opportunities.

Fig. 4.8: Daily chart of Asian paints with monthly CPR levels

MONTHLY CPR ↑ | WEEKLY CPR ↓

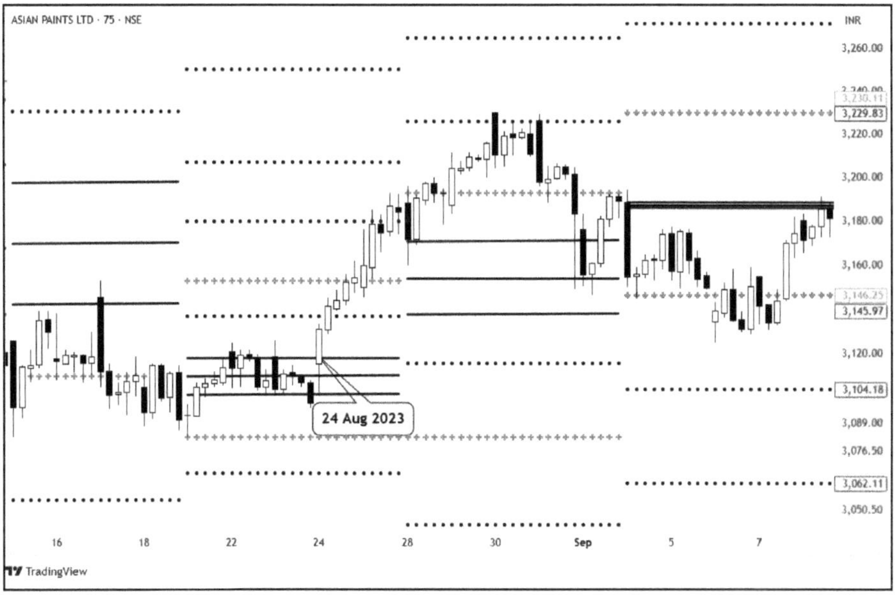

Fig. 4.9: 75-minute chart of Asian paints with Weekly CPR levels

This structure reflects a conflicted scenario. Price is holding above the Monthly CPR, indicating that the broader trend remains bullish. However, it is trading below the Weekly CPR, which shows short-term selling pressure and resistance from intermediate players.

This is not the time to go aggressive.

The structure suggests that you're trading with the tide but against the wind. In this case, the safest approach is to reduce position size and stay cautious. Look for signs of strength, such as price reclaiming the Weekly CPR, before scaling up. Until that happens, treat the setup as low conviction.

Fig. 4.10: Daily chart of HINDUSTAN AERONAUTICS LTD with monthly CPR levels

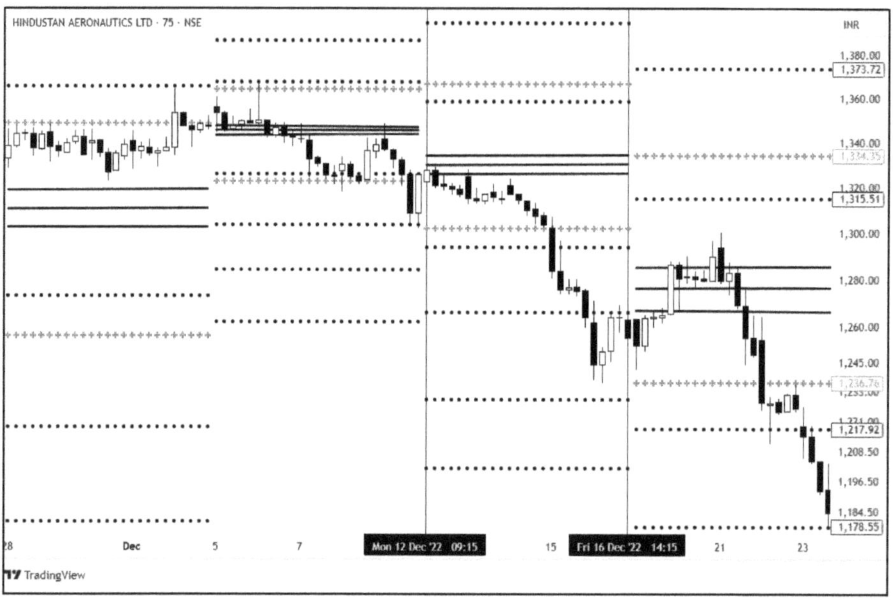

Fig. 4.11: *75-minute chart of HINDUSTAN AERONAUTICS LTD with Weekly CPR levels*

MONTHLY CPR ⬄ | WEEKLY CPR ⬆

In this setup, price trades above the Monthly CPR, suggesting strength in the broader context. However, it remains below the Weekly CPR, which acts as a ceiling in the short term. This creates a zone of hesitation where momentum is not yet fully supportive.

In this setup, price trades above the Monthly CPR, suggesting strength in the broader context. However, it remains below the Weekly CPR, which acts as a ceiling in the short term. This creates a zone of hesitation where momentum is not yet fully supportive.

Given this mixed structure, traders should avoid taking full-size positions. It's safer to trade with reduced position size, treating the setup as low conviction.

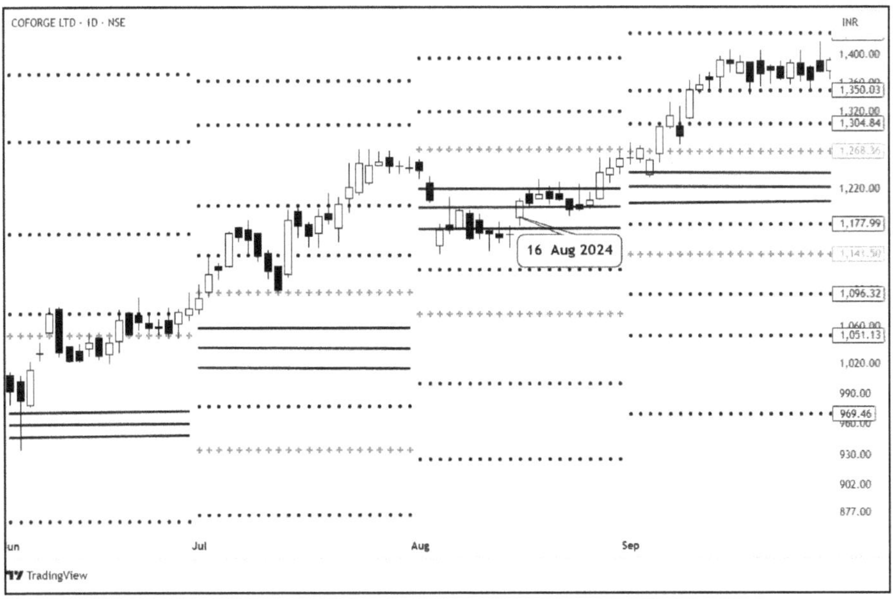

Fig. 4.12: Daily chart of COFORGE LTD with monthly CPR levels

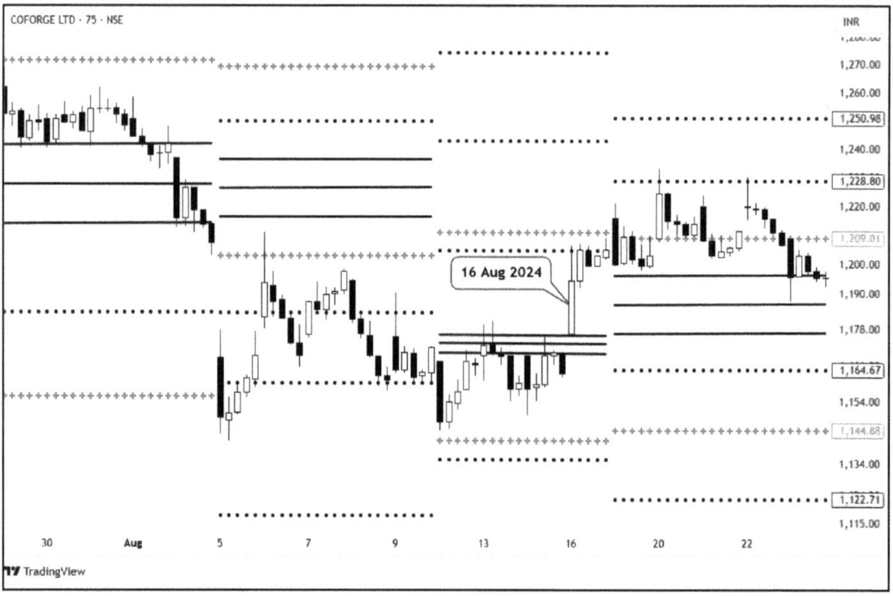

Fig. 4.13: 75-minute chart of COFORGE LTD with Weekly CPR levels

MONTHLY CPR | WEEKLY CPR

When both CPRs are inside, it reflects low conviction and indecision at both the higher and medium timeframes. There is no directional edge, and any move within this zone is likely to be erratic or short-lived.

For traders, this is a clear no trade condition.

Avoid taking trades during this structure. Any entry taken here is likely to get trapped within noise. It's better to protect capital and wait patiently for the breakout. Let the market show its hand. Once price breaks out of these inside structures with volume and strength, only then consider entering.

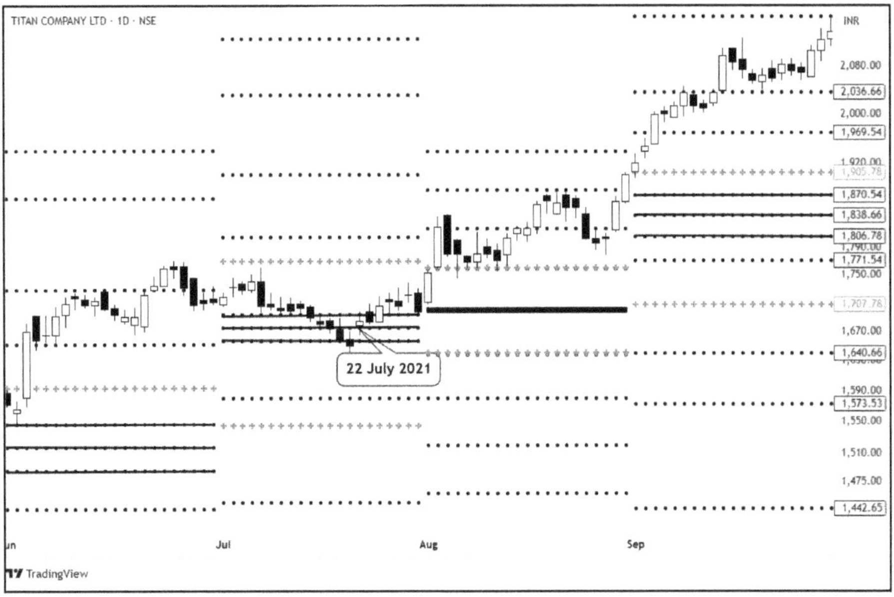

Fig. 4.14: Daily chart of TITAN COMPANY LTD with monthly CPR levels

Fig. 4.15: 75-minute chart of TITAN COMPANY LTD with Weekly CPR levels

Intraday Trading Strategy: Quick Execution with Precision

After building a strong foundation with conservative swing trading and gaining experience with aggressive swing trading, you will naturally develop a better ability to filter out the noise of intraday movements. With this foundation, you are now ready to step into the faster world of intraday trading using the 5-minute timeframe with daily CPR levels. Now we enter the T20 zone, intraday trading. Here, speed matters, but structure still leads. The table 4.4 below will help you decide how to approach intraday setups using Daily CPR, guided by the bigger picture of weekly and monthly trends.

Before diving into intraday trades, it is important to first understand the broader structure. The monthly and weekly CPR trends set the larger direction, while the daily CPR levels guide your entries and exits with precision.

Table 4.4: *Day Trading Using Daily CPR with weekly and monthly bias*

Monthly CPR	Weekly CPR	Daily CPR	Setup	Suggested Position Size
Above	Above	Above	Strong Bullish	Full Position (100%)
Below	Below	Below	Strong Bearish	Full Position (100%)
Any	Below	Above	Bullish	Medium Position (50-75%)
Any	Above	Below	Bearish	Medium Position (50-75%)
Any	Inside	Above/Below	Weak Bullish/ Bearish	Less Position (25-50%)
Any	Inside	Inside	No Clear Signal	Avoid Trade

However, if the monthly CPR trend points one way, the weekly trend points another, and the daily CPR points yet another direction, the market is in a state of conflict. In such situations, it is best to avoid aggressive trades. Reduce your position size heavily or stay out completely, as the odds of clean moves are low and intraday setups can fail quickly.

MONTHLY CPR ↑ | WEEKLY CPR ↑ | DAILY CPR ↑

When the monthly, weekly, and daily CPR structures all align in the same direction, it creates the highest quality setups for intraday trading. These are the trades where you can go with full confidence and normal position size. When the monthly, weekly, and daily CPR structures align, it is like a T20 power play where you can play freely and go for big shots. But when the structures are mixed, it is like facing tight bowling early on and the pitch is not good, you must play carefully, wait for the right ball, and protect your wicket.

Fig. 4.16: Daily chart of STATE BANK OF INDIA with monthly CPR levels

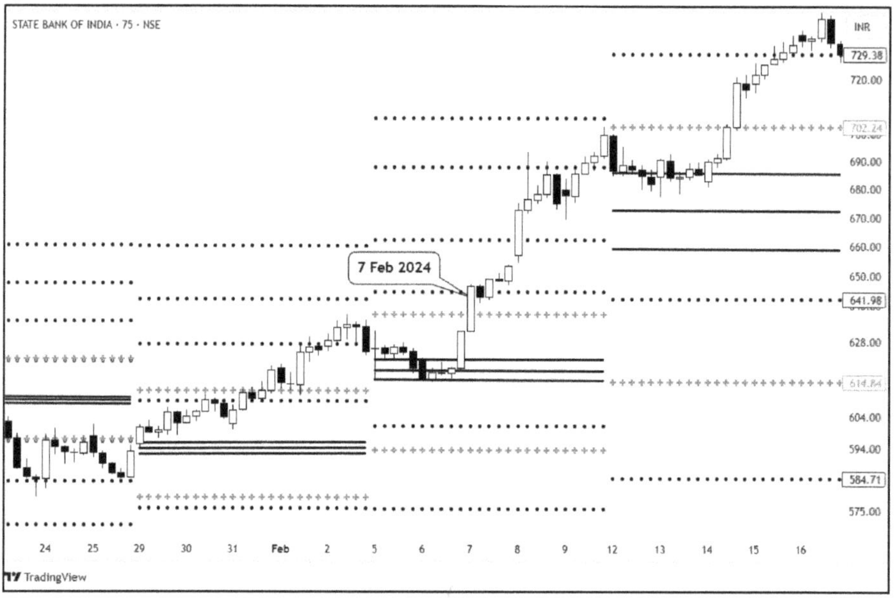

Fig. 4.17: *75-minute chart of STATE BANK OF INDIA with Weekly CPR levels*

Fig. 4.18: *5-minute chart of STATE BANK OF INDIA with Daily CPR levels*

MONTHLY CPR ⬇ | WEEKLY CPR ⬇ | DAILY CPR ⬇

When the Monthly, Weekly, and Daily CPR (Central Pivot Range) structures all align pointing downward, it signals one of the most potent shorting opportunities for intraday traders. This rare but powerful alignment indicates that selling pressure is consistently dominant across all major timeframes, ranging from the broader, long-term outlook to the immediate, intraday perspective. Such uniformity in trend direction strengthens the conviction that the market is firmly under bearish control.

This alignment simplifies the trader's decision-making process. The structure is unmistakably clear, eliminating any ambiguity that might cloud judgment. The bearish bias is not just present; it's overwhelming, reinforced by the congruent signals from multiple timeframes. Momentum, an essential element in trading, is fully tilted in favor of the bears, creating an environment where downtrends can accelerate rapidly.

Fig. 4.19: Daily chart of AVENUE SUPERMARTS LTD with monthly CPR levels

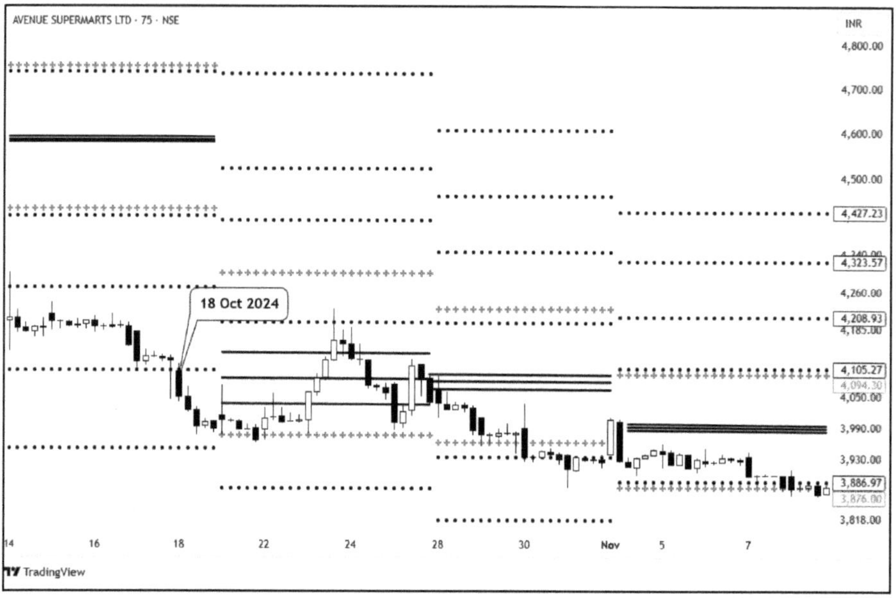

Fig. 4.20: *75-minute chart of AVENUE SUPERMARTS LTD with Weekly CPR levels*

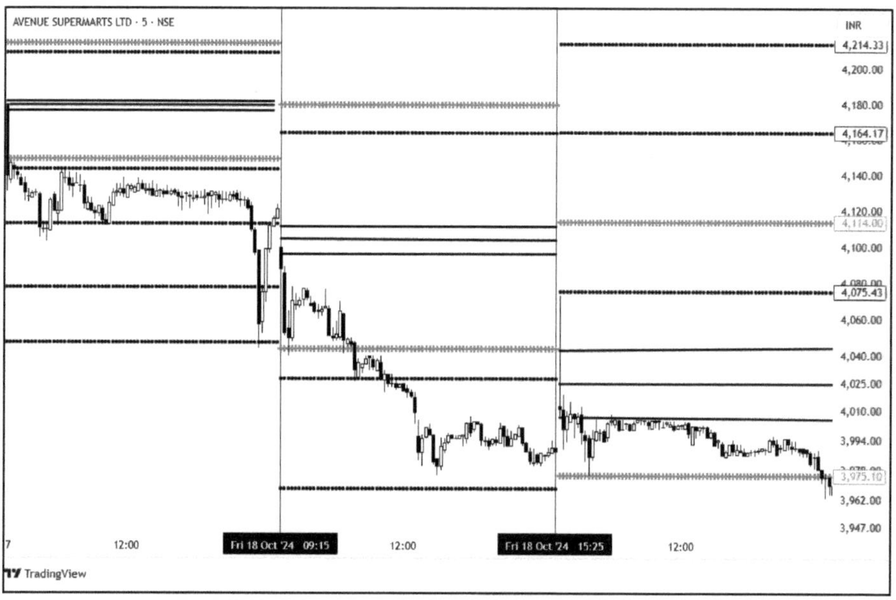

Fig. 4.21: *5-minute chart of AVENUE SUPERMARTS LTD with Daily CPR levels*

WEEKLY CPR ⬇ | DAILY CPR ⬆

If you observe that the monthly CPR trend is not perfectly in sync with the weekly and daily CPR trends, do not be discouraged. In fact, if the weekly and daily CPRs are moving cohesively in the same direction, it signals that the short to medium-term market momentum is favoring that direction. This alignment between the daily and weekly CPRs can provide a strong basis for trade decisions, even if the broader monthly trend appears neutral or slightly divergent.

In such scenarios, traders should proceed with cautious optimism. The key strategy here is to slightly reduce your position size to manage risk effectively. This conservative approach helps mitigate potential adverse impacts that could arise from the lack of monthly trend support.

Fig. 4.22: 75-minute chart of TATA CONSULTANCY LTD with Weekly CPR levels

Fig. 4.23: 5-minute chart of TATA CONSULTANCY LTD with Daily CPR levels

WEEKLY CPR ↑ | DAILY CPR ↓

When the Weekly CPR is up but the Daily CPR is down, follow the Daily CPR. Intraday trades should respect the short-term structure. The immediate pressure is on the downside, and that's where the edge lies.

In the first chart (Weekly CPR), price is clearly trading above the Weekly Central Pivot Range. This shows that over the last few sessions, buyers have been in control. The structure is strong, and the market has been respecting higher lows and breakouts. The weekly trend is bullish.

However, the second chart (Daily CPR) tells a different story. Here, price is trading **below** the Daily CPR. This indicates short-term weakness. Sellers have stepped in at the start of the session, and the immediate momentum has shifted to the downside.

Fig. 4.24: 75-minute chart of MUTHOOT FINANCE LTD with Weekly CPR levels

Fig. 4.25: 5-minute chart of MUTHOOT FINANCE LTD with Daily CPR levels

WEEKLY CPR ⇔ | DAILY CPR ↓

This setup presents a clear opportunity for intraday traders leaning toward the short side. The Weekly CPR is inside, indicating that the broader market is still in a consolidation phase, and no strong trend direction has emerged at the intermediate level. However, the Daily CPR is sloping downward, revealing fresh short-term weakness.

When this combination occurs, the market is showing signs of preparing for a breakout, and the daily structure is hinting it may break lower. Price action below the Daily CPR confirms that sellers are active today, even though the weekly trend hasn't yet expanded.

In this case, traders can go with a short bias, but should keep position size moderate. Since the Weekly CPR is inside, expect possible reversals or fake moves, so entries must be sharp and exits decisive.

Fig. 4.26: 75-minute chart of HAVELLS LTD with Weekly CPR levels

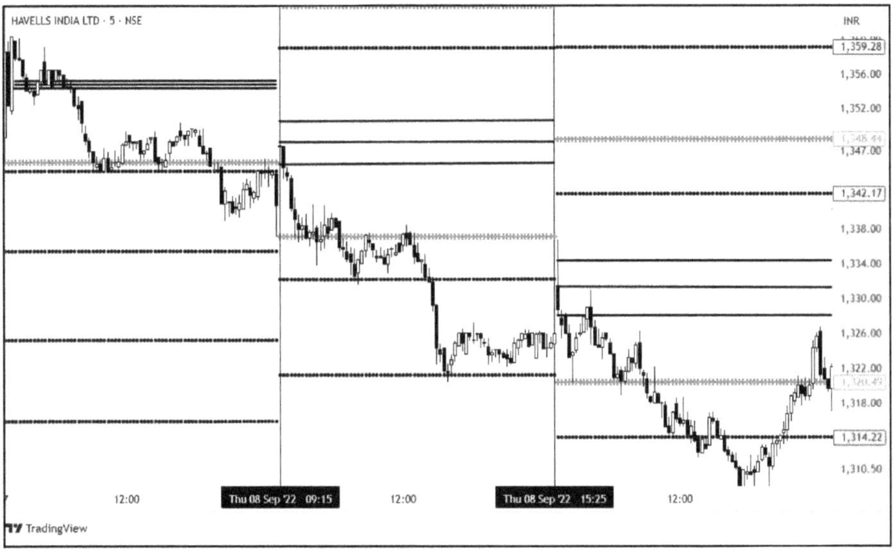

Fig. 4.27: *5-minute chart of HAVELLS LTD with Daily CPR levels*

WEEKLY CPR ⬌ | DAILY CPR ⬌

When both the Weekly and Daily CPR are inside their previous ranges, the market is in clear compression mode. This is a phase where volatility is low, direction is unclear, and momentum is missing. Price is trapped in a tight zone with no clear breakout or breakdown in sight.

For intraday traders, this is a no trade condition.

Any trade taken here is likely to get stuck in chop, fizzle out, or reverse quickly. The best move is to stay patient, observe, and wait for price to escape this compression zone. Once it breaks out of the Daily CPR with strength, especially if it also moves outside the Weekly range, that's when the real opportunity begins.

Fig. 4.28: *75-minute chart of BHARTI AIRTEL LTD with Weekly CPR levels*

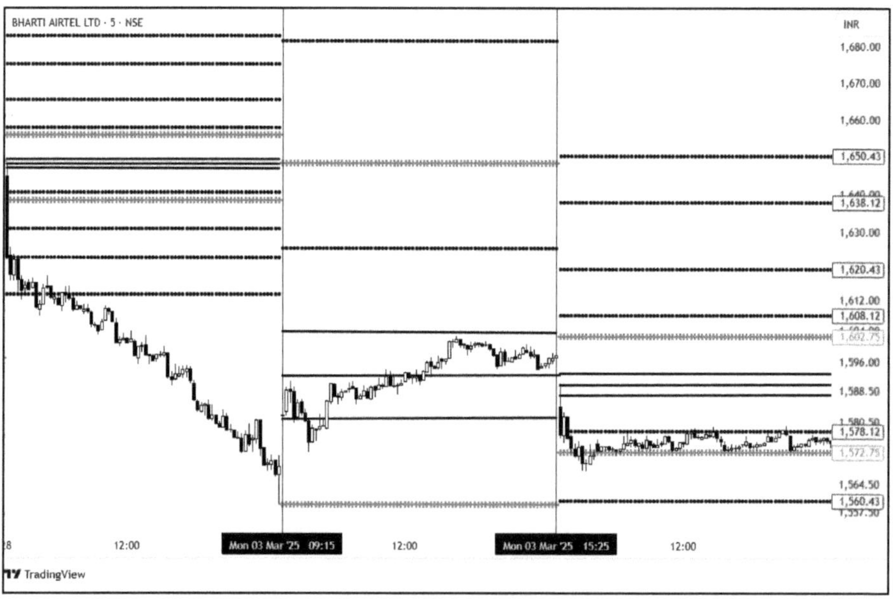

Fig. 4.29: *5-minute chart of BHARTI AIRTEL LTD with Daily CPR levels*

Modified CPR Techniques for scalping

After you have practiced and gained comfort with intraday trading using the 5-minute chart and daily CPR, you naturally build the reflexes needed for quicker decision-making. Some traders at this stage seek even faster opportunities. This is where scalping comes into play. Scalping takes the speed and precision of intraday trading to the next level, focusing on capturing very small price movements within extremely short timeframes. While the principles of CPR remain the same, the execution becomes sharper, quicker, and more disciplined. Let us now explore how Modern CPR techniques can be adapted for high-speed scalping setups. This table 4.5 breaks down how to trade these high-speed setups using Hourly and Daily CPR to stay on the right side of momentum.

Table 4.4: *Scalping Using Hourly CPR with Daily bias*

Daily CPR	Hourly CPR	Setup	Suggested Position Size
Above	Above	Strong Bullish	Full Position (100%)
Below	Below	Strong Bearish	Full Position (100%)
Below	Above	Bullish	Medium Position (50-75%)
Above	Below	Bearish	Medium Position (50-75%)
Inside	Above/Below	Weak Bullish/Bearish	Less Position (25-50%)
Inside	Inside	No Clear Signal	Avoid Trade

DAILY CPR ↑ | HOURLY CPR ↑

For scalping, we shift to even shorter time frames like the 3-minute charts, while anchoring our decisions using the CPR levels from the 75-min chart. Before entering any scalp trade, it is important to quickly check two key structures: the daily CPR and the hourly CPR.

If both are aligned with your intended trade direction, it adds extra strength to your setup. For example, if you are planning a quick long scalp, it is better if the price is trading above both the daily and hourly CPR levels. In scalping, we do not need to check the monthly or weekly CPR, because trades are opened and closed within a few minutes. Our focus is purely on the immediate structures that influence short bursts of momentum. This simple alignment increases the probability of success by ensuring you are trading with the immediate momentum rather than against it. Even though scalping happens at high speed, taking a few seconds to check this alignment can save you from chasing weak trades and improve your win rate over time.

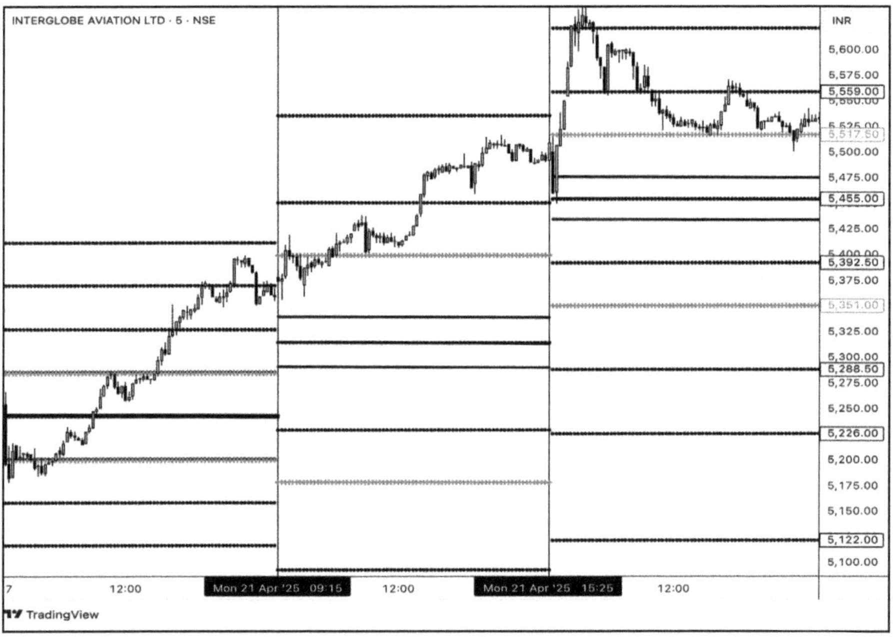

Fig. 4.30: 5-minute chart of INTERGLOBE AVIATION LTD with Daily CPR levels

Fig. 4.31: 3-minute chart of INTERGLOBE AVIATION LTD with Hourly CPR levels

DAILY CPR | HOURLY CPR

Similarly, if you are looking to execute a short scalp trading strategy, it is ideal to identify price points that are positioned below the Central Pivot Range (CPR) levels. This is because prices trading below these CPR levels often indicate a bearish trend or downward momentum in the market. In such conditions, there is a higher probability of quick price drops, which can be advantageous for short-term traders aiming to capitalize on small price fluctuations. By targeting entries below these critical levels, traders can enhance their chances of making profitable trades while minimizing potential risks associated with sudden market reversals.

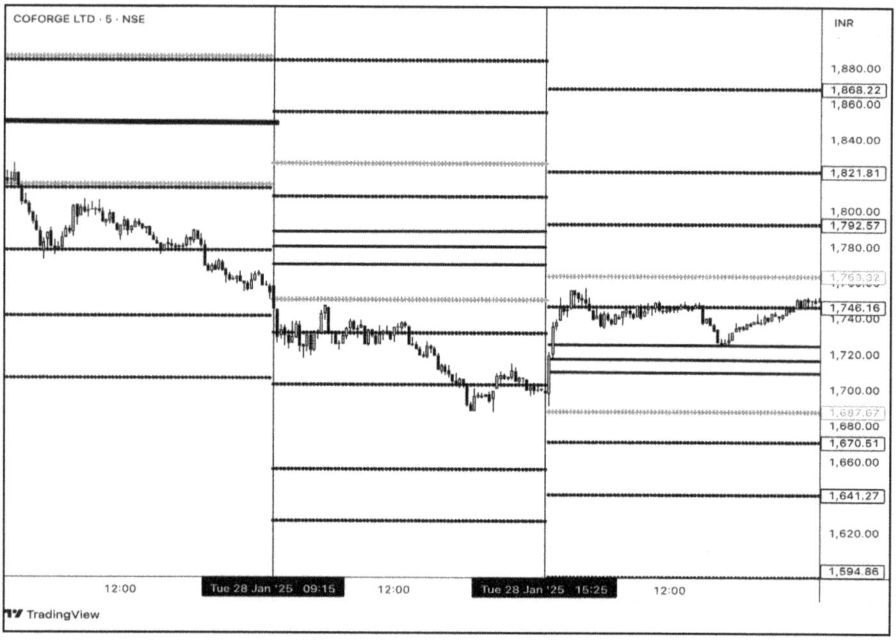

Fig. 4.32: 5-minute chart of COFORGE with Daily CPR levels

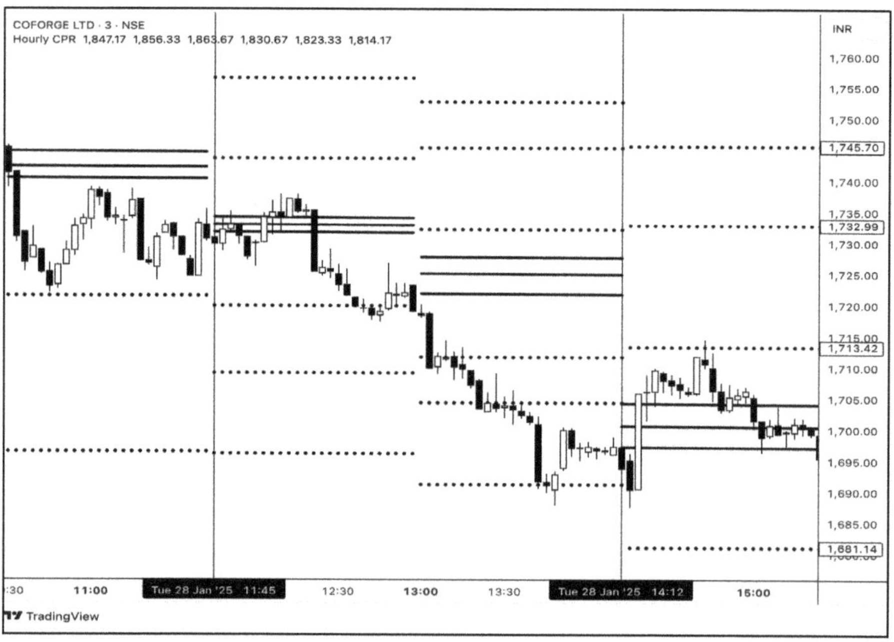

Fig. 4.33: 3-minute chart of COFORGE with Hourly CPR levels

DAILY CPR ⬇ | HOURLY CPR ⬆

In this setup, price is holding below the Daily CPR, showing overall intraday support. But at the same time, it is trading above the Hourly CPR, which signals long. Go with small position size to reduce the risk of this conflict.

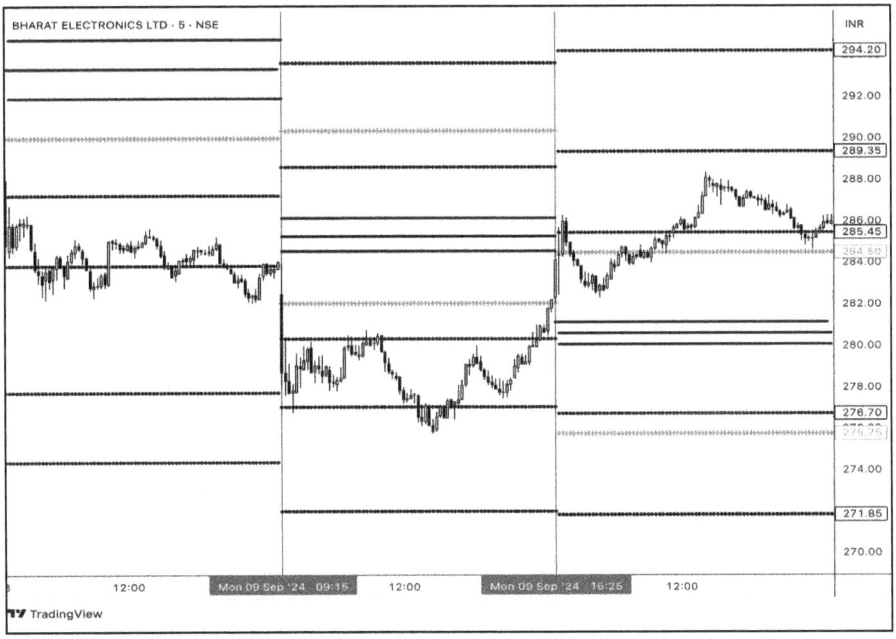

Fig. 4.34: 5-minute chart of BHARAT ELECTRONICS with Daily CPR levels

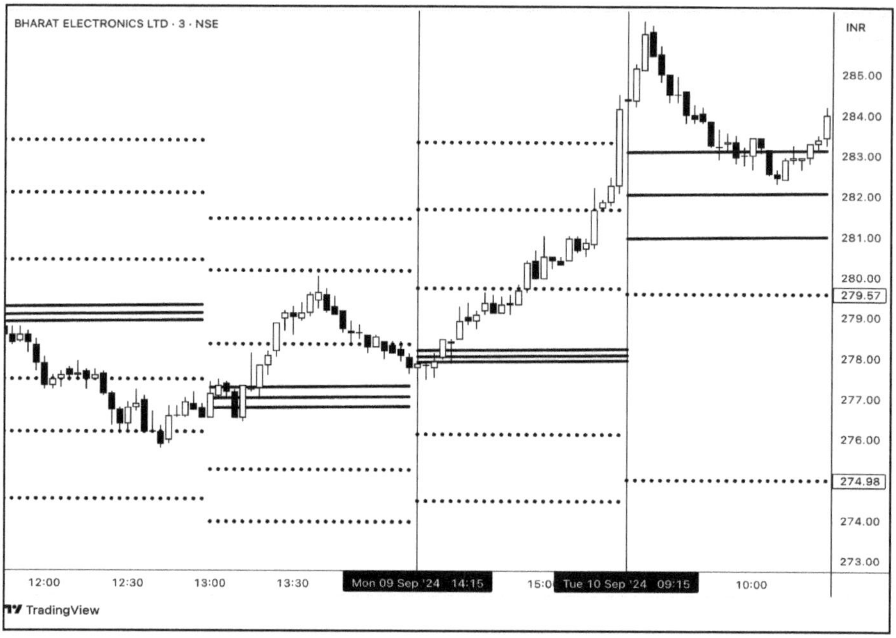

Fig. 4.35: 3-minute chart of BHARAT ELECTRONICS LTD with Hourly CPR levels

DAILY CPR ⬆ | HOURLY CPR ⬇

In this setup, price is holding above the Daily CPR, showing overall intraday support. But at the same time, it is trading below the Hourly CPR, which signals short. Go with small position size to reduce the risk of this conflict.

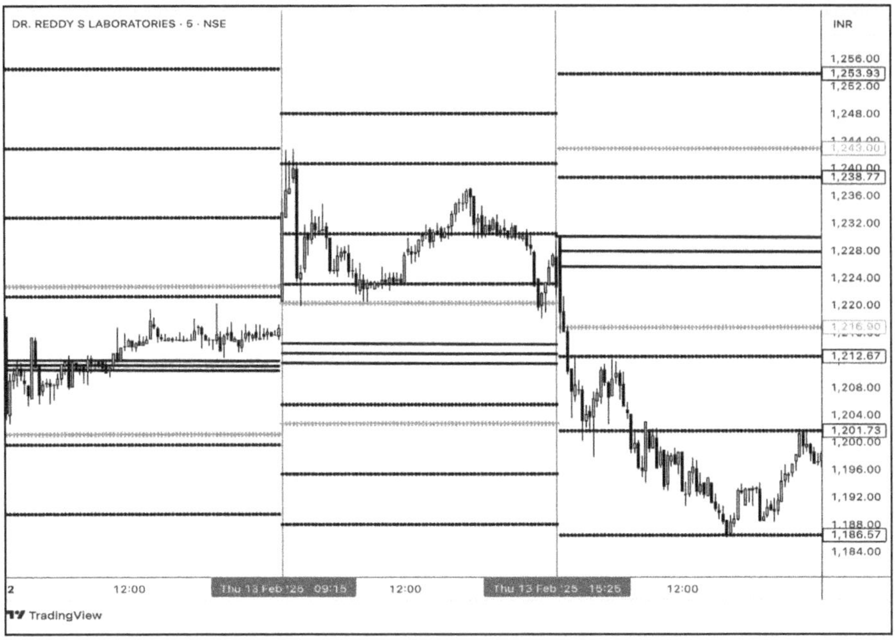

Fig. 4.36: *5-minute chart of DR.REDDY LABORATORIES with Daily CPR levels*

Fig. 4.37: *3-minute chart of DR.REDDY LABORATORIES with Hourly CPR levels*

DAILY CPR ⬄ | HOURLY CPR ⬆

This setup suggests quiet buildup with early signs of bullish intent. The Daily CPR is inside, which indicates a compressed structure, the market is waiting. However, the Hourly CPR is rising, showing that price is beginning to lean upward in the lower timeframe.

In this case, the best approach is to stay alert but not go aggressive. The market hasn't fully broken out, but the hourly structure gives a hint. You may consider small long scalps with tight stops, treating them as test trades. If price breaks above the Daily CPR range and holds above the Hourly CPR, that's your cue to scale up.

Until then, trade light and let the breakout confirm.

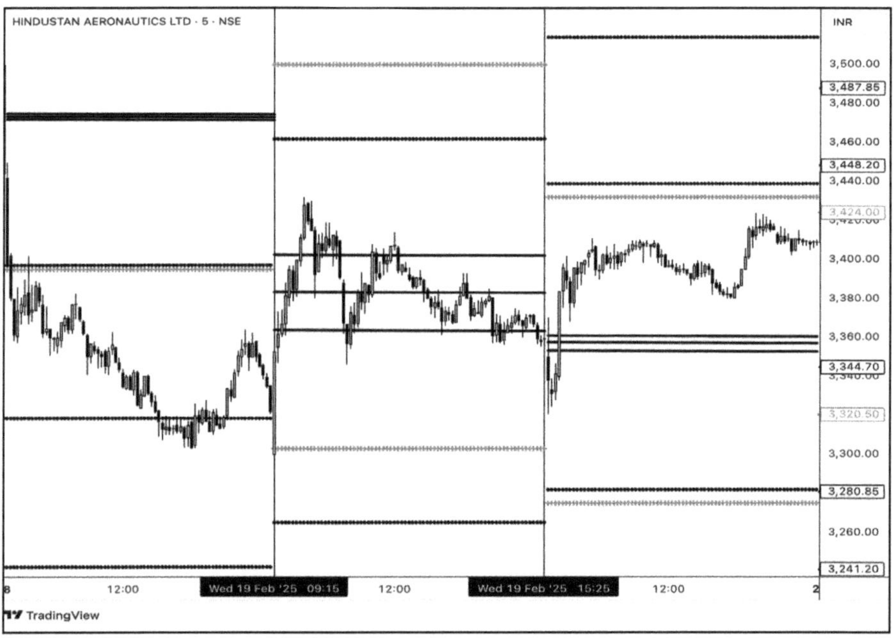

Fig. 4.38: 5-minute chart of HINDUSTAN AERONAUTICS LTD with Daily CPR levels

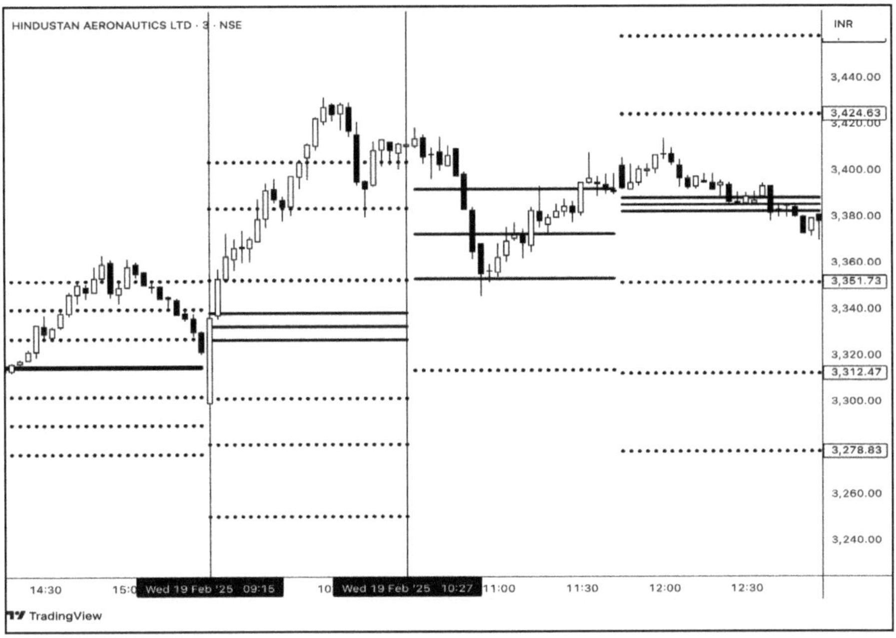

Fig. 4.39: *3-minute chart of HINDUSTAN AERONAUTICS LTD with Hourly CPR levels*

The Practice Session Begins

The CPR doesn't change. But how you approach it must. Whether you're holding for days or reacting in seconds, your time frame shapes not just your entries, it shapes your mindset. What looks like noise on a 3-minute chart might reveal structure on a daily one. The skill is in knowing when to zoom in, when to step back, and how to stay clear in both.

You now have the setup. You've learned how to align CPR with different formats. Now it's time to test it. But knowledge without practice means nothing. Before the big match, every player hits the nets. And now, it's your turn.

In the next chapter, we enter the practice session. Real charts. Real conditions. Clean setups. No pressure, just preparation. This is where you test what you've learned and build confidence through repetition.

Let's put CPR to work, and get ready for the real game.

Chapter 05

LEARNING THROUGH MARKET CASE STUDIES

The charts look clean on the weekend. The strategies make sense. Everything falls into place when the market is paused. But once the session begins, that clarity is the first to disappear. The market doesn't come with labels like "Narrow CPR breakout" or "Ascending structure, go long." No alerts. No signals. Just raw price ticking and shifting with no warning. In those early minutes, even seasoned traders find themselves hesitating, rushing, or reacting without structure. Because real trading is not just about knowing the setup. It's about executing it when everything is uncertain.

This chapter isn't here to reintroduce CPR. You already have the tools. The real test now is whether you can use them when the market is live and messy. Chapter 1 gave you a compass through market structure, the rhythm of higher highs and lower lows, and how demand and supply shape direction. Chapter 2 brought CPR into focus as the heartbeat of the market, where balance is tested and breakouts are born. Chapter 3 translated CPR structures into stories such as Narrow, Inside, Ascending, and Descending, each with its own message. And in Chapter 4, you discovered how CPR adapts across formats, from the calm of daily charts to the speed of scalping, helping you find your natural trading style.

Now, in Chapter 5, everything comes together. This is the bridge between knowing and doing. You've trained with net practice long enough. It's time to step into the middle. Pads on. Real deliveries coming at you. The setups you're about to see are not textbook diagrams. They are live-market moments. Setups that formed, failed, or flourished in real time. Our goal is not just to show what happened. It is to walk you through the exact lens a trader must carry. **What do I see? Where is the price? Is the structure helping me or warning me? What's my plan?** Here's the flow we'll follow:

To bring this to life, we'll walk through four real-world market scenarios, one each from NIFTY and SENSEX. Each chart tells a story of how CPR speaks in real time.

Case study 1 - NIFTY

STEP 1: Identify the market trend

From January to March, NIFTY stays in a clear downtrend. Lower highs and lower lows, just like we learned in Chapter 1 through Dow Theory. Sellers are in control and price keeps breaking previous lows without any real fight from buyers. But in April, that changes. Price stops making lower lows and starts forming higher highs and higher lows. That's our first clue. The downtrend is losing strength and a fresh uptrend is beginning to take shape. The structure is shifting and buyers are slowly stepping in.

Fig. 5.1: *NIFTY 50 showing trend direction*

STEP 2: Find the CPR type - Descending Trend Reversal

This shift is also clearly reflected in the CPR. From January to March 2023, CPR keeps forming lower each month, confirming the bearish sentiment. But April tells a different story. For the first time in months, price begins to stay above the CPR, signaling a possible trend reversal. Not just that, April forms a narrow CPR, which often signals a strong move. With this structure and behavior lining up, a bullish rally looks likely from here.

Fig. 5.2: *Nifty 50 Descending Trend Reversal on Daily Timeframe with Monthly CPR (Jan–Apr 2023)*

STEP 3: Choose your trading Style - Conservative Swing trader (Day chart - Monthly CPR)

We are having a narrow CPR and we are expecting a trending market. Now, in general, when prices are above CPR, our entry locations will be a bull candle taking support above CPR, or an R1 breakout, or an R2 breakout. In this scenario, the second day/candle of the month is slightly above CPR, which could be our entry aiming for a target at R1. Stop-loss can be planned below CPR or even below the entry candle.

If you're comfortable with conservative swing trading, you can stop with this Step-3. The structure has delivered its move, and the targets are achieved. There is no need to push further if your plan was to play it safe. Remember, a conservative swing trade holding period will be up to 20 trading days. If you feel the holding period is quite long and you want to be more active even as a swing trader, then you can shift to the next gear and become an aggressive swing trader.

***Fig. 5.3:** Ascending CPR Formation in Daily Timeframe with Monthly CPR (April–June 2023)*

STEP 4: Choose your trading Style - Aggressive Swing trader (75 mins - Weekly CPR)

As an aggressive swing trader, we are getting our entry in the last week of the April month. The CPR is not too narrow or too wide, a medium-sized CPR is in place, and the prices are comfortably taking support above the Weekly CPR, which will be our entry point for a target at Weekly R1, with a stop-loss below the Weekly CPR or below the entry bull candle. For someone who missed the entry at CPR, you can plan your entry once the Weekly R1 and PWH zone is broken, for a target at Weekly R2 and stop-loss below PWH or below the entry candle. In the latter entry, we are planning our stop-loss below PWH and not below Weekly R1 because your stop-loss might become big, and you may lose a huge chunk of money in case the trade goes wrong.

If you're comfortable with aggressive swing trading, you can stop with this Step-4. The structure has delivered its move, and the targets are achieved. There is no need to push further if your plan was to play it safe. Remember, an aggressive swing trade holding period will be up to 5 trading days. For someone who's only an intraday player, then proceed to the next step.

Fig. 5.4: *Ascending CPR Formation in 75-Minute Timeframe with Weekly CPR*

STEP 5: Choose your trading Style - Intraday Trading (5 mins - Daily CPR)

Now we shift gears into intraday mode. In a month, there are usually 20 trading days. You can take intraday trades almost every day, but not every day gives a quality setup. That's where structure helps. Days that open with a narrow CPR or an inside CPR can offer a big edge. These are the days where the market is preparing for a strong move, and if you're ready, you can catch it early.

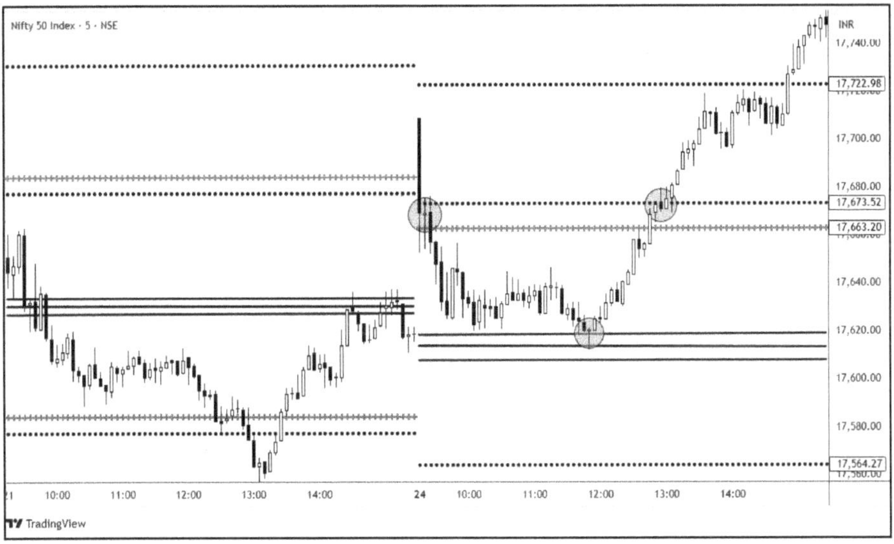

***Fig. 5.5:** Nifty 50 on 5-Minute Timeframe with Daily CPR*

The session opens above R1 with a gap-up, initially signaling strength. However, the bullish momentum fails to hold. A strong bearish reversal candle forms and closes below R1, creating a clear "CPR attract candle" setup, as explained in Chapter 3. The inability to sustain above R1, along with the sharp reversal, indicates that price is likely to move back toward the CPR. In this scenario, the target shifts to the CPR zone, and the stop-loss sits just above R1. This is not the only opportunity the market presents. After some time, a bullish engulfing pattern forms at the CPR zone, signaling renewed buying interest. This setup offers a second entry point, with R1 as the immediate target. If momentum picks up, the position can be trailed further toward R2, allowing the trade to capture extended upside potential.

If you're comfortable with intraday trades, you can stop with this step. The structure is complete, the entry is logical, and the plan is clear. No need to look beyond the session if your strategy is built for day trades. For intraday traders, positions are closed within the same day. But if you're someone who wants even more speed, tighter entries, and quick exits within an hour, then you're stepping into the scalper's zone.

STEP 6: Choose your trading Style - Scalping (3 mins - Hourly CPR)

This is where trading becomes rapid-fire. Scalping isn't for everyone. It demands sharp focus, real-time decision-making, and tight risk control. But for traders who thrive in the fast lane, this is the zone where opportunity meets intensity.

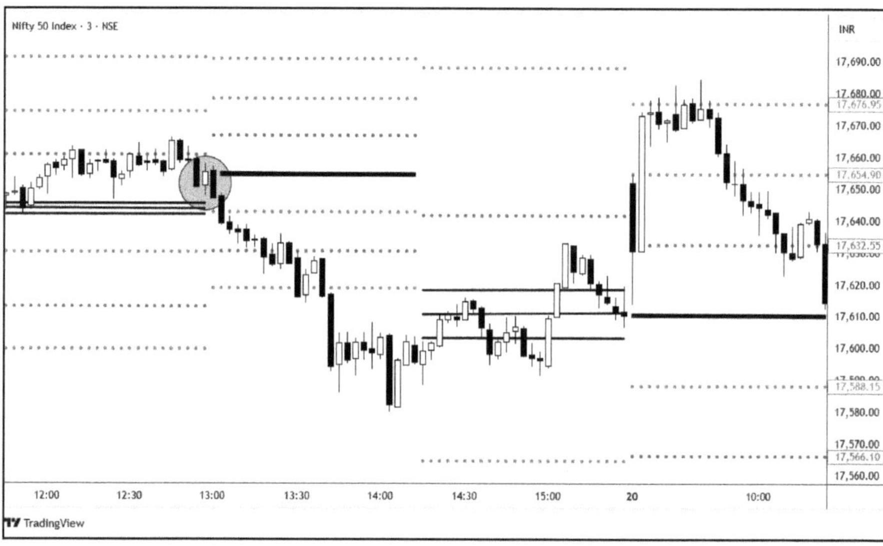

Fig. 5.6: Nifty 50 on 3-Minute Timeframe with Hourly CPR

A narrow CPR forms, indicating a potential for a sharp move, which is ideal for a scalping setup. On the 3-minute chart, a bearish candle closes below the CPR, signaling a possible breakdown. This candle provides the entry trigger. The stop-loss is placed just above the high of the entry candle to manage risk tightly. With CPR acting as a resistance zone and momentum building to the downside, the trade aims for extended intraday targets, first S2, and if selling pressure continues, a move toward S3 becomes likely. This setup aligns with the principles of CPR-based momentum scalping: quick entry, defined risk, and fast execution.

Case study 2 - SENSEX

STEP 1: Identify the market trend

From December to March 2024, SENSEX followed a clear downtrend. Price moved lower with ease, forming a clean series of Lower lows and lower highs. Each fall broke previous support levels, and every rise found strong selling interest. The momentum was with the bears, and the market structure supported it.

Fig. 5.7: *Sensex showing trend direction*

STEP 2: Find the CPR type - Descending CPR

The CPR signaled a shift before most traders noticed. In December and January, it had been falling steadily, aligning perfectly with the ongoing downtrend. Price continued to trade below the CPR, confirming bearish strength.

But in February, the CPR was narrow and descending, indicating potential for a strong move, but still in line with the overall bearish trend.

Fig. 5.8: *Sensex Descending Trend Reversal on Daily Timeframe by Monthly CPR (Jan–Mar 2025)*

STEP 3: Choose your trading Style - Conservative Swing trader (Day chart - Monthly CPR)

In the first week of February, the monthly candle opened above the CPR with a strong bullish push, tempting many traders to consider long entries. But despite that early move, the CPR was descending, a clear signal that the broader structure was still bearish.

As traders, we avoid going against the dominant direction. Unless price breaks above R1 or the previous month's high, there's no reason to chase a reversal. That early bullish move was likely a trap, a false breakout meant to shake out weak shorts. The real confirmation came in the second week. Price closed below the CPR with a strong bearish candle. That was our entry, with a target at S1 or S2, and a stop-loss placed just above the high of the bearish candle.

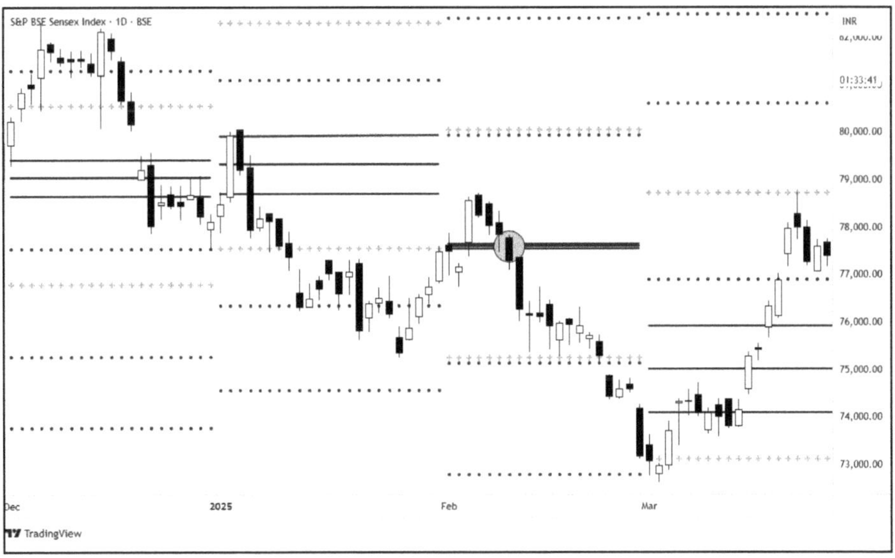

Fig. 5.9: *Sensex February Downtrend Confirmation on Daily Timeframe and Monthly CPR*

STEP 4: Choose your trading Style - Aggressive Swing trader (75 mins - Weekly CPR)

For an aggressive swing trader, February offered a clear opportunity on the 75-minute chart. The Monthly CPR was descending, and the overall trend remained bearish, even though the first few sessions showed strength. In the second week, price began to weaken. On the 75-minute chart, it closed below the Weekly CPR, signaling a shift in short-term momentum. That became the entry point, with a stop-loss just above the candle high and a target at Weekly S1. If momentum continued, the trade could extend toward Weekly S2. The move played out over 2 to 3 sessions, offering a clean, structured trade in the direction of the broader downtrend.

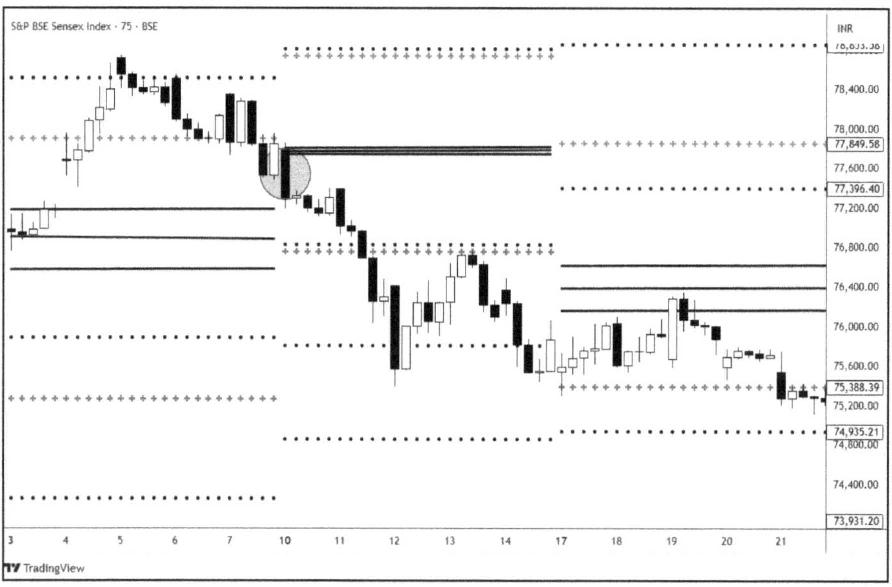

Fig. 5.10: Sensex on 75-Minute Chart with Weekly CPR (February)

STEP 5: Choose your trading Style - Intraday Trading (5 mins - Daily CPR)

Now we shift gears into intraday mode.

When the Monthly and Weekly CPRs are both bearish, your intraday bias should remain on the short side. The structure is aligned, and your job is to wait for price to offer a clean opportunity. When price opens below the Daily CPR, the bias is already negative. Watch how price behaves near the Previous Day Low (PDL). If PDL gets broken with a strong bearish candle, that becomes your entry point. The trend is continuing, and momentum is in your favor. Place your stop-loss just above the high of the breakdown candle. Your first target is S2, and if the price continues to fall, extend your target to S3. This way, you're trailing your profits.

If you're entering late near S2, adjust your plan. Don't enter with full size, reduce your position size because the reward-to-risk ratio has compressed. You're closer to the target and your stop might be wider.

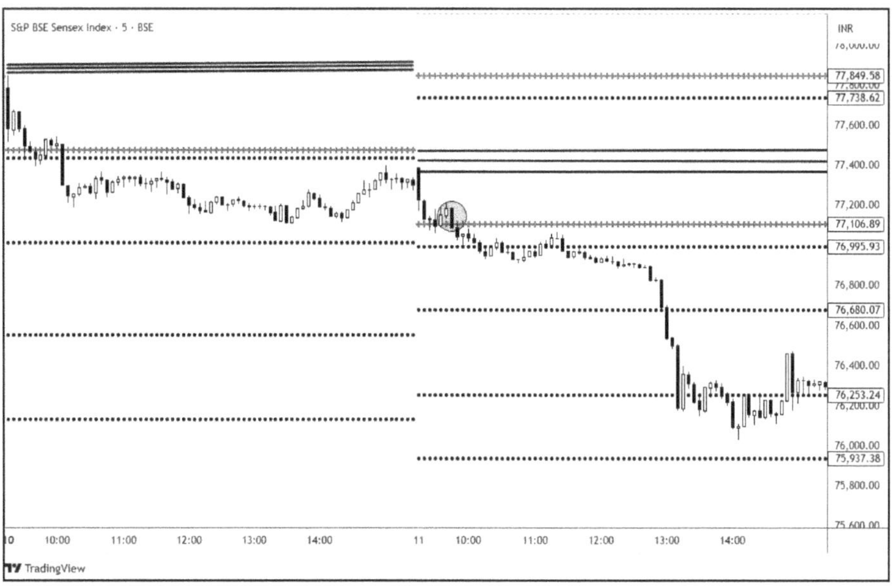

Fig. 5.11: *Sensex on 5-Minute Timeframe with Daily CPR*

STEP 6: Choose your trading Style - Scalping (3 mins - Hourly CPR)

When the Daily CPR is bearish, the structure favors shorts, and as a scalper, it's better to stay on the short side. You're not here to fight the trend, you're here to catch the quick, decisive moves that happen in its direction. On February 11, the price opened below the CPR and immediately began to slide. On the 3-minute chart, it broke below the CPR cleanly in the opening minutes, offering an early scalping entry. The setup was simple: enter on breakdown, keep a tight stop-loss above CPR, and aim for S2 or even S3 as targets.

This early move gave a strong start to the session, but it wasn't the only opportunity. Around mid-day, Price once again pulled back and tested the CPR zone from below. It failed to break through and formed a weak rejection candle. That became the second scalping opportunity. Entry was taken below the candle, stop-loss stayed above the CPR, and the trade once again moved cleanly toward support levels.

Fig. 5.12: Sensex on 3-Minute Timeframe with Hourly CPR

Case study 3 - NIFTY IT

STEP 1: Identify the market trend

Through November and December, NIFTY IT moves in a strong uptrend. Price forms higher highs and higher lows, with buyers staying in control. Every pullback finds support, and momentum continues to build as the index climbs steadily.

But in January, the pace begins to slow. Price starts reacting near previous highs, and the clean upside rhythm loses strength. Breakouts turn weak, and candles show hesitation. The trend doesn't reverse sharply, but it shifts. What looked like a confident move now starts to flatten, showing early signs of exhaustion.

Fig. 5.13: *Nifty IT showing trend direction*

STEP 2: Find the CPR type - Ascending Trend Reversal

The strong uptrend from November to January is also reflected in the CPR structure. CPR keeps shifting higher each month, forming a clean ascending pattern. Price moves in sync, staying above CPR zones and reacting with strength. The setup remains healthy, and buyers stay in control throughout this period.

But in January, the rhythm starts to break. The market turns choppy. Price begins hovering around the CPR instead of bouncing cleanly. There's hesitation near the highs, and the candles lose their earlier momentum. Even though CPR continues to rise, price no longer shows the same conviction.

And in February, the structure shifts again. CPR starts forming lower, marking the beginning of a descending pattern. This confirms what the price action had already been hinting. The uptrend has lost steam, and the market is now showing early signs of a trend reversal.

Fig. 5.14: *Nifty IT Ascending Trend Reversal on Daily Timeframe with Monthly CPR (Nov - Feb 2025)*

STEP 3: Choose your trading Style - Conservative Swing trader (Day chart - Monthly CPR)

With price losing momentum in January and CPR still rising, this becomes a classic ascending trend reversal setup. The structure shows strength, but the price stops following through. When the February CPR opens lower for the first time in months, it confirms the shift. The market is no longer in a strong uptrend.

On the daily chart, price breaks below the monthly CPR zone in early February. That break, combined with a lower CPR, gives us the entry trigger. A strong bearish candle closing below the CPR becomes the confirmation. Entry is planned on that close, with a stop-loss just above the CPR zone or above the high of the entry candle. The first target is the support zone near S1, and if momentum continues, a further move toward S2 can be expected.

Fig. 5.15: Nifty IT Downtrend Confirmation in February on Daily Timeframe with Monthly CPR

STEP 4: Choose your trading Style - Aggressive Swing trader (75 mins - Weekly CPR)

The shift that starts on the daily chart becomes even clearer on the 75-minute timeframe. In the second week of February, price begins to trade below the Weekly CPR. After a brief pullback toward the zone, price fails to reclaim it and starts moving lower. That breakdown confirms the weakness already seen in the broader structure.

Entry is planned once price slips below the CPR zone, with a stop-loss just above the CPR or above the recent swing high. The first target is Weekly S1, and if momentum builds, the trade can be extended toward S2. The 75-minute chart offers a balanced view, fast enough to react early but still clear enough to follow the structure. The holding period stays short, typically 3 to 5 trading days, making it an ideal setup for active swing traders.

Fig. 5.16: Nifty IT on 75-Minute Chart with Weekly CPR

STEP 5: Choose your trading Style - Intraday Trading (5 mins - Daily CPR)

Now it's your turn to read the pulse and respond.

Price opens below the Daily CPR and then comes the break. S1 is taken out with a strong red candle. This is not a casual dip. It's intent. That's your moment.

You take the short position just below S1 and stoploss just above the high of the breakdown candle or above S1, keeping the risk tight and focused. Once the trade is active, the chart starts doing its job. There's no dramatic reversal or noisy reaction. Price flows downward with momentum, moving steadily toward S2. You begin to trail your stop, locking in partial gains as the market continues to reward your structure-based entry. Eventually, the move extends all the way to S3, delivering a full-range intraday breakdown.

Fig. 5.17: Nifty IT on 5-Minute Timeframe with Daily CPR

STEP 6: Choose your trading Style - Scalping (3 mins - Hourly CPR)

The Daily CPR is already sloping down, and the Hourly CPR confirms the weakness. The first hour shows a wide, indecisive range, but in the second hour, the CPR tightens, revealing built-up pressure and setting the stage for a sharp breakout.

A strong bearish candle below CPR. You enter short just below this candle, with a stop-loss just above the hourly CPR.

What follows is fast and clean. Price breaks S2 and keeps going. No pause, no hesitation. The momentum takes it straight to S3, but the story doesn't end there. This isn't a standard move. This is a momentum extension, and NIFTY IT continues sliding beyond S3. As a scalper, you trail your stop, book partial profits at every level, and let the rest ride the fall.

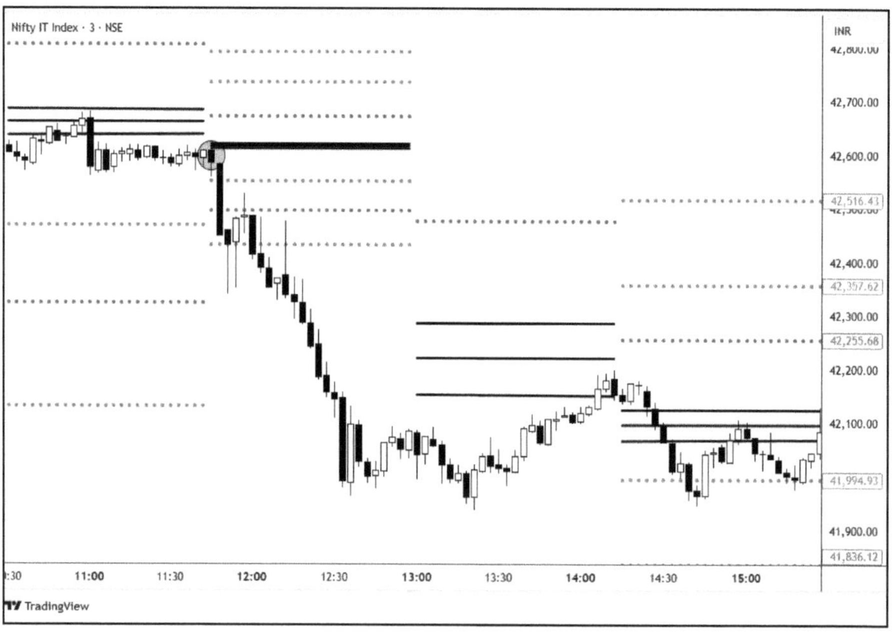

Fig. 5.18: Nifty IT on 3-Minute Timeframe with Hourly CPR

Case study 4 - NIFTY FMCG

STEP 1: Identify the market trend

From August to mid-September, the Nifty FMCG Index moves with strength, carving out higher highs and higher lows. Buyers stay firmly in control, and each dip finds eager support, pushing prices higher with confidence. But as September ends, something shifts. The rally stalls, and the index fails to reach new highs. What once looked like a strong uptrend begins to unravel. October brings deeper drops, with each bounce fading faster than the last. Lower highs and lower lows start to take shape, and the momentum clearly tilts in favor of the sellers. By mid-November, there's a flicker of hope, a sharp bounce from the lows, but it doesn't last. Price only climbs back to earlier breakdown levels, meets resistance, and stalls. Rejection sets in, and the index slips once more, continuing its descent with the downtrend firmly intact.

Fig. 5.19: *Nifty FMCG showing trend direction*

STEP 2: Find the CPR type - Ascending Trend Reversal

From the chart, we observe that August and September show an ascending CPR, with candles consistently forming above it, indicating strong bullish momentum. In October, the shift begins. The CPR continues to rise, but candles start forming below it, signaling early signs of trend exhaustion and a possible reversal. The price action changes, and the CPR says the same, both hinting at a weakening trend.

Fig. 5.20: *Nifty FMCG Ascending Trend Reversal on Daily Timeframe by Monthly CPR (Aug – Nov 2024)*

STEP 3: Choose your trading Style - Conservative Swing trader (Day chart - Monthly CPR)

As a conservative trader, the key entry signal appears in October when a shooting star candle forms after price crosses below the CPR zone. This pattern forming below the CPR aligns with a potential trend reversal. The entry point is just below the low of the shooting star candle, and the stop-loss is set above its high.

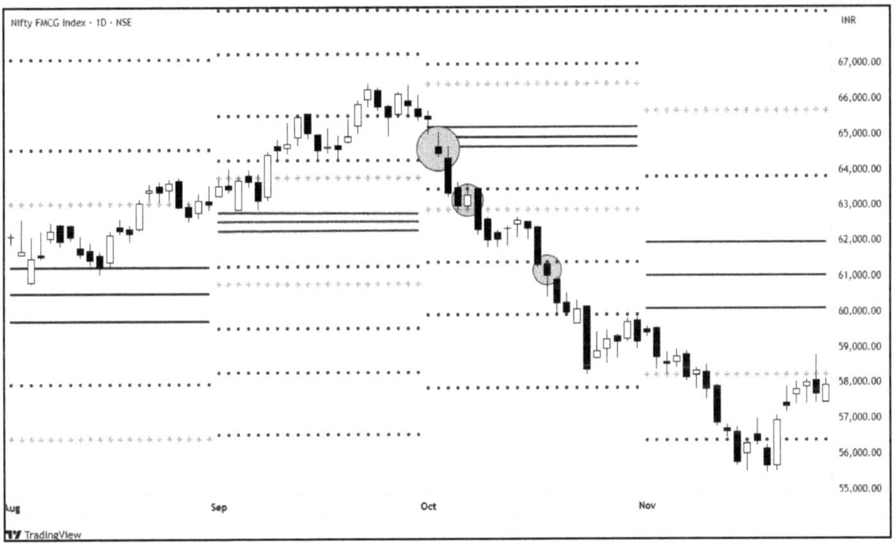

Fig. 5.21: *Nifty FMCG Downtrend Confirmation in October on Daily Timeframe with Monthly CPR*

STEP 4: Choose your trading Style - Aggressive Swing trader (75 mins - Weekly CPR)

For the aggressive swing trader, the opportunity came earlier than it did for the conservative setups. Price broke down below a narrow Weekly CPR, a structure that signaled built-up pressure ready to release. The entry was taken on the close of the 75-minute bearish candle that broke below the Weekly CPR. Stop-loss was placed just above the high of that breakdown candle or slightly above the CPR zone to protect against false reversals. At this point, while conservative traders were still waiting near the Monthly CPR for confirmation, the early structure had already offered a clean edge. With momentum in place, price continued its fall and extended all the way to S3, delivering a solid move for traders who trusted the structure and acted without hesitation.

Fig. 5.22: Nifty FMCG Swing Trade Setup on 75-Minute Chart by Weekly CPR

STEP 5: Choose your trading Style - Intraday Trading (5 mins - Daily CPR)

The structure was clear right from the open. Price started trading below the CPR, showing early signs of bearish intent. The breakdown came around mid-morning. Price slipped below S1 with a strong red candle, marking the first clean intraday short. The CPR was narrow, the path to the downside was open, and the structure fully supported the move. Entry was taken below S1, with stop-loss placed just above S1 or above the breakdown candle's high. The move extended lower, and by the time price approached S2, traders had two options. If you entered near S1, this was a perfect zone to book partial profits. If you missed the first entry, this was your second chance. Price hovered near S2 with a tight structure, offering a reduced-risk entry. Trade was taken near S2, with smaller position size and a stop-loss just above the minor pullback.

From there, price didn't just stop at S3, it continued sliding further, making it a strong day for structured intraday trading.

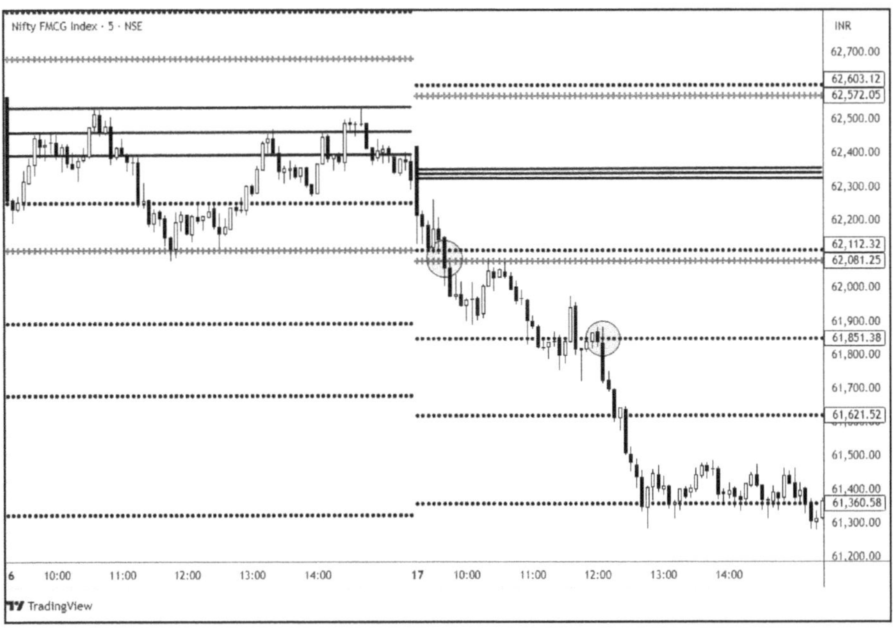

Fig. 5.23: *Nifty FMCG on 5-Minute Timeframe with Daily CPR*

STEP 6: Choose your trading Style - Scalping (3 mins - Hourly CPR)

The day began with a narrow Hourly CPR on the 3-minute chart, a clear sign to get ready. But despite the compression, the surrounding levels told a different story. Support and resistance levels were far apart. The structure had gaps, the range was too wide, and price had too much room to roam without a clean entry. For a scalper, this meant one thing: wait. No early triggers, no forced trades. Then came the second hour. Again, a narrow CPR formed, but this time, the structure was tighter. Price had coiled closer to key levels, and the space between CPR and support zones had compressed. The breakout was clean. A sharp bearish candle sliced below the second Hourly CPR. This was the entry.

The setup aligned perfectly. Entry was taken just below the CPR, with stop-loss placed just above the candle high or above the CPR. Momentum kicked in quickly. Price dropped straight to S2, and it extended all the way to S3 and didn't stop there. It extended even further, offering scalpers a clean, high-reward trade within minutes. This is the kind of move where structure, timing, and speed come together. If you were ready, the market rewarded you without hesitation. Two narrow CPRs in a row don't always mean back-to-back action. Sometimes, the first builds tension and the second delivers the breakout. Scalping is all about knowing the difference and waiting for the one that's ready to move.

Across NIFTY, SENSEX, NIFTY IT, and NIFTY Pharma, you've now seen how CPR guides traders at every level, from calm monthly swing setups to rapid-fire scalps. Each example told a different story, but the message stayed the same: structure leads, not emotions. The patterns are real, the decisions are grounded, and the outcomes are shaped by clarity, not guesswork.

***Fig. 5.24:** Nifty FMCG on 3-Minute Timeframe with Hourly CPR*

Final Thoughts: CPR Doesn't Just Guide, It Leads

This chapter proves that the best traders aren't the ones who guess right. They're the ones who prepare right. CPR doesn't predict the future. It organizes the present. It shows you where to wait, where to watch, and where to act. When you combine CPR with structure and timeframes, trading stops being noise and starts becoming narrative. Every setup becomes a story. Your job isn't to predict the ending, it's to read clearly and respond with precision.

So, is CPR a team player?

Absolutely. It doesn't just stand beside other tools, it leads them. Think of CPR as the captain. It sets the field, calls the direction, and guides the entire team with clarity. Indicators like Super trend, RSI, or MACD? They're the supporting players. They don't lead the strategy, they follow it. When CPR gives the green signal, they step in to offer confirmation, not confusion. CPR brings discipline to the chart. It builds the foundation.

In the next chapter, you'll see how this captain forms a team, turning structure into setup and setups into execution. When the leader is strong, the rest fall in line. That's how consistent trades are built.

Chapter 06

THE POWER OF CONFLUENCE: CPR MEETS OTHER INDICATORS

There comes a point in every trader's journey when simplicity becomes power. In the early days, it's easy to believe that the secret to success lies in having more indicators, more setups, and more signals. It feels like the more tools we add, the safer we become. But real trading teaches a different lesson. It shows us that clarity wins. And one tool, when deeply understood, can be enough to trade with skill and confidence. For most traders who learn to trust CPR, it is more than sufficient.

We don't add indicators to fill space. We use them to sharpen clarity, not to seek confirmation out of fear, and not to create doubt, but to reinforce confidence built on structure. Tools like Super trend, RSI, and MACD do not replace CPR. They act as silent companions, offering supporting evidence when a trade is setting up or providing additional comfort when holding a position. They are not crutches. They are used to sharpen what CPR already shows, without disturbing the clarity of the original setup. Use them wisely. Apply them only when necessary. And always let CPR lead the way.

One of the biggest mistakes traders make when trying to combine tools is overloading the chart. The goal is not to find more reasons to enter a trade, but to build conviction around the existing setup. Think of CPR as the framework. Once that structure is clear, ask a simple question: "Does any other tool agree with what CPR is showing me?"

If the answer is yes, you've added strength. If the answer is no, you don't need to force it. Adding indicators should never override what CPR is already suggesting. The best combinations happen when structure and momentum speak the same language.

CPR and Super Trend - To Ride the Trend

Before we dive deeper, let's understand what Super trend really is.

Super trend is a trend following indicator that reacts to price volatility. It plots a line, either above or below the price, depending on whether the trend is bearish or bullish. When the price closes above the Super trend line, the trend flips bullish. When it falls below, the trend turns bearish. The color change on the chart, usually green for bullish and red for bearish, makes trend direction visually easy to track.

But here's the key, it works best when combined with a solid setup, not on its own. Super trend is especially effective on lower time frames like the 5-minute or 15-minute chart, which makes it a preferred choice for intraday traders. When a CPR breakout is followed by a Super trend flip, it is not a signal to enter. It is a green light to stay in. It says, "Yes, the momentum agrees with your setup." This gives you emotional comfort, especially during volatility when your instincts might tell you to exit too early.

But remember this golden rule:

Super trend follows CPR, not the other way around. Let CPR show you the trade. Let Super trend give you the confidence to ride it longer. To better understand how CPR and Super trend complement each other, the following charts illustrate this combination in real market conditions. These examples highlight how Super trend strengthens CPR-based setups, offering clarity during volatile phases and helping traders stay confidently in the trade.

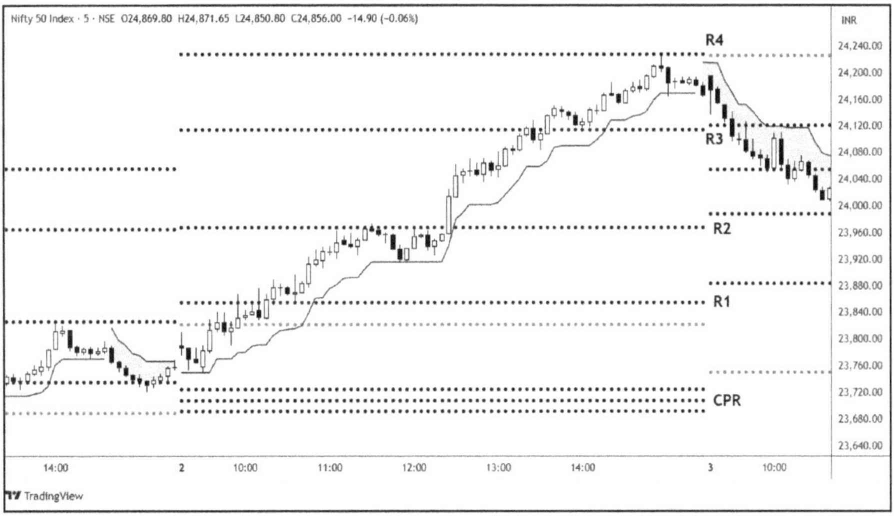

***Fig. 6.1:** NIFTY 50 Breakout Above R1 in 5 Min Time Frame with Daily CPR*

The market opened strong, right above the Central Pivot Range. That alone was a sign to pay attention. When price starts above the CPR, it often means buyers are holding the early advantage. In the opening candles, price stayed firm, refusing to dip back into the CPR zone. That kind of behavior tells you the bulls are not just present but they are in control. During this early move, Super trend quietly flipped from red to green. It didn't scream for a trade. It simply agreed with what CPR was already showing.

Then came the real confirmation. Price broke above the previous day's high with clean momentum. For a trader watching this unfold, everything was lining up.

> ***The CPR gave structure,***
> ***the breakout gave the entry,***
> ***and Super trend offered quiet support, a nudge that said,***
> ***"Yes, you're on the right side."***

Such a combination increases conviction. Traders who waited for CPR structure first, followed by Super trend confirmation, and then the previous day's high breakout, were rewarded with a high-probability move supported by momentum and structure.

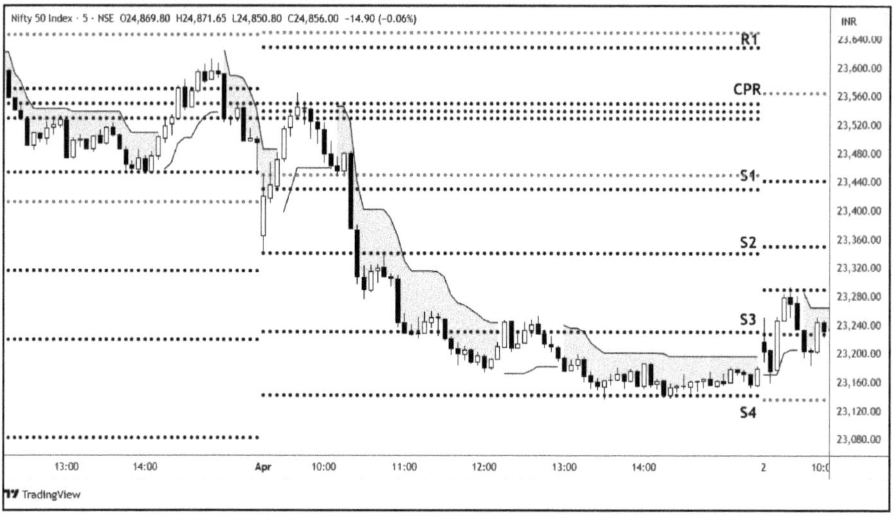

Fig. 6.2: *NIFTY 50 Breakdown Below CPR in 5 Min Time Frame with Daily CPR*

The price opened with a gap-down, below the CPR, which usually means sellers are in control. But the first 5-minute candle was bullish. It looked like the bulls were trying to make a comeback. For a moment, it felt like they had woken up after a short nap and were ready to fight back. But once Price touched the CPR, it struggled. The zone acted like a strong barrier. Sellers took control again, and the price started falling.

Soon after, it broke below the previous day's low, and Super trend flipped red, adding more weight to the bearish move. The breakdown was clear. CPR had done its job as resistance, and the trade setup became strong.

This setup teaches an important lesson. Don't get fooled by the first candle alone. Focus on the structure. In this case, CPR stayed above, the previous day's low gave way, and Super trend aligned with the breakdown. All signs pointed in one direction, down.

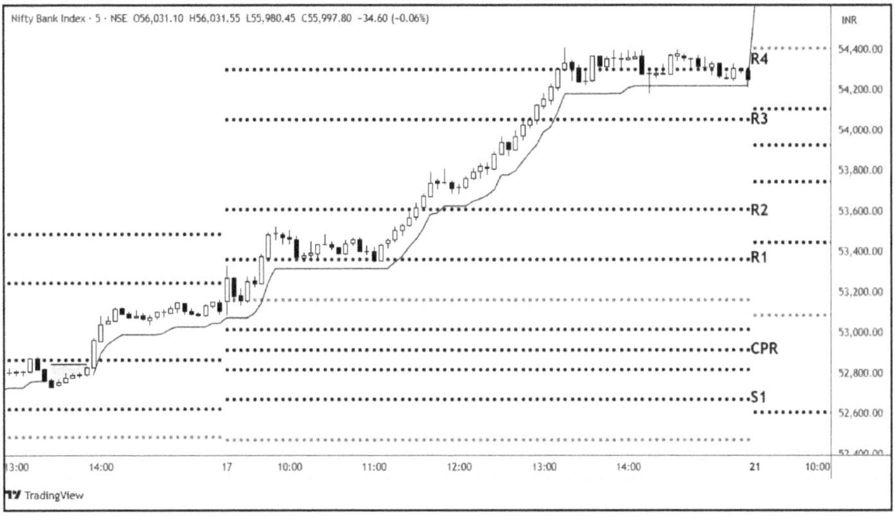

Fig. 6.3: *NIFTY 50 Breakout Above R1 in 5 Min Time Frame with Daily CPR*

The market opened with strong momentum, not just above the Central Pivot Range, but also above the previous day's high. That kind of open instantly puts traders on alert. It signals that buyers are already in control and the market may be gearing up for a trend day.

From the very first candle, price stayed above both the CPR and the previous day's high. There were no signs of weakness or any pullback to test support. The breakout had already started at the open, and price was simply continuing its upward path.

As the session progressed, the stock did pause and consolidate for a while, but what stood out was that even during this sideways phase, price remained above the CPR and R1. That told us the trend was not broken, just taking a breather. No breakdown, no panic, just controlled movement within strength.

Super trend remains green throughout, silently tracking the uptrend. In such scenarios, Super trend becomes a helpful tool to trail your stop loss. It allows you to stay in the trade longer and manage risk as the trend unfolds.

CPR and RSI - To Spot the Reversal

RSI (Relative Strength Index) is a simple momentum tool. It doesn't give trade signals by itself, but it does offer valuable insight into how strong or weak the price action is when it interacts with CPR levels.

Unlike Super trend, which helps with trend-following and trailing stop clarity, RSI is about internal strength. It tells us whether price moves are happening with real power or just fizzling out.

Here's how we use it:

- When RSI climbs above 70 and price approaches key resistances like R1 or the previous day's high, it often signals that the buying pressure is stretched. If the price fails to sustain above those levels, CPR attracts candle gets activated, and price starts drifting back toward the CPR zone.
- Likewise, when RSI dips below 30 and price nears S1 or the previous day's low, it hints at seller exhaustion. If the price shows hesitation or a reversal near these supports, CPR once again begins to attract the candles, pulling price back toward equilibrium.

The key point is that RSI doesn't lead the trade. It plays a supporting role. It helps us assess the quality of the move happening around CPR levels. While CPR defines the zones, RSI shows us the energy behind price as it reaches those levels. This dynamic between CPR structure and RSI strength gives traders a clear map, not just of where price might go, but whether it has the energy to stay there.

In this chart, price was in a clear downtrend and steadily moved toward the S1 support level. The sellers looked in control, and the move seemed strong on the surface. But a closer look revealed something important. RSI was already near oversold territory.

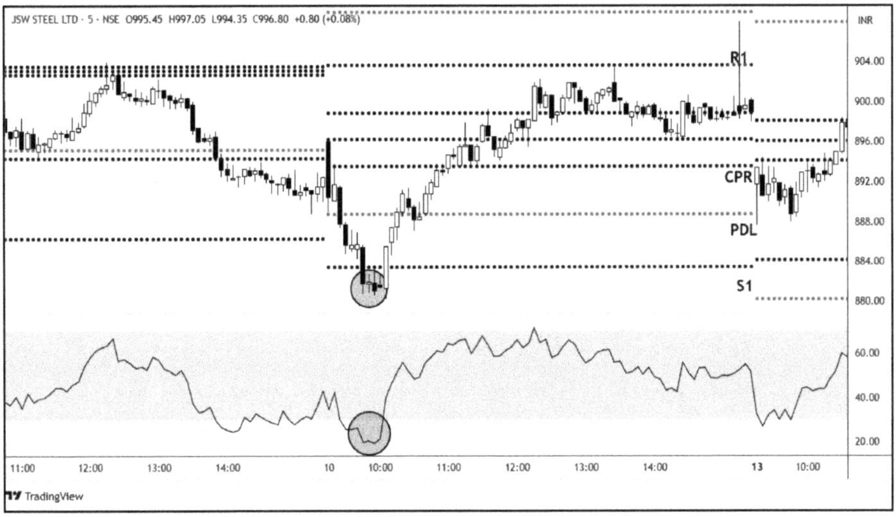

***Fig. 6.4:** BANKNIFTY reversal from S1 in 5 mins time frame with daily CPR*

As price reached S1, RSI dipped below 20, signaling that the selling pressure might be losing steam. Shortly after, a bullish candle formed right at the S1 level. This was not just a technical bounce, it was a moment where structure and momentum came together.

CPR had already mapped out the broader market bias, but S1 acted as a strong intraday support. The oversold RSI added weight to the idea that a reversal could be on the table. Traders who observed this confluence had a high-probability long setup, with a clear entry, stop below S1, and targets toward CPR or higher.

This example shows how RSI does not trigger trades on its own, but when paired with key support levels like S1, it helps confirm when the market might be ready to turn.

Fig. 6.5: NIFTY Reversal from R1 in 5 mins time frame with daily CPR levels

In this chart, the stock had been trending upward through the morning, making higher highs with strong momentum. Price eventually approached the R1 level, which often acts as an intraday resistance point. This move looked strong at first glance, but the internal strength was telling a different story.

As price neared R1, RSI was already in the overbought zone. It had climbed above 70, signaling that the market might be stretched. While candles were still green, the strength behind them was fading. The move started to slow down, with smaller candles and wicks forming near the top. Then came the turning point. Price failed to close convincingly above R1, and a bearish candle appeared, rejecting the level. At the same time, RSI began to fall back below 70, confirming that momentum was weakening.

This is where CPR and RSI together told the full story. CPR provided the structure, a market that had already moved far from its base. R1 acted as a barrier. RSI exposed the exhaustion within the trend. For traders, this was a cue to shift their mindset. Instead of chasing the trend, it was time to look for signs of reversal. Whether taking profits on longs or preparing for a potential short, the message was clear. The uptrend was losing steam. And when such exhaustion sets in, price often starts drifting back toward its base. CPR attracts candles, acting like a magnet that pulls price back toward equilibrium when momentum fades.

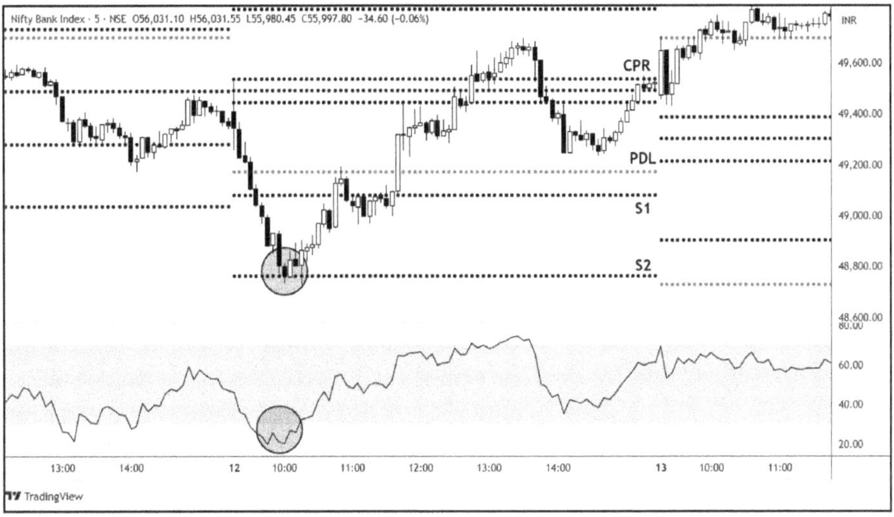

Fig. 6.6: *BANKNIFTY reversal from S2 in 5 mins time frame with daily CPR*

In this session, the market opened on a weak note and continued to slide during the initial phase. Within the first hour, price dropped rapidly and tested the S2 support level. The fall was steep, and on the surface, it appeared as though the day might turn into a complete breakdown.

But RSI was telling a different story.

While price action looked aggressive, RSI had already entered the oversold zone. This was an early sign that the sellers might be running out of strength. The candles were red, but the energy behind them was fading.

At the S1 level, the price printed a decisive bullish candle, a clear rejection of the downside. This was not a random bounce, but one that came after a deep drop, near a known support, and with momentum exhaustion showing through RSI.

For a trader watching closely, this was a moment to pause, not panic. The market had dropped fast, but instead of chasing the fall, this setup gave a reason to look the other way. The reversal was supported by context, behavior, and confirmation, a solid base for a long opportunity back toward CPR levels.

This move is a reminder that structure shows us where to look, but momentum helps us decide when to act.

CPR and MACD - To Confirm Momentum Shift

MACD (Moving Average Convergence Divergence) is a momentum indicator that helps us understand the strength and direction behind price movements. It doesn't generate trades on its own, but when combined with CPR, it adds powerful confirmation to our analysis.

Unlike Super trend, which follows trend direction visually, and RSI, which gauges strength based on overbought or oversold zones, MACD focuses on momentum shifts. It reveals whether a breakout has strength behind it or if a move is losing steam.

Here's how we use it:

When MACD shows a bullish crossover and the histogram begins expanding as price breaks above the CPR or approaches key resistances like R1 or the previous day's high, it signals strong upward momentum. This confirms that the breakout has energy, and traders can hold the position with confidence.

However, if MACD starts to flatten or show a bearish crossover near these resistance zones, even if price is still above CPR, it acts as an early warning. If momentum fades and the breakout lacks follow-through, CPR attracts candle gets activated, and price often pulls back toward the central pivot zone.

Likewise, when MACD shows a bearish crossover and the histogram turns negative near S1 or the previous day's low, it reinforces the bearish structure. But if price nears these supports and MACD starts showing signs of recovery, like a bullish crossover or shrinking negative histogram, it hints that sellers are losing grip. In such cases, CPR again begins to attract the candles, and price may start rising back toward the CPR zone.

The key point is that MACD doesn't give entries. It filters noise and reveals the quality of momentum. While CPR defines the structure, MACD helps us measure the strength behind the move. This alignment gives traders clarity, not just about direction, but about whether the move has the fuel to continue.

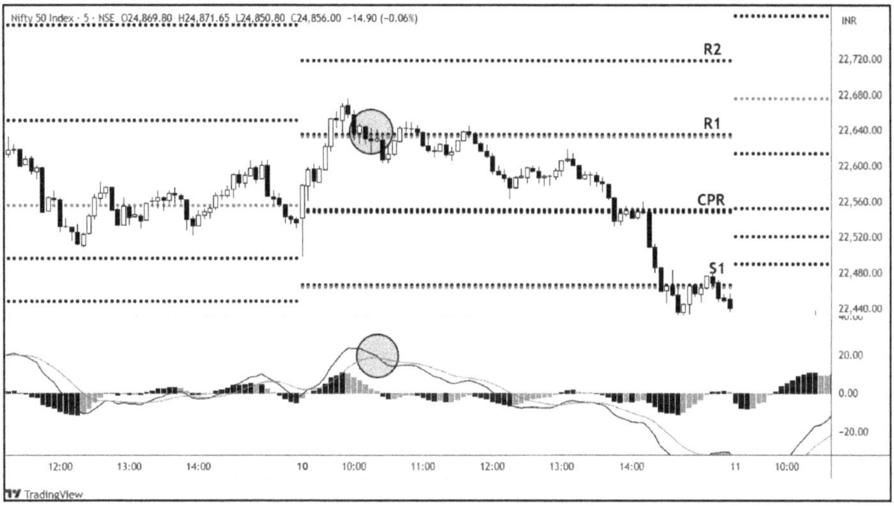

Fig. 6.7: NIFTY Reversal from R1 in 5 mins time frame with daily CPR

At first glance, this looked like a strong bullish setup. The stock had already broken above the CPR, moved past R1, and even cleared the previous day's high. For many traders, this would seem like a solid uptrend in progress.

But the price told a different story.

Despite crossing these key levels, there was no follow-through. The candles started shrinking, volume faded, and price began to slow down. While it looked like a breakout on the surface, MACD revealed the truth early. As price hovered near the highs, MACD showed a bearish crossover, and the histogram began to fade. This was a clear warning. Momentum was not supporting the breakout. It was a sign that the up move was weakening from within. Not long after, the price failed to hold above the previous day's high and started drifting back down.

For traders, this wasn't just a failed breakout, it was a potential shorting opportunity. Once the weakness was confirmed and price began to slip back below key zones, the short setup was clear. With CPR above acting as resistance and MACD backing the down move, the trade had structure and momentum on its side. This setup shows the power of combining CPR and MACD. When a breakout lacks energy, and MACD starts to turn, it's often better to step back from long trades or even flip the bias and go short.

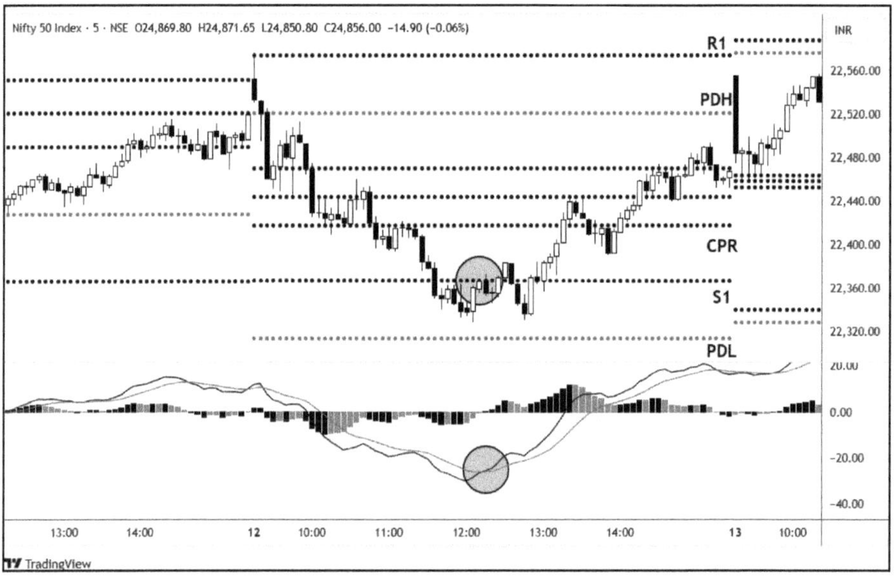

Fig. 6.8: NIFTY Reversal from S1 in 5 mins time frame with daily CPR

The session began with a gap-up, and price opened above the Central Pivot Range. After the open, price moved higher and approached the S1 resistance level. It even managed to break above S1 briefly, but the move lacked follow-through. Candles started to shrink, upper wicks appeared, and momentum clearly began to fade. This was a sign that buyers were losing strength. MACD supported this observation. The histogram began to flatten, and the MACD lines moved closer together. There was no strong expansion to confirm the breakout, which hinted that the upward move might not hold. This is a classic example of how MACD helps validate CPR-based setups. CPR gave the structure. S1 served as a resistance checkpoint. And MACD showed that momentum wasn't on the breakout's side.

For traders, this was a signal to be cautious. When price breaks key levels without strength, it's often better to wait or reassess the bias. Momentum and structure must align, otherwise the move might fade as quickly as it started.

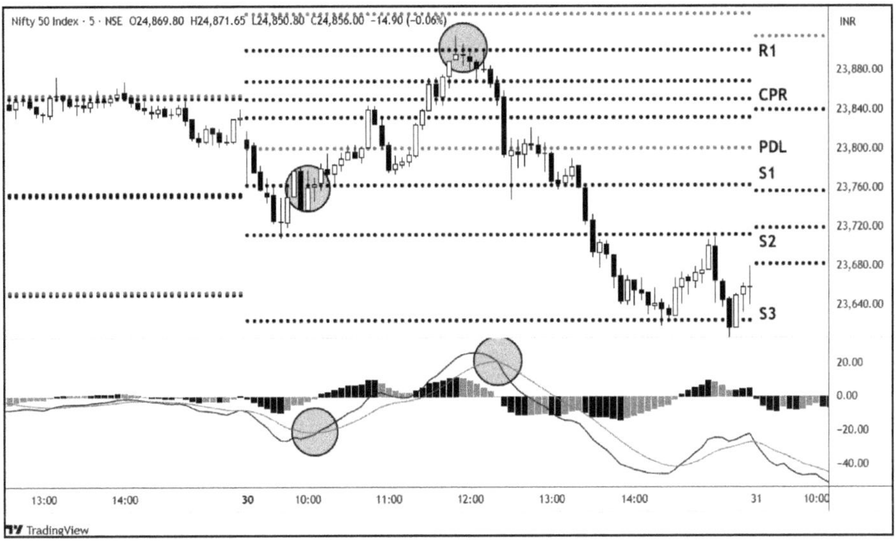

Fig. 6.9: NIFTY Reversal from S2 in 5 mins time frame with daily CPR

The day began just below the Central Pivot Range, and price quickly slipped into a downtrend. Sellers drove the market lower, and it reached the S2 level within the first leg of the session. At that point, it looked like the bearish momentum might continue.

But something shifted.

As price hovered near S2, a bullish crossover appeared on the MACD, and the histogram started to rise. This was the first sign that selling pressure was weakening and buyers were stepping in. Soon after, a strong bullish candle confirmed the reversal. Price then rallied sharply, crossed the CPR zone with strength, and headed toward R1. MACD remained bullish during this move, confirming that the upward momentum was supported.

However, once the price reached R1, the tone changed again. Candles near R1 were small and lacked conviction. MACD showed a bearish crossover, and the histogram started to fade. This was the clue that the upside move had lost strength. It wasn't just a pause, it was the beginning of a reversal.

From there, price dropped sharply, breaking through the CPR and S1, and continued falling all the way to S3. MACD remained bearish throughout the fall, giving traders the confidence to hold their short positions or exit longs early. This chart is a great example of how CPR and MACD together can guide a trader through both the reversal and the trend, from the lows of S2 to the highs of R1, and all the way back down to S3. Structure and momentum worked hand in hand to map the entire session.

More Than Indicators, It's About Clarity

As you've seen, CPR does the heavy lifting. It gives the structure, the map, the framework. But when momentum tools like RSI, MACD, and Super trend align with CPR zones, they add clarity to the chaos.

Super trend helps you stay in a move when your emotions want to bail out.

RSI shows you when strength is fading, even if price is still pushing.

MACD quietly confirms whether the market truly has momentum or is just bluffing.

Each tool speaks a different language, but when they all say the same thing around CPR, that's your moment. That's where conviction builds. But here's the bigger truth: CPR isn't just a tool for Indian equities. It's a language. And this language doesn't change when you switch markets.

So even if the chart in front of you belongs to gold, crude oil, EUR/USD, or Bitcoin, CPR doesn't lose meaning. It finds rhythm. Because price may belong to different markets, but the way it moves, reacts, and respects key zones is often the same. Let's see how CPR performs on a global stage

THE UNIVERSALITY OF CPR IN TRADING

Chapter 07

The world is quiet, but the charts are not. Crude moves on supply. Gold moves on sentiment, bitcoin responds to fear. Different trains, different speeds, but all moving on the same track. Most of the time, that track is CPR. It does not predict headlines or react to emotion. Instead, it highlights where price is balanced, where it is moving, and where traders begin to take action.

> ***"Markets may vary, Instruments may differ,***
> ***Time zones may shift, But CPR behaves the same."***

What makes CPR truly universal is how naturally it adapts to any chart. It builds structure from price itself, no matter what you're trading. It doesn't rely on external data or complex algorithms. Its strength comes from its simplicity. To see CPR in action, there's no better place to start than with commodities. These markets don't wait. A headline drops, a supply shift hits, and price reacts. But often, CPR shows the story before the news does.

Commodity Trading with CPR: A Global Perspective

Every major move in commodities has a story behind it. It could be a conflict disrupting oil supply, a policy change affecting gold prices, or a weather event shaking up agriculture. These markets are closely tied to global events, and their prices often shift well before the news becomes obvious. This is where CPR becomes a trader's advantage. It doesn't rely on assumptions or headlines. Instead, it shows how the market is reacting in real time. A strong bounce from a CPR zone or a clean breakdown through it can reveal what traders are expecting, sometimes before the rest of the world catches on.

Crude Oil: The Market That Moves Everything

Every day, crude oil fuels the ships, planes, and trucks that keep the world moving. But its influence doesn't stop at the ports or highways. When oil prices rise or fall, that change quietly spreads, pushing up shipping costs, nudging inflation higher, and even steering interest rates. In nearly every corner of the economy, the ripple begins with crude. It's no wonder traders everywhere keep a close eye on crude, making it one of the most closely watched and sensitive commodities on the planet. A sudden conflict in the Middle East, an OPEC production cut, or even a shift in US inventory data can send prices soaring or crashing. And often, by the time the news becomes public, the price has already reacted. But here's the edge. While most traders wait for headlines to make sense of the move, CPR traders already see the signs on the chart. Here's how CPR captured those moves before the headlines did.

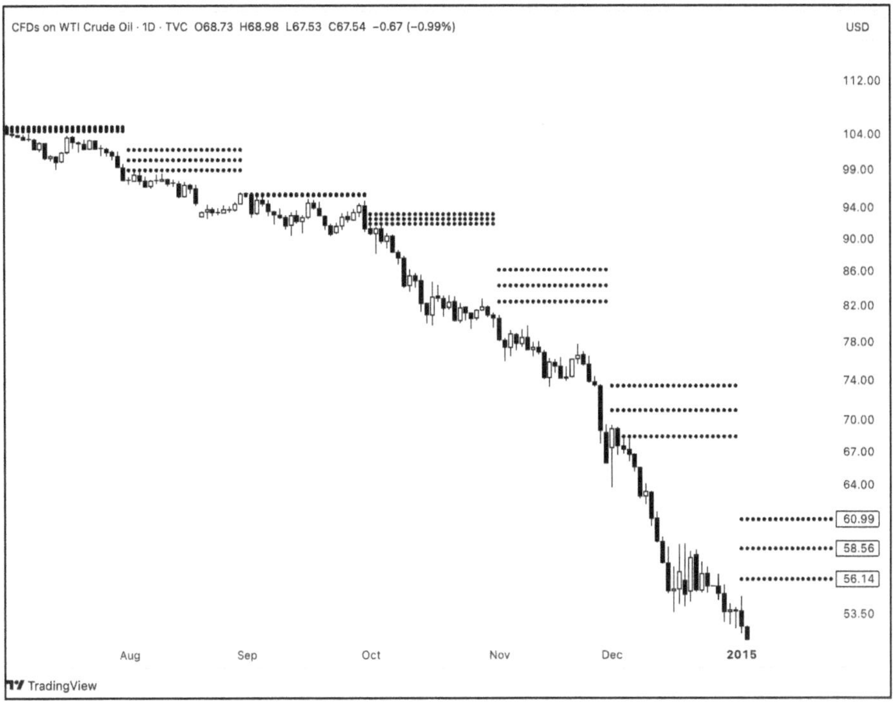

Fig. 7.1: Crude Oil Price Fall below CPR Zones in the Daily Chart (July 2014 to January 2015)

During the sharp decline in crude oil between mid-2014 and early 2015, price stayed below the CPR almost every session. Each rally ran into resistance near the zone, and lower highs kept confirming the bearish mood. As seen in Chapter 3, a descending CPR was not just a technical detail, it was a warning that weakness was still in control. For traders following structure, CPR made the downtrend clear. It helped them to avoid long trades and stay focused on shorting opportunities. Even when the market turned volatile, CPR kept the roadmap clear, often revealing the story before the headlines could catch up.

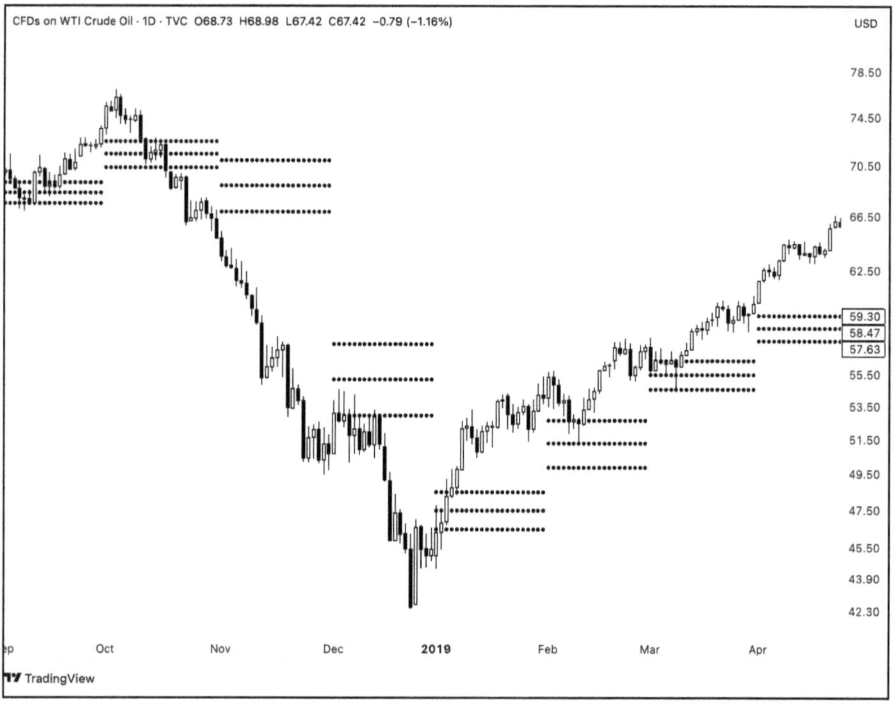

Fig. 7.2: *CPR Structure During Crude's Fall and V-Shaped Bounce in daily timeframe (2018–2019)*

Late 2018 brought another steep drop in oil, with CPR zones capping every rally and reinforcing the decline. But in early 2019, the story flipped. Price surged back above the same CPR levels, turning what was once resistance into support and setting up a sharp V-shaped recovery. This smooth transition revealed CPR's true power, guiding traders through both the final stretch of a downtrend and the swift turnaround that followed. As highlighted in earlier chapters, CPR adapts as the market shifts, giving structure whether the trend continues or reverses. In wild swings or sudden reversals, it remains the anchor traders can trust.

Fig. 7.3: *Crude Breaks CPR and Drops Below Zero in daily timeframe (April 2020)*

In early 2020, the world came to a halt. The COVID-19 pandemic shut down borders, grounded flights, and froze economic activity across continents. Demand for crude oil vanished almost overnight. With storage facilities full and no buyers in sight, prices collapsed. On April 20, 2020, for the first time in history, crude oil futures traded below zero. But before the headlines captured the shock, the charts had already started revealing it. A clean breakdown below CPR levels had already marked the shift, warning traders that this wasn't just another dip. It was the start of a historic collapse.

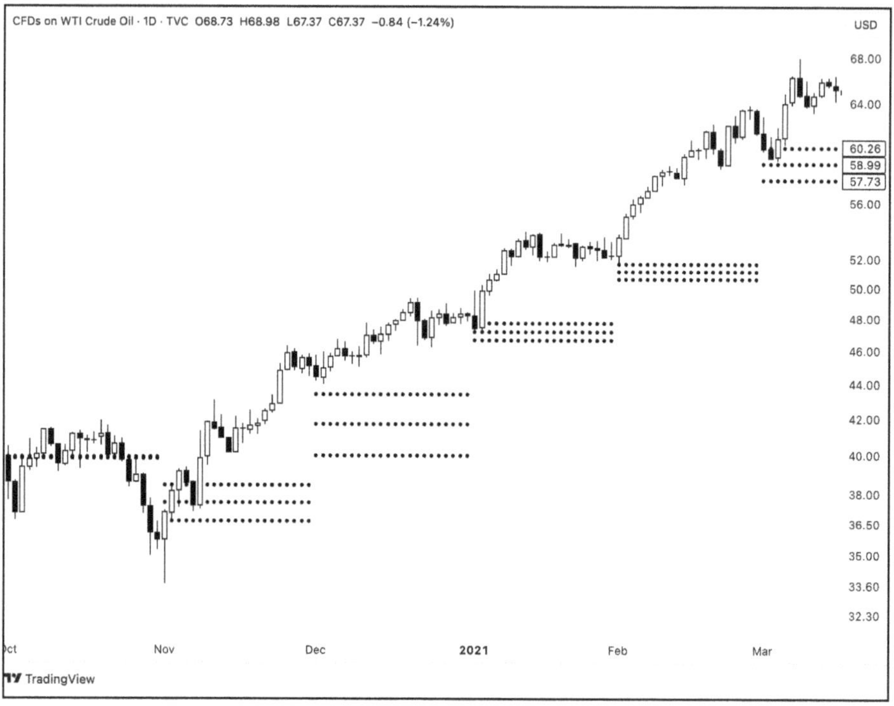

Fig. 7.4: Crude Recovery Aligned with CPR – 2020 in daily timeframe

After crude oil prices crashed below zero in April 2020, they slowly started to recover. As demand returned and the market began to stabilize, the price began to move in line with CPR zones. These CPR levels helped traders identify key support and resistance areas on the chart. The price respecting CPR again showed that the market was becoming more stable. Even after such a big shock, CPR gave traders clear levels to watch and make decisions with more confidence.

Gold: A Sentiment-Driven Market

From the age of kings to modern markets, gold has always held power beyond its shine. In times of crisis, it wasn't paper money or stocks that people ran to, it was gold. A timeless refuge. Whether it was war, inflation, or economic collapse, gold stood as a symbol of safety. It is not just a metal, it is a message. A message about inflation, currency weakness, policy shifts, and rising uncertainty. Unlike crude, which reflects activity and demand, gold moves with emotion. It reacts to central bank decisions, sudden volatility, and cracks in financial confidence. And long before fear shows up in the headlines, gold often begins to move.

Fig. 7.5: *Gold Breaks CPR in daily time frame and Rallies (September to December 2009)*

Between September and December 2009, gold entered a strong bullish phase, marked by its repeated respect for the Central Pivot Range (CPR). During this period, the price consistently used the CPR as a launchpad, bouncing cleanly from the zone each time it was tested. As global economic uncertainty lingered post 2008, gold's rally was not just emotional, it was technical, guided by a structure that brought clarity to every move.

***Fig. 7.6:** CPR Breakdown in daily timeframe Triggers Gold Decline (Apr–Sep 2018)*

From April to September 2018, gold slipped into a steady downtrend, and the first warning came in early April with an inside-CPR formation. The month's CPR band was narrow and nested inside the prior band, a sign that energy was coiling. When price finally broke below that inside CPR, momentum flipped decisively to the downside. After the break, every approach to the central pivot zone failed. CPR repeatedly rejected each rally, offering clear short entries as lower highs formed beneath the band. The decline unfolded in measured steps rather than sudden crashes.

For traders who rely on structure over speculation, the inside-CPR break was the trigger, and the series of rejections was the conviction to hold, or even add to, shorts. This phase showcased CPR's value not only in spotting breakout moments but also in confirming sustained weakness. By respecting those repeated knock-backs, traders stayed on the right side of the move as gold fell, session after session.

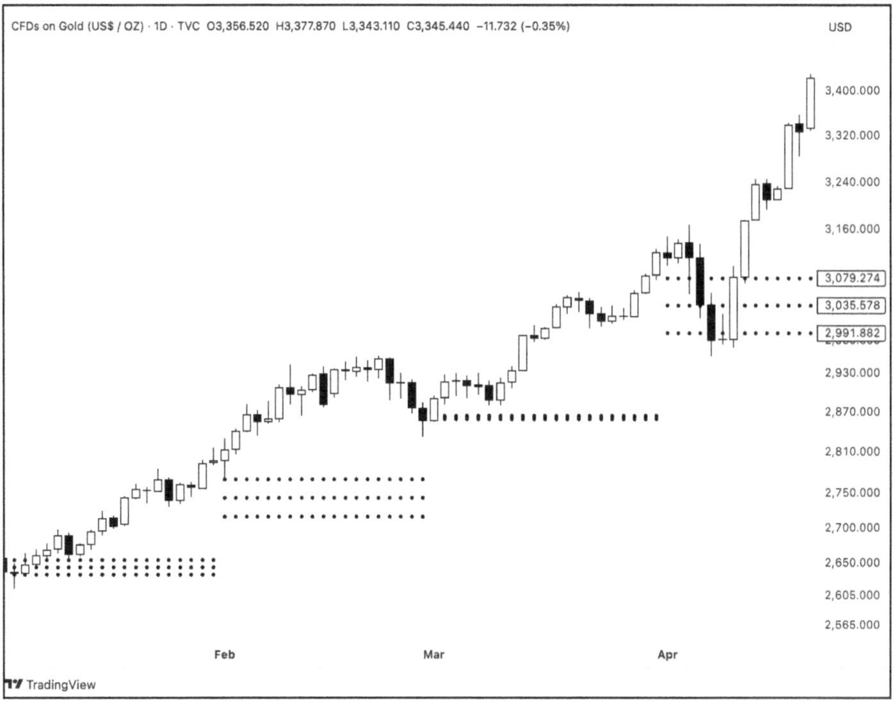

Fig. 7.7: *Gold Launches a Strong Rally After CPR Breakout in daily timeframe (2025)*

In 2025, as inflation fears and monetary policy uncertainty gripped global markets, gold began forming a base around its CPR zone. Eventually, a clean breakout above the upper band of the CPR triggered a sharp bullish continuation, confirming buyer control. Traders who had been tracking the structure were able to position themselves early, ahead of the momentum. The rally that followed was steady and disciplined, session after session, with each day printing a slightly higher CPR, an ascending CPR that confirmed buyer strength was still building. This move stood as a textbook example of how CPR can guide traders through volatile macro conditions, offering clarity and early signals when the rest of the market is still uncertain.

Commodities like oil and gold show how CPR spots the subtle cues behind major moves. But the story doesn't end with physical goods. Next, we turn to the world of currencies – where money itself becomes the commodity – to see how CPR holds up in the global foreign exchange arena.

Forex Trading with CPR: Mastering Currency Movements

The forex market never sleeps. It runs around the clock, five days a week, with traders reacting to news the moment it drops, no matter the time zone. It is the largest and fastest market in the world, with trillions traded every single day. Forex trading revolves around sessions such as Asian, London, and New York. Each session carries its own rhythm, with the London to New York overlap often being the most active and volatile. During these periods, news releases, policy statements, and employment data can trigger sharp movements. Even in these fast conditions, price often respects structure. Recognising these levels helps traders stay focused and make decisions based on what the market is actually doing.

EUR/USD: The Global Financial Barometer

EUR/USD links the world's two largest economies, making it the most traded currency pair on the planet. This pair acts as a barometer of global financial sentiment. When European growth or risk appetite improves, the euro tends to strengthen; when uncertainty rises or the U.S. dollar is in demand as a safe haven, this pair often falls. Major decisions by the European Central Bank or the U.S. Federal Reserve can set the tone for EUR/USD's direction, and those shifts ripple into markets worldwide. With such massive liquidity and attention, technical levels like the CPR carry significant weight – many eyes are watching, and price behavior around the CPR often reflects that collective focus.

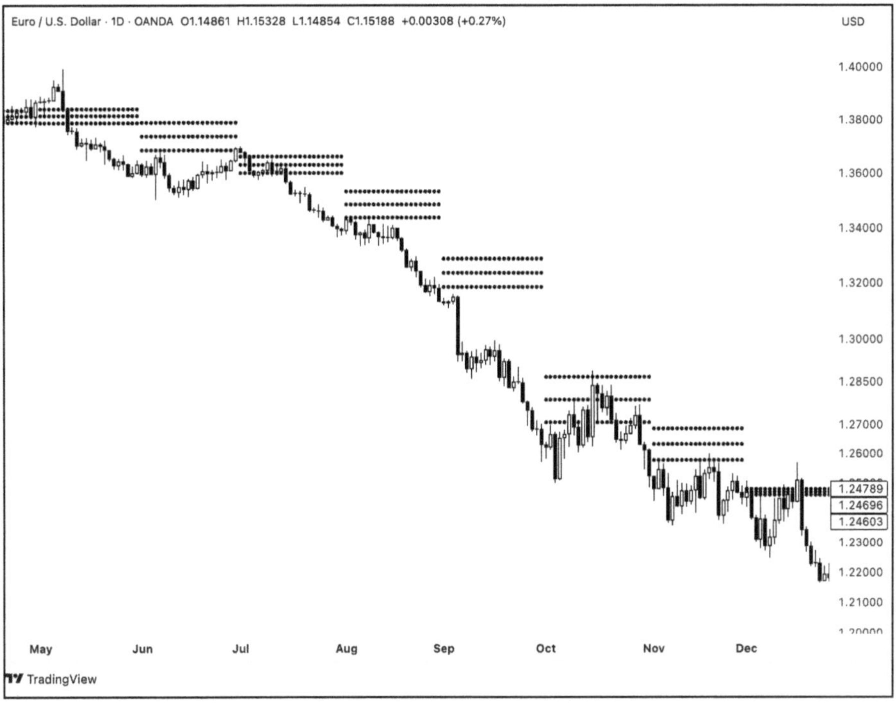

Fig. 7.8: *CPR Structure During EUR/USD Breakdown in daily timeframe (Jul–Nov 2014)*

Repeated attempts to move above the CPR failed, and a sustained bearish phase took hold in EUR/USD. Each approach to the zone was rejected, a clear sign that sellers remained in control while buyer confidence steadily faded. The CPR itself trended lower, a descending CPR that signalled continuing weakness and pointed to a deeper slide ahead. With each bounce failing near the CPR, price kept forming lower highs below the pivot. It was a quiet but clear sign that the downtrend was still in control and gaining strength. For traders, CPR offered not only precise entry cues but also the conviction to stay with the move as EUR/USD drifted lower day after day.

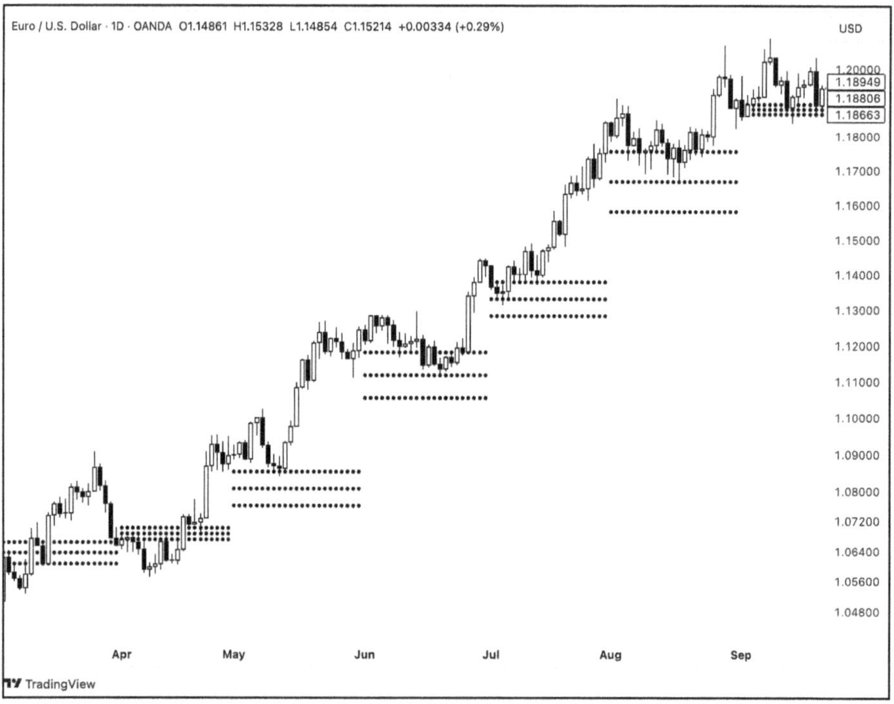

Fig. 7.9: EUR/USD Rally Respecting CPR Zones in daily time frame (April to Sep 2017)

Between April and September 2017, EUR/USD charted a steady uptrend, guided by the Central Pivot Range acting as dynamic support. Each time the price approached the CPR zone, it responded with strength, forming clean rejections and higher lows. The CPR structure remained intact throughout the rally, offering traders reliable re-entry points to ride the trend. This phase showcased how CPR doesn't just define support, but reinforces conviction during long directional moves in the forex market.

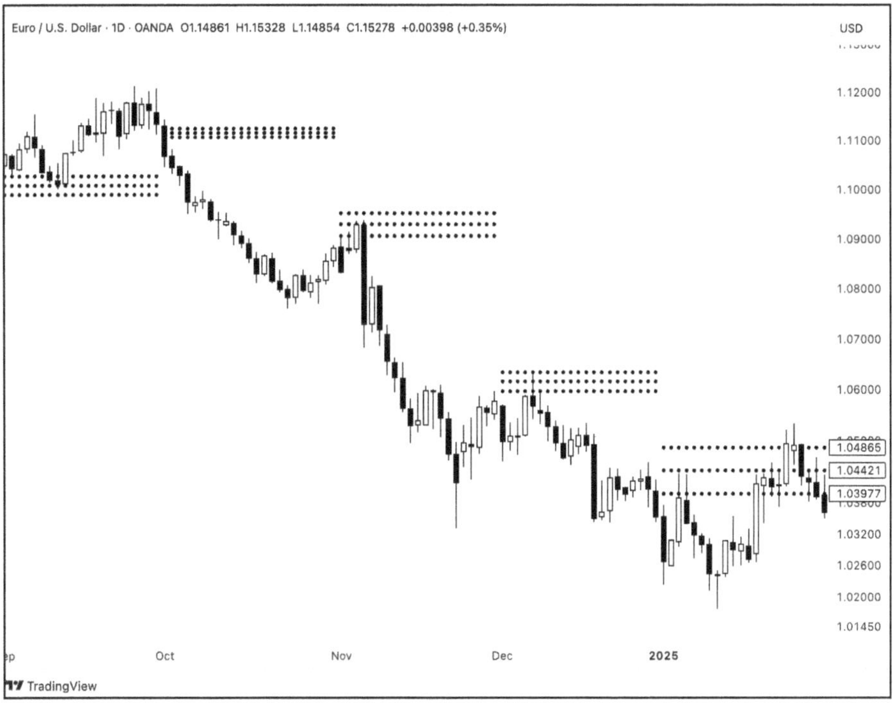

Fig. 7.10: *EUR/USD Slide Along CPR Zones from Oct 2024 to Jan 2025*

From October 2024 to January 2025, the EUR/USD pair followed a disciplined downtrend, with price consistently respecting the CPR as a resistance barrier. Each time the pair attempted to climb, it was met with rejection at or near the central pivot zone, reinforcing the presence of strong selling pressure. These repeated failures to breach the CPR led to the formation of lower highs, a classic sign of trend strength in bearish markets. The structure gave traders clear confirmation to stay with the trend, using each CPR retest as an opportunity to re-enter or add to short positions. This period highlighted how CPR can act not only as a trend confirmation tool, but also as a guide for timing entries during prolonged downtrends in the forex market.

USD/JPY

USD/JPY connects two major global economies, the United States and Japan, and reflects key market trends. Traders watch this pair closely, as it often moves due to differences in interest rates between the two countries. When markets are optimistic, traders typically prefer the higher returns offered by the US dollar, pushing USD/JPY upward. However, during times of market stress or uncertainty, traders seek safety in the Japanese yen, causing USD/JPY to fall. This ongoing push-and-pull makes USD/JPY sensitive to sudden shifts and reversals. CPR helps traders clearly see these movements, providing valuable signals about market direction, whether influenced by central bank decisions or global economic concerns.

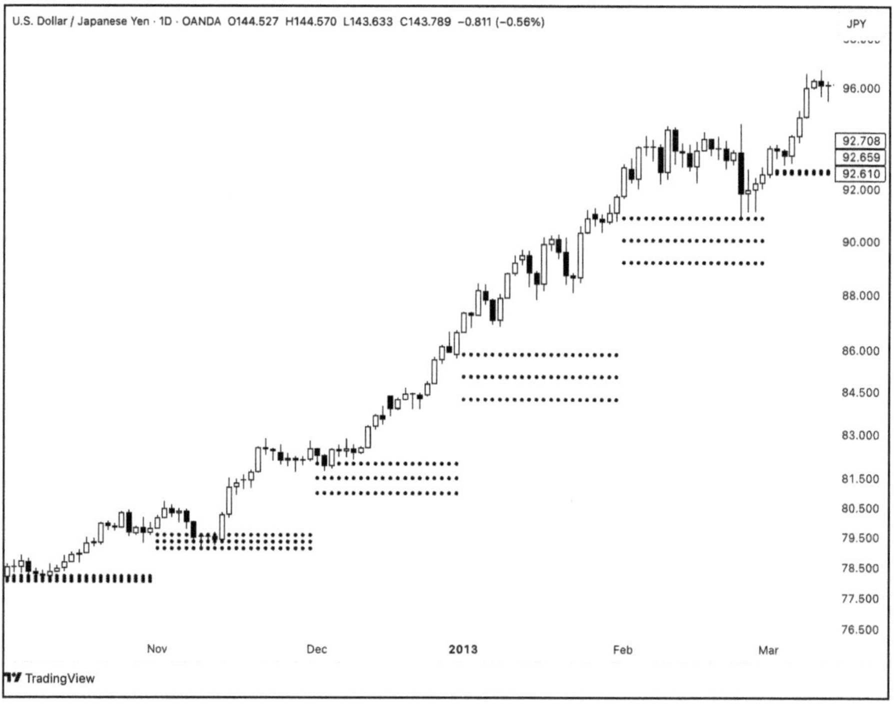

Fig. 7.11: *USD/JPY Respecting CPR Structure in daily time frame (Oct 2012 to Mar 2013)*

From October 2012 to March 2013, USD/JPY displayed a textbook uptrend, with price consistently holding above the CPR zone.

Every pullback into the range was met with fresh buying, reinforcing the strength of the structure. The CPR acted as a reliable base throughout the rally, allowing traders to trail stop-losses with confidence and even scale into positions on dips. This sustained respect for the pivot zone showcased the power of CPR in trend confirmation and position management across longer timeframes in the forex market.

Fig. 7.12: USD/JPY Fall Triggered Near CPR Levels in daily time frame (2025)

In 2025, USD/JPY attempted to push above the CPR zone but met strong resistance, leading to a decisive rejection. This failure to break out was the first sign of shifting sentiment. What followed was a sharp reversal, as price broke below key intraday levels and confirmed the start of a clean downtrend. The CPR acted as a clear turning point, offering traders early warning that bullish momentum had stalled. The move highlighted how even a single rejection at the CPR can signal a complete sentiment shift in currency markets, setting the stage for high-probability setups.

Currencies may be the lifeblood of global finance, but even they have competition when it comes to volatility. As intense as forex can be, an even wilder frontier has emerged in recent years: cryptocurrency. How does CPR fare in a market that never sleeps and knows no borders? Let's find out.

Cryptocurrency Trading with CPR: Navigating the High Volatility

What makes crypto different from other assets is that it is not tied to any government, central bank, or physical economy. It is built on code, maintained by decentralised networks, and traded globally without borders. It does not sleep, does not wait for earnings reports, and does not follow traditional financial calendars. This independence is why many see it as revolutionary. For the first time, value can be created, transferred, and stored digitally, without a middleman. It challenges how we think about money, ownership, and even trust. Some believe it could replace traditional systems entirely. Others see it as just a pump and dump. Whether it lives up to that promise or not, one thing is certain. Crypto may be wild, but it still has structure, and price continues to respect it.

Bitcoin (BTC): The Digital Gold Rush

Launched in 2009 in the aftermath of a financial crisis, Bitcoin pioneered an entirely new asset class. Often called "digital gold," it sparked a modern gold rush among traders and investors. Its dramatic booms and busts have made headlines worldwide. One year Bitcoin can skyrocket on a wave of euphoria; another year it can crash back to earth as fear takes over. Yet beneath those extreme swings, Bitcoin's price still respects technical structure. CPR has proven to be a valuable guide for navigating Bitcoin's trends – helping traders catch its big rallies and heed early warnings when the tide turns.

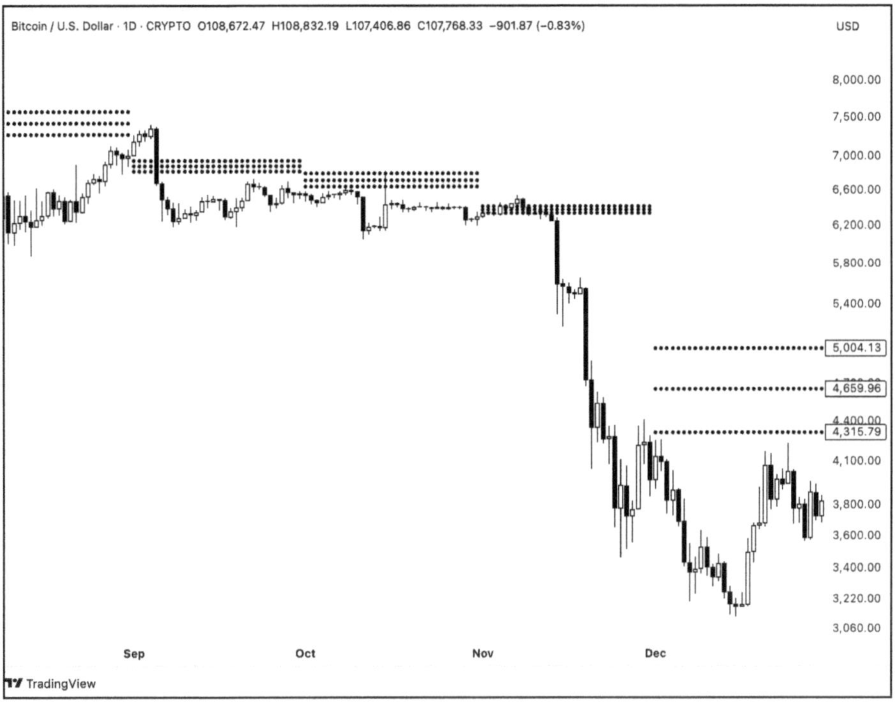

Fig. 7.13: CPR Gives Early Sign Before Bitcoin Crash in 2018

In early 2018, before the full extent of the Bitcoin crash unfolded, CPR levels began to flash early warnings. Price struggled to stay above the central pivot zone, with each attempt met by selling pressure. Eventually, Bitcoin broke below the CPR with conviction, forming lower highs and rejecting re-entry attempts. This clean breakdown was not just technical noise, it was a structural shift in market sentiment. The CPR, calculated purely from price action, picked up on this shift before the news cycle caught on. While headlines focused on hype and speculation, the chart told a different story, one of distribution. Traders who respected the CPR signal had the opportunity to reduce exposure or flip short early. It was a classic case where the market structure spoke first, and fundamentals lagged behind. The fall that followed wiped out billions in value, but it didn't happen without clues. CPR once again proved its value as a leading indicator during a major trend reversal.

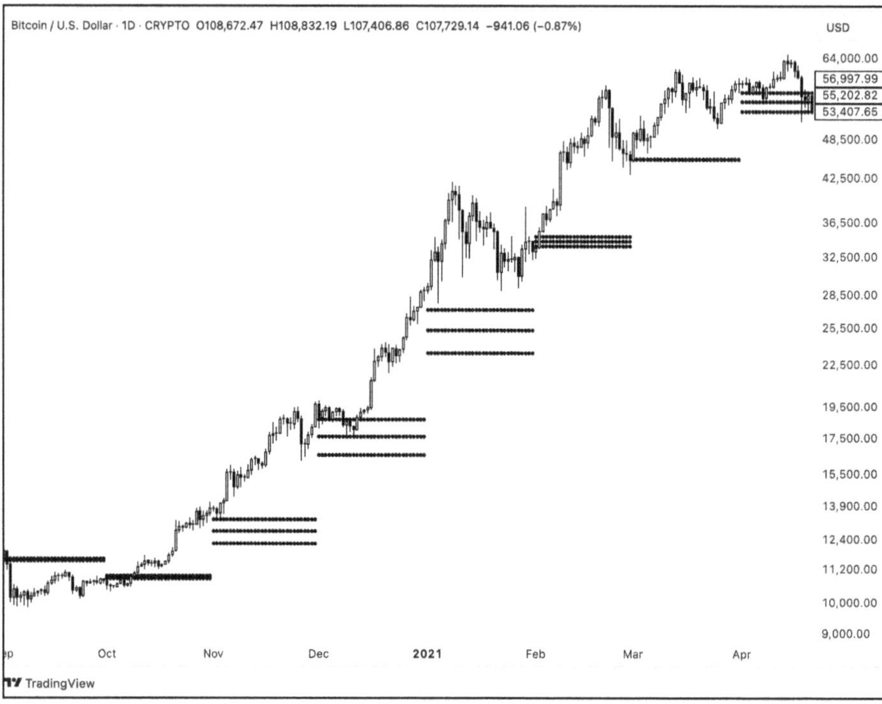

Fig. 7.14: Bitcoin's Historic Rally from $10,000 to $50,000 (Daily Time Frame, 2020 to 2021)

CPR levels consistently held as support during Bitcoin's historic bull run. Traders used the zone to manage entries and exits throughout the rally. During Bitcoin's legendary bull run from $10,000 to $50,000, the CPR consistently acted as a reliable support zone. Each pullback into the range offered fresh entry opportunities, while the structure helped traders manage their positions with discipline. The CPR levels served as a guiding framework throughout the rally, allowing traders to ride the trend confidently and adjust stops or scale positions without losing alignment with the broader move.

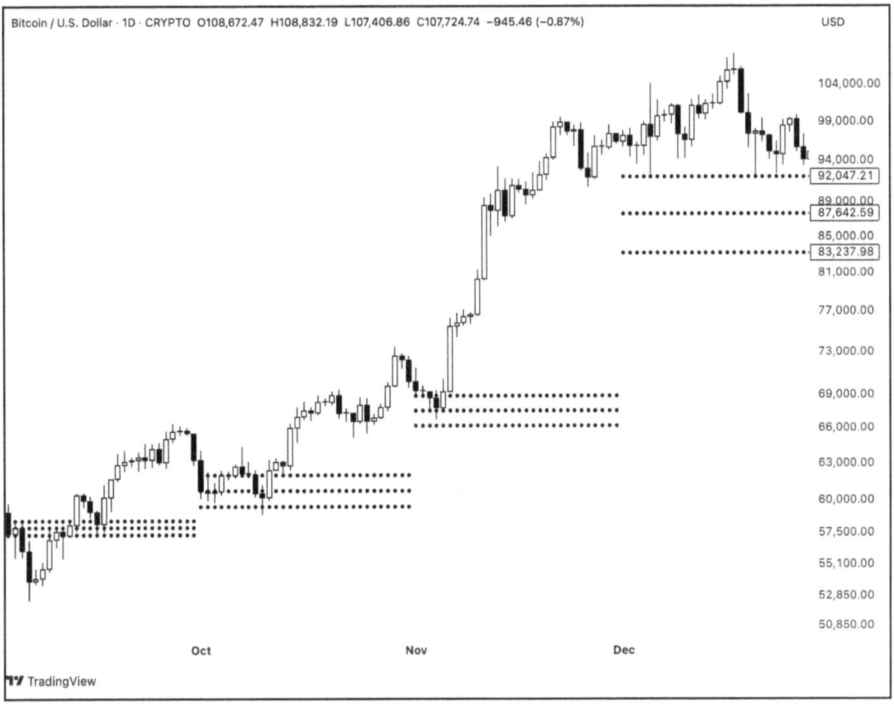

Fig. 7.15: CPR Breakout in daily timeframe Fuels Bitcoin Rally to 100K

Bitcoin ignited a powerful rally after breaking above the CPR resistance near 58,000. The breakout was clean, backed by strong momentum and clear follow-through, leaving no room for doubt. Each candle that held above the CPR added conviction, and price surged toward the 100,000 mark in a sustained trend. For traders tracking structure, this move was a perfect example of CPR acting as both a launchpad and a guidepost during high-momentum phases in crypto markets.

Ethereum (ETH): Fueling the Decentralized Revolution

If Bitcoin is digital gold, Ethereum is often likened to digital oil – it fuels an entire ecosystem of decentralized applications. Launched in 2015, Ethereum introduced smart contracts and the foundation for things like DeFi and NFTs, earning it the nickname "the world computer." Its value is driven not just by monetary policy or supply and demand, but by innovation and network usage. Ether (ETH), the native token, powers transactions on the network, so its price rides on both speculative fervor and real utility. Ethereum's market tends to move in tandem with Bitcoin's, though it can be even more explosive during periods of innovation or congestion. Through wild swings of its own, CPR remains just as relevant on Ethereum's charts, helping traders interpret its volatile dance of technology and speculation.

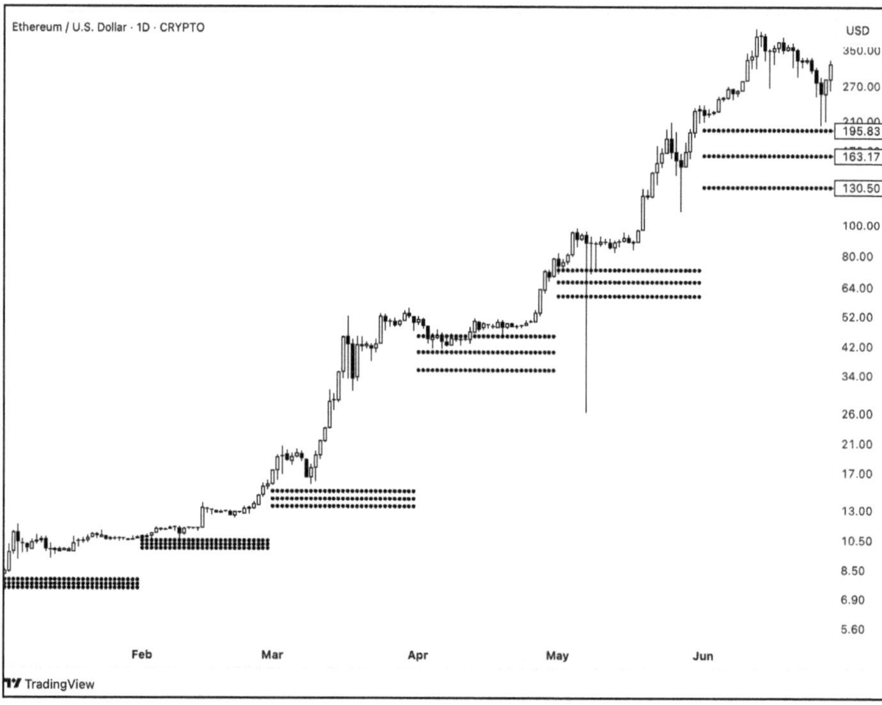

Fig. 7.16: ETH Respects CPR During Its Early Trend in 2017

In 2017, Ethereum (ETH) began its parabolic run, but if you look closely at its earlier breakout phase, price action repeatedly respected the Central Pivot Range on the daily timeframe. Every pullback into CPR was met with buying pressure, indicating accumulation by strong hands. This kind of price behavior, respecting CPR and bouncing from it, is a clear signature of trending phases where CPR acts as dynamic support. Traders using CPR during this period could have confidently added positions or trailed their stops with each higher CPR formation.

This shows how even in the volatile world of crypto, CPR remains relevant as a structure for swing or positional setups.

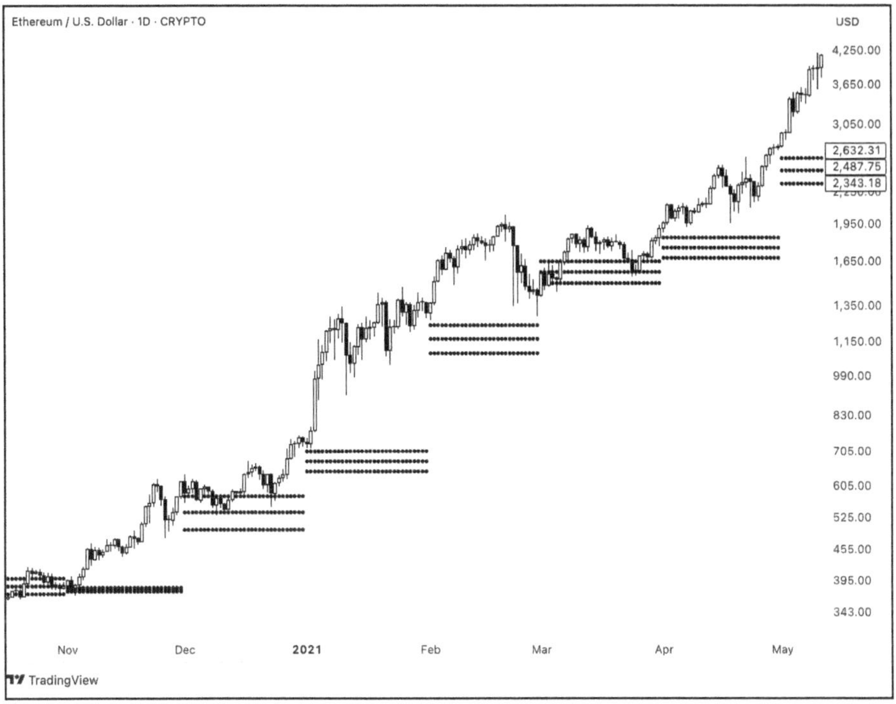

***Fig. 7.17:** ETH Breaks CPR to Begin Historic Bull Run (2020)*

Ethereum broke through CPR resistance, marking the start of a major rally. Price respected structure throughout the move, giving clarity to trend followers. In 2020, Ethereum broke decisively above the CPR zone, signaling the start of a historic bull run. The breakout wasn't just a single spike, it was backed by strong candles and sustained follow-through. Each time price retested the CPR, it held firm, offering confirmation of trend strength. This structure became the foundation for the move that took ETH from consolidation into price discovery. For trend-following traders, CPR acted like a map, showing where to enter, where to stay, and where to manage risk. The clean respect of structure gave clarity amidst the growing hype and volatility. Even during minor pullbacks, price continued to bounce from the CPR, never breaking the rhythm. Momentum aligned with structure, and the rally picked up pace without looking back. This wasn't just luck, it was a textbook example of how CPR can frame powerful moves. Ethereum's rise in 2020 stood as a reminder that when price and structure speak together, trends can unfold with conviction.

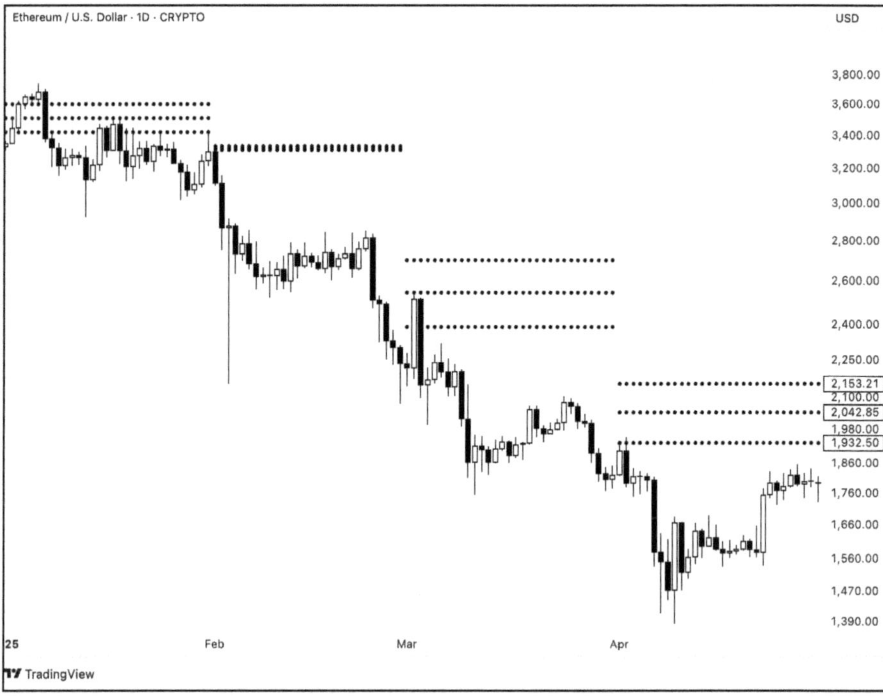

***Fig. 7.18:** Ethereum Fails to Hold CPR and Declines (2025)*

In 2025, Ethereum began showing signs of weakness as it repeatedly failed to hold above the CPR zone. Each attempt to reclaim the range was met with firm rejection, as price failed to close decisively within the structure. They revealed steady selling pressure. This shift in behavior marked the early stages of a bearish reversal. Traders observing the structure could see that ETH was losing strength session after session. Momentum confirmed what CPR had already suggested, the bulls had lost control. For disciplined traders, the structure offered multiple opportunities to exit longs or initiate shorts. The fall wasn't a surprise for those who trusted price over hope.

The Final Piece

Throughout this chapter, we have seen CPR act as a truly universal tool. Whether it is crude oil, gold, forex pairs, or cryptocurrencies, price continues to respect structure. CPR adapts across asset classes, regions, and market conditions. It does not rely on prediction but reflects how traders are positioned. What makes CPR even more powerful is its longevity. It is not a method that works for a short period and becomes irrelevant. The examples in this chapter, from as early as 2009 to recent market moves, show that CPR has remained effective over the years. It has held up during rallies, crashes, recoveries, and even in fast-moving assets like crypto.

CPR is not tied to a specific timeframe, trend, or news cycle. It reflects how price behaves around balance zones. That principle stays consistent regardless of the asset or time. And that is what makes CPR one of the most reliable tools a trader can keep on their chart. But CPR can only guide. It can't decide.

That part? That's on the trader.

Because even the best structure means nothing if you don't follow your process. If your mindset isn't ready. If your actions don't match your plan. When the market opens, it's not the tool that gets tested, it's the trader behind it. Your routine. Your mindset. Your ability to stay focused when the chart is alive and uncertain.

Let's find the final piece of the puzzle.

Chapter

08

BEYOND SETUPS, THE DISCIPLINE OF DOING IT

Think back to your school days. It's a sports day. You're standing at the starting line, barefoot, maybe a little nervous. The white lines are drawn on the dusty ground. The sun is bright. Your PT master raises his whistle. He shouts, "On your mark, get set," and raises the whistle. One sharp blow. That was the "Go." The whistle echoed through the field and You blast forward like your life depends on it. It's dusty. Your breath is heavy. You don't care who's watching. You run.

Your legs aren't trained. Your arms swing wide. You don't think about the crowd. There's no calculation, no strategy. You just run. All you care about is that finish line. You didn't win because of skill. You didn't lose because of weakness. You showed up. You gave everything. And for those few seconds, the world disappeared. That was you. Untrained, full of spirit, running with everything you had.

That's how every journey begins. Not polished. Not perfect. Just present and ready to give it everything. And one such boy started the same way. School field. Chalk track. No shoes. But even back then, he moved differently. There was rhythm in his steps. He didn't run for cheers. He ran to beat himself.

Years later, when he stood under the Olympic lights and the world waited in silence, the gunshot cracked through the air. It cracked like a thunderstorm. But unlike a real storm where lightning comes first and sound follows, this time it was the lightning-fast Usain Bolt who chased the sound. This time, the entire world was watching. Even the crowd's eyes didn't blink ten times. And in under ten seconds, he didn't just win a race. He validated everything he had practiced for years in the dark. The time on the board flashed, but in his mind, the race was already won long before the gun fired. It wasn't magic. It was a memory, muscle, mentality. He didn't run that race on race day. He ran it every day before it. That's how champions are born. Not in the spotlight but in the silence of repetition. That journey from raw instinct to refined execution is the same rhythm CPR gradually builds into your trading.

Where Preparation Meets Execution

Once the bell rings, the market begins to move. This is the market's language. You don't chase it, you listen to it. A narrow CPR? That's your 100-metre starting line. A breakout with structure? That's your starting gun sound. You don't react to every move. You wait for your setup, just like a runner waits for the exact millisecond to push off the blocks. Look for confirmation through price behaviour, such as retests or clear directional strength. Avoid conflicting signals. Don't trade against the trend on a trending day. CPR and overall structure should support the same directional bias.

This isn't just about clicking "Buy" or "Sell." It's about being precise. Wait for the zone. Wait for the candle to close. Let the pattern confirm. Set the stop loss just beyond the structure, not based on fear, but logic. Pre-define the target. It could be a resistance or support level, or the previous day's high or low. Never move the target mid-trade unless structure demands it.

You don't look at the crowd when you're running. You look at the track, the lane, the line ahead. Every athlete knows when to sprint and when to pause. You can't run full throttle for hours. Neither can the market. After a strong morning move, the market often takes a breather. Price might chop around CPR or between two levels.

This is not the moment. This is the rest zone. Review the trades. Avoid overtrading. Preserve energy for tomorrow's run.

"Even Bolt doesn't sprint all day. He rests, resets. That's what keeps him sharp." The market is no different. Some days won't offer a clean setup. No trade days aren't failures, they are part of the process. Patience is as much a skill as execution. Use that time to reflect. Review the entries and exits. Was the setup valid? Was the plan followed? Did emotion creep in, or did execution stay clean? Update the trade journal. Screenshot key CPR reactions. This builds the memory bank. This is the cooldown phase, the part where muscles recover, but the mind sharpens.

You are not here to chase green candles. You are here to chase your best version. A version that does not panic. Do not rush. Do not doubt when the setup is clear. Because trading is not about one trade. It is about showing up every day, warming up, listening for the signal, and then executing without hesitation. "You do not win on race day. You win on the days you train in silence." And now, the rhythm is in place. CPR is the pulse. The market is the track. The tools are ready. The structure is known. Now, it is time to practice.

Risk Management: The Bedrock of Consistent Performance

If an athlete does not know whether he is running a 100-metre sprint or a marathon, how can he finish strong or even finish at all? Trading without understanding risk and position size is the same. The setup might be perfect, but without knowing how much to risk, the race ends before it begins. Position sizing gives you that clarity. It tells you how far to push and when to pull back. Without it, you might go too big or too small. Stick to your limits.

In trading, you'll usually face one of four outcomes:

1. Big profit
2. Small profit
3. Small loss
4. Big loss

Your job isn't to avoid all losses; it's to avoid the one that can knock you out of the game i.e., big losses. A sprinter might win. Some may finish slow But the worst outcome is a foul start, stepping off the line too early. No chance to run. Just disqualified before the race even begins. Trading is similar. Entering a trade without proper risk control or position size is like that false start. It's not just losing a trade, it's being thrown out of the game before you even begin. The one outcome you must avoid to survive in the market is losing big. Everything else can be managed, learned from, or recovered. But losing big can take you out of the game. That's why risk management is not just a technique. It is your protection.

Let's Take a Breather... and a Peek Through the Window

Visualize this: two traders, same capital, same stock, same day, but very different mornings. One is sipping coffee with a trading journal open, the other is already yelling at the screen five minutes into the market open. No, this isn't a meme. It's real life. We won't bore you with fancy theories. Let's peek into their worlds, no spy cams, just good old storytelling. On one side, we've got Arjun, who treats the market like a game show buzzer. On the other hand, Ravi, who trades like he's defusing a bomb, is calm, methodical, and with his stop-loss in place.

ARJUN VS RAVI

VS

	ARJUN	RAVI
	RISK TAKER	RISK MANAGER
CAPITAL	10,00,000	10,00,000
RISK PER TRADE	NO IDEA	10,000(1% of CAPITAL)
ENTRY PRICE	800	800
STOP LOSS	NO STOPLOSS	790
POSITION SIZE	1250 SHARES	1000 SHARES
CAPITAL USED	10,00,000	8,00,000
EXECUTION STYLE	EMOTIONAL	RULE BASED
OUTCOME	25,000 LOSS , PANICKED EXIT	10,000 LOSS , CALM EXIT

Now, pause for a moment and ask yourself:

What exactly separated these two traders? Was it skill, luck, or something else entirely?

Or was it the way they managed their risk?

Same chart. Same setup. But two completely different outcomes. One exits with control. The other with regret. Here's a clear look at how both traders approached the same situation, and how mindset shaped their decisions:

Concept	Arjun (Emotional Trader)	Ravi (Disciplined Trader)	Key Principle
Risk Management	Jumped in without knowing the risk	Planned his loss before the trade	Risk per trade = 1% of Capital
Position Sizing	No sizing logic, just random quantity	Calculated position size based on risk and stop-loss	Position size = Risk ÷ Risk per share
Money Management	Went all-in. No reserve, no cushion. Couldn't handle tough days	Always traded with a buffer, never with full capital	Diversify risk and preserve capital

That morning, both of them entered the same breakout trade. But when the price reversed, things unfolded very differently. Arjun couldn't take the hit. The loss shook him, and with emotions running high, he walked away from the screen in frustration. The day wasn't over, but for him, it was.

Ravi, on the other hand, absorbed the loss, reviewed it, and stayed focused. His risk was planned, his mindset was steady. When the next setup appeared, he was still there. Calm, composed, and ready to act.

Later that day, another stock triggered a clean breakout setup. Ravi stayed focused. He risked ₹10,000 again. This time, the trade worked and hit the target perfectly. He booked a ₹50,000 profit.

→ Net gain = ₹50,000 – ₹10,000 = ₹40,000

That's a 4% gain on capital, but more importantly, a 100% win in mindset.

Because in trading, the difference isn't who wins every trade. It's who stays long enough to let discipline do the heavy lifting.

How the Big Boys Stay Rich: Risk Discipline Decoded

Risk and money management are foundational pillars for both hedge funds and proprietary trading firms, forming the invisible scaffolding behind every successful trade and long-term performance. Hedge funds approach risk from a macro perspective by diversifying across asset classes, geographies, and investment strategies. This diversification helps them minimize the impact of any single market event. To optimize capital usage, many hedge funds pledge their investments through prime brokers, using portfolio margin and securities lending to gain leverage while maintaining control. Their risk oversight is highly quantitative, relying on tools like Value at Risk (VaR), stress testing, and scenario analysis to simulate worst-case outcomes and manage exposure in real time.

In contrast, proprietary trading firms focus on micro-level control. Each trader is assigned strict position sizing rules and maximum daily loss limits to prevent individual blow-ups. Risk is monitored continuously with real-time dashboards and automated alerts, ensuring that any breach of discipline is instantly addressed. Most prop firms also enforce stop-loss and take-profit orders as mandatory, making sure risk is capped even if the trader hesitates. Beyond systems and numbers, these firms invest heavily in trader education, teaching the psychology and principles of disciplined execution. Traders who fail to respect risk guidelines are quickly filtered out.

Despite their different approaches, both hedge funds and prop firms share one core belief: success is not about eliminating risk, but about controlling it intelligently. They know that no strategy can avoid losses altogether. But with strong money management, the losses are small, the wins are meaningful, and the process remains sustainable. Risk management is not a backup plan, it's the reason to stay in the game.

So the next time you're tempted to double your position because "this one feels right," remember, hedge funds don't rely on vibes. They rely on VaR.

The Mental Framework Behind Every Trade

Even if your strategy and risk plan are in place, your mindset decides whether you follow through. The market is uncertain, always shifting. You don't need to predict the next move, you need to stay ready to respond without hesitation. It's not about certainty. It's about managing risk within a game of probabilities.

Most traders don't fail because their setup is wrong. They fail because their mindset isn't ready. The best traders treat each trade as one of many. They don't judge success based on a single outcome, but on how well they follow their process over time. What breaks that process? Fear. Greed. The urge to be right. These emotions cause hesitation, overreaction, or abandoning the plan mid-trade. You don't overcome emotion by ignoring it. You overcome it by trusting your process. Confidence grows not by winning one trade, but by knowing your edge works over the long run.

Think in terms of process, not outcome. Define your edge. Stick to your risk. Execute with focus. Success is not measured by profit on a single trade, but by consistency in action. That's your real edge: calm, control, and commitment to the process.

Common Mind Traps: FOMO and Bias

Not every setup needs your action. One of the biggest traps traders fall into is FOMO, the fear of missing out. You see a candle spike, and suddenly you feel like you're being left behind. But reacting without structure is like sprinting just because the crowd moves. It's not your race unless it matches your plan.

Another trap is bias. If you walk into a session already convinced of direction, you might bend every price move to fit your opinion. That's not trading, that's guessing. The market doesn't care what you think. It only responds to your preparation.

The moment you force trades out of fear or cling to bias, you lose your edge. Stay neutral. Let the market speak. Your job is not to be right. It's to be ready.

The Next Frontier: Automating the CPR Indicator

Imagine a trader sitting at their desk at 9:15 AM, coffee in hand, charts glowing, CPR levels drawn. They've done their analysis, set their alerts, even whispered a small prayer to the market gods. Now begins the waiting game. The price dances near the top CPR line, hesitates, fakes a move, reverses, and breaks out for real, right after the trader blinks. They miss the entry. Again. Sound familiar?

This is the story of thousands of traders who know their strategy works but find themselves caught in the human trap: hesitation, overthinking, late entries, early exits. This is where the future of the CPR indicator is headed, not to replace traders, but to free them from the noise.

CPR, by its very design, offers structure. But the true power comes when it's blended with other indicators like VWAP, Super trend, RSI, or Moving Averages. These combinations act like filters, confirming breakouts, rejecting false moves, and giving traders confidence. For instance, a CPR breakout with VWAP crossover and Super trend support? That's not a trade. That's a green carpet entrance to a high-probability setup. But even great strategies suffer if the trader second-guesses the system. That's why automation is the natural next step. Whether you're a novice just learning CPR or an experienced trader managing multiple instruments, automation brings structure to execution. Alerts for CPR breakouts, scripts to identify narrow CPR days, even auto-calculated position sizing can now be built into simple bots or trading systems. No more blinking at the wrong time. No more missed entries because the dog barked or the kettle whistled.

The beauty of CPR automation lies in its scalability. It doesn't demand machine learning or hedge-fund budgets. A beginner can use alert-based setups, while a pro can build full-fledged execution bots. Either way, the strategy stays the same; it just becomes cleaner, faster, and emotionally detached. And here's the funny part: while you automate your CPR strategy to avoid emotional trading, your bot doesn't panic when there's a red candle. It doesn't cheer when it's green. It doesn't call its friend to ask, "Bro, should I exit now?" It just follows rules, something we traders promise to do but often forget the moment a candle winks at us.

So, as CPR evolves, it's no longer just a technical level. It's the base layer of a disciplined, smart, and scalable trading system. In the world of trading, where chaos is the norm, CPR offers structure. And in the future, that structure will power systems that think less, react faster, and trade better.

Every Journey Has a Beginning

This journey began with learning how to trade. Along the way, it became about something more. It became about structure, discipline, and finding calm in the middle of chaos. CPR was the starting point, but what truly made the difference was the mindset built around it. Over time, the charts became familiar, the process became second nature, and trading stopped feeling like a gamble. It became a craft. One that's practiced quietly, refined daily, and respected deeply.

And now, you're no longer just learning.
You're becoming a trader.

But before all this, before the structure, the routines, and the charts, there was a reason behind my journey. A personal one. The moment that set everything in motion. And that's what comes next.

THE MAN BEHIND CPR BY KGS

While accepting the **Dadasaheb Phalke Award** at the 67th National Film Awards ceremony, superstar **Rajinikanth** stood before the nation and said:

> ***"I dedicate this award to my friend in Karnataka, bus driver and my colleague Raj Bahadur. When I was a bus conductor, he was the one who identified acting talent in me and encouraged me to join cinema"***

A thunderous applause followed, for all Rajini fans, **Raj Bahadur** is a cherished name. A humble man from Chamrajpet in Bengaluru, he was no ordinary friend; he was the *guardian angel* who pushed **Shivaji Rao Gaekwad** to become the iconic **Rajinikanth**. It was Raj Bahadur who insisted he go to Chennai, join acting school, and even taught him to speak Tamil fluently. That one act of belief changed cinema history forever.

In my own life, I too had a Raj Bahadur whose name was **Venkatesh**.

It was the year **2014**, We were just two friends, talking casually like we always did. That day, Venkatesh happened to mention something I'd never really heard before the **share market**. That one phrase didn't mean much to him but it changed everything for me. A whole new world opened up. Venkatesh had unknowingly ignited a spark in me, one that would grow into a full-blown passion for trading. He was the first to show me there was something beyond traditional careers, something dynamic, challenging, and deeply fascinating. While most were discussing job interviews and corporate ladders, he opened a window to price charts and market psychology. I didn't realize it then, but that moment became the turning point of my life. He didn't guide me step-by-step, and he didn't have to. He simply *planted the idea,* and that was enough. That was everything.

Venkatesh is no longer with us, but his memory lives on not just in my mind, but in every trade I take, every chart I analyze, and every student I mentor. He may be gone, but his role in my journey is eternal. This book, in many ways, is a result of the spark he lit over a decade ago. **Thank you, Venkatesh. You gave me direction before I even knew I needed one.** *May your soul rest in peace.*

Inspired by that spark Venkatesh lit in me, I entered the market with raw enthusiasm but absolutely no knowledge. I began trading in penny stocks, thinking they were the quickest way to make big money. I had no clue about technical analysis, no understanding of fundamentals, and even less awareness of risk management. I was simply buying because something looked "cheap" or because someone said it was going to fly. As expected, the market taught me its first lesson the hard way. I blew up my trading account more than once. Each time, I'd promise myself it wouldn't happen again and each time, it did because I still didn't know what I was doing.

But instead of quitting, I grew more curious. I started reading blogs and books. That's when I came across an article from Hindu BusinessLine and Zerodha's Z-Connect blog. Those stories of real traders making disciplined, intelligent decisions fascinated me. It gave me hope that profitability wasn't about luck, it was about skill, structure, and study. I committed myself to learning. I started diving deep into technical analysis, candlestick patterns, chart patterns, indicators etc. I also began to explore fundamental analysis, how to read balance sheets, track sector performance, and analyze business models. Most of the top-level traders in our country were my mentors. I had attended their workshops and webinars, which directly and indirectly had a big impact on helping me understand market concepts at a fast pace. Along the way, I got the opportunity to work with some of the most respected names in the industry, Karvy Stock Broking, where I began understanding client behavior and market operations. Spider Software Pvt Ltd, where I got hands-on experience with professional charting tools. And finally, Zerodha, India's most innovative brokerage, where I immersed myself in the evolving ecosystem of modern trading. Each place became a learning ground shaping me, challenging me, and slowly transforming me from a reckless trader into a rule-based, process driven market participant.

The journey was far from easy, but it was worth every fall, every mistake, and every long night of self-doubt. Even after gaining industry experience, studying technical and fundamental analysis, and working with reputed brokerage firms, making consistent money from trading still felt out of reach. I understood how markets moved, I knew the theory but the execution, the conviction, the edge it was still missing. Every time I looked at an indicator, I found myself thinking:

> ***"If everyone is seeing the same thing, how can this work for everyone? The market clearly doesn't reward the majority. Only a few seem to win consistently".***

That question stayed with me. Like a disciple searching for his guru, I was searching for something deeper, a trading style that resonated with me, that made sense logically, visually, and emotionally. That's when another turning point arrived.

My trading friend, **Amit**, introduced me to something I had never taken seriously before the **CPR indicator**. Just like how the word *share market* fascinated me when Venkatesh first mentioned it, this time, it was the word *CPR* that pulled me in with equal intensity. There was something about it clean, structured, yet full of depth that made me want to give it a try. Until then, I had learned about pivot points in theory, but never used them in my trading. I thought they were too basic or too widely known. But CPR felt different. It had layers. It had meaning. It had *zones* not just lines and it felt alive on the chart.

So, I went deeper. I started studying the works of those who had modernized the pivot point concept **Mark Fisher**, author of *"The Logical Trader"* and **Frank Ochoa**, author of *"Secrets of a pivot boss"* who brought structure and clarity to pivot based strategies. Their insights helped me understand that trading is not about predicting it's about preparing. And CPR, as a tool, was built for preparation. That moment was the start of something powerful. I had finally found my trading edge and with it, a new chapter in my journey began. The amount of effort I had put into learning other indicators moving averages, RSI, MACD, Bollinger Bands nowhere came close to the effort I poured into understanding the CPR indicator. I went all in. I back tested thousands of charts, meticulously saving them into folders, labeling setups, marking entries and exits. I wasn't just observing, I was *learning CPR like a language*. I took live trades, noted how price behaved around the central pivot, and journaled every win, loss, and emotional reaction. The deeper I went, the clearer everything became. Suddenly, trading didn't feel like a gamble anymore; it felt like a well rehearsed game plan. It started feeling like a cakewalk, not because trading became easy, but because *I finally knew what I was looking for*. And then came a realization that changed everything for me:

> ***"Every indicator works, if you understand its true character across different timeframes".***

Maybe the reason other indicators didn't work for me wasn't because they were flawed. Maybe I wasn't mentally ready. Looking back, I now understand that the *optimistic mindset* I carried while exploring CPR, my excitement, my dedication, my belief was missing when I was trying out other tools. Had I approached RSI or Bollinger Bands with the same attitude, perhaps I would have found success there too. And perhaps I would've never explored CPR. And this book wouldn't be in your hands right now. But life has a way of leading us to where we're meant to be. Everything happens for a reason. And my reason was CPR.

As my conviction in CPR deepened and the results began to speak for themselves, something remarkable happened. I found myself constantly making 2x of my monthly salary through trading alone. What once felt like an uncertain side hustle was now showing signs of becoming a full-fledged career. And in November 2019, I made a bold, life defining decision. I left the safety net of a paycheck and embraced trading full time. Little did I know that just a few months later, the world would change. The COVID-19 crash of 2020 brought chaos to the markets. But for a prepared, directional trader, it brought opportunity. I had clarity in my process, the discipline of CPR, and the mental readiness to act decisively. I not only navigated the crash I captured it, and equally, I rode the recovery that followed. That phase helped me grow my capital at a pace I never imagined possible.

People often ask me, "What do you do in trading?"

My answer? That's the wrong question.

A better question would be:
"What haven't I done in trading?"

Because the truth is, I've done it all.

- Scalping, Intraday, Swing trading
- Option buying and selling
- Momentum investing and value investing

I've done it all. Every style taught me something. Every phase of the market taught me something new. Every style added a layer to my understanding and also to mitigate my risk And CPR? It remained my constant companion through it all.

As I started to see consistent success, one thought kept echoing in my mind:

> ***"This concept of CPR should reach every retail trader who's struggling to survive in this noisy, chaotic market".***

I had experienced the confusion. The overwhelm. The endless indicator hopping. And I knew that if CPR could bring clarity to me, it could do the same for countless others. That's when I decided to start my YouTube channel "**Gomathi Shankar (CPR by KGS)**". The goal was simple, to explain CPR strategies in a lucid, beginner friendly manner, without the jargon or hype. I didn't aim for fame. I just thought maybe 10 or 20 people might watch, and if even one of them found clarity, it would be worth it. But life, again, had other plans. To my surprise, the CPR concept itself started trending. It resonated with traders across the country who were searching for structure and logic amidst the chaos. My videos began gaining traction rapidly. Today, those videos have crossed over 8.5 million views. And something strange (and wonderful) happened along the way. People stopped calling me by my real name. They started calling me: **"CPR by KGS."** It became my identity not just a channel name, but a symbol of everything I had learned, lived, and shared. And that moment. when someone comes up to me and says, *"I learned CPR from your videos, and it changed the way I trade"* that is the real reward. Far more fulfilling than any profit booked.

Putting my journey into words in this book might read simple, maybe even effortless at times. But just like watching a cricket match on TV hides the hours of practice behind a straight drive or hearing a billionaire's success story masks their sleepless nights, this story too carries its share of pain and perseverance. There were countless ups and downs in my trading career and in my personal life too. Moments where life landed knockout punches to my mindset. Some of them took days, even weeks, to recover from. And during those phases, I wasn't just losing trades I was losing balance, losing direction. But every time I felt lost whether in the markets or in life I'd remind myself of a verse from the **Bhagavad Gita** that never fails to ground me:

> ***"What have you lost that you cry for?***
> ***What did you bring that you have lost?***
> ***What did you create that was destroyed?"***

Those words gave me perspective. They lifted me out of despair, reminded me that nothing truly belongs to us and that even in trading, we are just instruments playing our part. Though trading is everything to me, I've made it a rule:

> ***"Without a healthy mindset, I never sit in front of the screen".***

For me, healing and clarity always came from one sacred place, **Tiruvannamalai**. That holy mountain, **Lord Arunachala**, has been my spiritual anchor. When the noise of the world gets too loud when losses overwhelm or emotions take over I go back there. I sit in silence. I walk in Girivalam. And I return stronger. I cannot write this book without acknowledging the transformative power of meditation in my life. If meditation hadn't entered my path, If I hadn't learned to sit with myself, I may not have survived the storms. Forget being a trader I would have been emotionally and mentally disabled.

Would you believe me if I told you, **I started writing this book in 2021?** And now finally it's in your hands. By now, you can probably imagine the hardships I've endured, both as a trader and as a human being. Life tested me. Markets tested me. My own mind tested me. But through it all, I held on with faith, with effort, and with the hope that one day, I would complete this book. And today, that day has come. The wait is over. It's time to enjoy the fruit.

This book is all and only about the CPR indicator, because it is what changed my life. It's what gives me my bread and butter every single day. This concept has worked for legends like Mark Fisher, Frank Ochoa, Ashwani Gujral, it has worked for me, and for countless price action traders across the globe. So there's no reason it shouldn't work for you too. But not just CPR, whatever technical tool or indicator you choose, if you truly understand its character, structure, and potential across different timeframes, it will work.

However, if there's one principle I wish someone had tattooed into my mind earlier, it is this:

"Position sizing is everything."

When you master your position sizing,
- your risk per trade stays under control,
- your emotions stay balanced,
- and your money management takes care of itself.

I've seen traders chase the perfect strategy, the best indicator, the next breakout setup. But none of it matters if your position sizing is reckless. Without it, you'll stay trapped in that endless loop of winning and losing, never truly compounding, never truly progressing. But with it even an average strategy becomes powerful.

This book is my truth.
And now, it's yours.
Thank you for reading.
Thank you for believing.

May your trading journey be filled with clarity, discipline, and peace.
"Together we grow as a price action trading community".
Gomathi Shankar (CPR by KGS)

APPENDIX A: CPR MASTER SHEET: TYPES, ENTRY TECHNIQUES, AND CAMARILLA FORMULA

This appendix brings together everything a trader needs to recall in the heat of action. It covers the most important CPR structures, how to read them, where to enter, and which designed for clarity and speed. This sheet offers a single, focused view of what matters. It's not built for theory, it's built for execution. Whether you're preparing before the market opens or quickly checking structure between trades, this reference keeps your approach sharp, confident, and ready. Every pattern here speaks a language, and every formula has a purpose. Keep this sheet close. It's made for moments when the market doesn't wait.

CPR Types

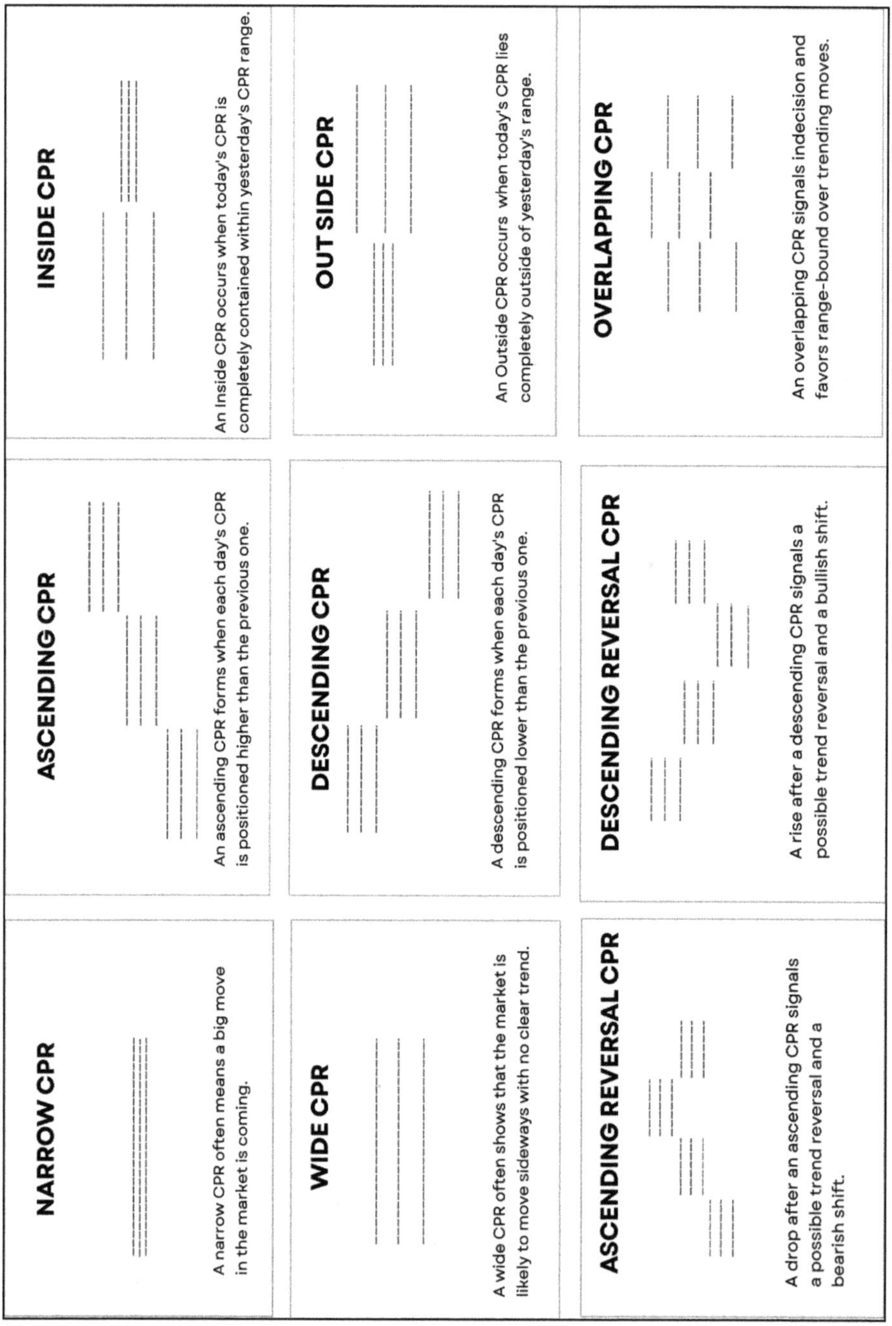
NARROW CPR
A narrow CPR often means a big move in the market is coming.
ASCENDING CPR
An ascending CPR forms when each day's CPR is positioned higher than the previous one.
INSIDE CPR
An Inside CPR occurs when today's CPR is completely contained within yesterday's CPR range.
WIDE CPR
A wide CPR often shows that the market is likely to move sideways with no clear trend.
DESCENDING CPR
A descending CPR forms when each day's CPR is positioned lower than the previous one.
OUT SIDE CPR
An Outside CPR occurs when today's CPR lies completely outside of yesterday's range.
ASCENDING REVERSAL CPR
A drop after an ascending CPR signals a possible trend reversal and a bearish shift.
DESCENDING REVERSAL CPR
A rise after a descending CPR signals a possible trend reversal and a bullish shift.
OVERLAPPING CPR
An overlapping CPR signals indecision and favors range-bound over trending moves.

CPR Based Entry Location

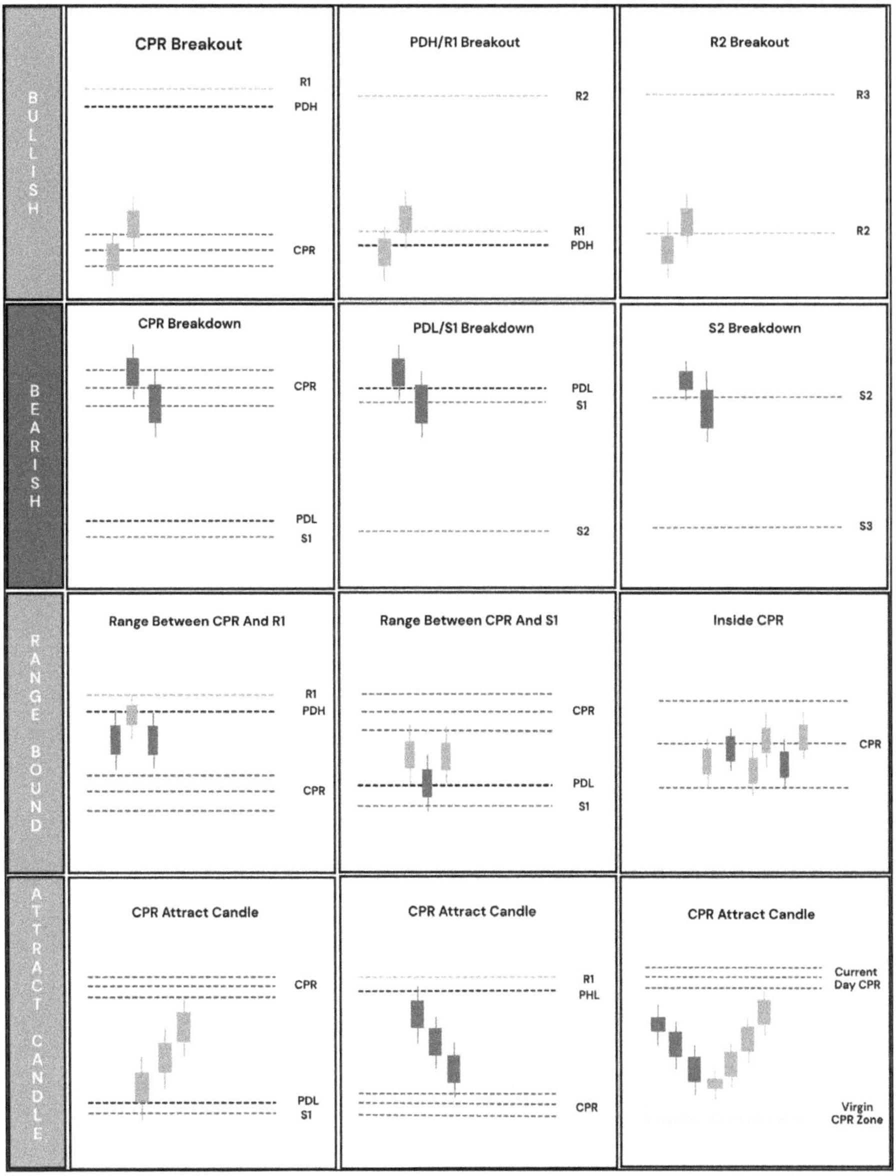

Key Reversal Levels in Camarilla Pivot Trading

The Camarilla pivot point method is a popular tool used by intraday traders to identify key support and resistance levels. Among the multiple levels it provides, R3 and S3 are particularly important because they often act as strong reversal points. Here's a breakdown of how they are calculated and used:

Component	Formula
Range	Previous Day High - Previous Day Low
Camarilla R3	Close + (Range) × 1.1 / 4
Camarilla S3	Close - (Range) × 1.1 / 4

APPENDIX B: PINE SCRIPT CODEBASE

This section serves as a comprehensive technical vault for the Pine Script logic used throughout the book. Each script included here is meticulously crafted to support the CPR-based trading strategies discussed in earlier chapters. Whether you're looking to visualize Daily, Weekly, Monthly, or Developing CPR levels, this codebase equips you with practical, ready-to-use tools that integrate directly into TradingView.

The objective is not only to help you replicate the visual setups but also to empower you to understand the underlying logic behind each level. From central pivot calculations to extended support and resistance zones like S4 and R4, every detail is included with clarity. You'll also find specialized modules such as Camarilla Pivots and Developing CPR, which provide dynamic structure and real-time adaptability during market hours. This appendix is designed for traders who wish to bridge theory with execution. Think of this section as your personal CPR script toolkit, a bridge between strategy and screen.

Mark Fisher Range

```
//@version=6
indicator('MARK FISHER ', overlay = true)

// Get previous day's high, low, and close from the Daily timeframe
prevHigh = request.security(syminfo.tickerid, 'D', high)
prevLow = request.security(syminfo.tickerid, 'D', low)
prevClose = request.security(syminfo.tickerid, 'D', close)

// 1. Calculate the Daily Pivot Price
dailyPivotPrice = (prevHigh + prevLow + prevClose) / 3

// 2. Calculate the Second Number
secondNumber = (prevHigh + prevLow) / 2

// 3. Find the Daily Pivot Differential
dailyPivotDifferential = dailyPivotPrice - secondNumber

// 4. Calculate the Daily Pivot Ranges
dailyPivotRange = dailyPivotPrice - dailyPivotDifferential
dailyPivotRange2 = dailyPivotPrice + dailyPivotDifferential

// Plot Daily Pivot Ranges on the chart
plot(dailyPivotRange, title = 'Daily Pivot Range', color = color.blue,
linewidth = 2, style = plot.style_circles)
plot(dailyPivotRange2, title = 'Daily Pivot Range 2', color = color.blue,
linewidth = 2, style = plot.style_circles)
```

CPR Indicator

```
//@version=6
indicator(title = 'CPR Indicator', shorttitle = 'CPR Indicator', overlay = true)

s75 = input.bool(true, title = 'Show 75min CPR')
showDailyTF = input.bool(true, title = 'Show Daily CPR')
showWeeklyTF = input.bool(true, title = 'Show Weekly CPR')
showMonthlyTF = input.bool(true, title = 'Show Monthly CPR')
```

```
// Calculation for 75/daily/weekly/monthly CPR levels with previous high/
low levels
getPivotData(_res, _index) =>
[h, l, c] = request.security(syminfo.tickerid, _res, [high[_index], low[_
index], close[_index]], lookahead = barmerge.lookahead_on)
pivot = (h + l + c) / 3.0
bc = (h + l) / 2.0
tc = pivot - bc + pivot
BCPR = math.min(bc, tc)
TCPR = math.max(bc, tc)
r1 = pivot * 2.0 - l
s1 = pivot * 2.0 - h
r2 = pivot + (h - l)
s2 = pivot - (h - l)
r3 = r1 + (h - l)
s3 = s1 - (h - l)
r4 = r3 + (r2 - r1)
s4 = s3 - (s1 - s2)
[pivot, BCPR, TCPR, r1, s1, r2, s2, r3, s3, r4, s4, h, l, c]

// Standard (Previous) Daily/Weekly/Monthly
[h75_Pivot, h75_BC, h75_TC, h75_R1, h75_S1, h75_R2, h75_S2, h75_R3, h75_S3,
h75_R4, h75_S4, h75H, h75L, h75C] = getPivotData('75', 1)
[dPivot, dBC, dTC, dR1, dS1, dR2, dS2, dR3, dS3, dR4, dS4, dH, dL, dC] =
getPivotData('D', 1)
[wPivot, wBC, wTC, wR1, wS1, wR2, wS2, wR3, wS3, wR4, wS4, wH, wL, wC] =
getPivotData('W', 1)
[mPivot, mBC, mTC, mR1, mS1, mR2, mS2, mR3, mS3, mR4, mS4, mH, mL, mC] =
getPivotData('M', 1)

// 75 mins
plot(s75? h75_Pivot: na, title='75 min Pivot', style=plot.style_circles,
color=color.blue, linewidth=2)
plot(s75? h75_BC : na, title='75 min BC', style=plot.style_circles,
color=color.blue, linewidth=2)
plot(s75? h75_TC : na, title='75 min TC', style=plot.style_circles,
color=color.blue, linewidth=2)
plot(s75? h75_R1 : na, title='75 min R1', style=plot.style_circles,
color=color.green, linewidth=2)
plot(s75? h75_R2 : na, title='75 min R2', style=plot.style_circles,
color=color.green, linewidth=2)
plot(s75? h75_R3 : na, title='75 min R3', style=plot.style_circles,
color=color.green, linewidth=2)
```

```
plot(s75? h75_R4 : na, title='75 min R4', style=plot.style_circles,
color=color.green, linewidth=2)
plot(s75? h75_S1 : na, title='75 min S1', style=plot.style_circles,
color=color.red, linewidth=2)
plot(s75? h75_S2 : na, title='75 min S2', style=plot.style_circles,
color=color.red, linewidth=2)
plot(s75? h75_S3 : na, title='75 min S3', style=plot.style_circles,
color=color.red, linewidth=2)
plot(s75? h75_S4 : na, title='75 min S4', style=plot.style_circles,
color=color.red, linewidth=2)
plot(s75 ? h75H: na, title="Prev 75 High", style=plot.style_circles,
color=color.black, linewidth=2)
plot(s75 ? h75L: na, title="Prev 75 Low", style=plot.style_circles,
color=color.black, linewidth=2)

// DAILY
plot(showDailyTF? dPivot: na, title="Daily Pivot", style=plot.style_
circles, color=color.blue, linewidth=2)
plot(showDailyTF? dBC : na, title="Daily BC", style=plot.style_circles,
color=color.blue, linewidth=2)
plot(showDailyTF? dTC : na, title="Daily TC", style=plot.style_circles,
color=color.blue, linewidth=2)
plot(showDailyTF? dR1 : na, title="Daily R1", style=plot.style_circles,
color=color.green, linewidth=2)
plot(showDailyTF? dR2 : na, title="Daily R2", style=plot.style_circles,
color=color.green, linewidth=2)
plot(showDailyTF? dR3 : na, title="Daily R3", style=plot.style_circles,
color=color.green, linewidth=2)
plot(showDailyTF? dR4 : na, title="Daily R4", style=plot.style_circles,
color=color.green, linewidth=2)
plot(showDailyTF? dS1 : na, title="Daily S1", style=plot.style_circles,
color=color.red, linewidth=2)
plot(showDailyTF? dS2 : na, title="Daily S2", style=plot.style_circles,
color=color.red, linewidth=2)
plot(showDailyTF? dS3 : na, title="Daily S3", style=plot.style_circles,
color=color.red, linewidth=2)
plot(showDailyTF? dS4 : na, title="Daily S4", style=plot.style_circles,
color=color.red, linewidth=2)
plot(showDailyTF ? dH: na, title="Prev Day High", style=plot.style_circles,
color=color.black, linewidth=2)
plot(showDailyTF ? dL: na, title="Prev Day Low", style=plot.style_circles,
color=color.black, linewidth=2)
```

```
// WEEKLY
plot(showWeeklyTF? wPivot: na, title="Weekly Pivot", style=plot.style_
circles, color=color.blue, linewidth=2)
plot(showWeeklyTF? wBC : na, title="Weekly BC", style=plot.style_circles,
color=color.blue, linewidth=2)
plot(showWeeklyTF? wTC : na, title="Weekly TC", style=plot.style_circles,
color=color.blue, linewidth=2)
plot(showWeeklyTF? wR1 : na, title="Weekly R1", style=plot.style_circles,
color=color.green, linewidth=2)
plot(showWeeklyTF? wR2 : na, title="Weekly R2", style=plot.style_circles,
color=color.green, linewidth=2)
plot(showWeeklyTF? wR3 : na, title="Weekly R3", style=plot.style_circles,
color=color.green, linewidth=2)
plot(showWeeklyTF? wR4 : na, title="Weekly R4", style=plot.style_circles,
color=color.green, linewidth=2)
plot(showWeeklyTF? wS1 : na, title="Weekly S1", style=plot.style_circles,
color=color.red, linewidth=2)
plot(showWeeklyTF? wS2 : na, title="Weekly S2", style=plot.style_circles,
color=color.red, linewidth=2)
plot(showWeeklyTF? wS3 : na, title="Weekly S3", style=plot.style_circles,
color=color.red, linewidth=2)
plot(showWeeklyTF? wS4 : na, title="Weekly S4", style=plot.style_circles,
color=color.red, linewidth=2)
plot(showWeeklyTF ? wH: na, title="Prev Week High", style=plot.style_
circles, color=color.black, linewidth=2)
plot(showWeeklyTF ? wL: na, title="Prev Week Low", style=plot.style_
circles, color=color.black, linewidth=2)

// MONTHLY
plot(showMonthlyTF? mPivot: na, title="Monthly Pivot", style=plot.style_
circles, color=color.blue, linewidth=2)
plot(showMonthlyTF? mBC : na, title="Monthly BC", style=plot.style_circles,
color=color.blue, linewidth=2)
plot(showMonthlyTF? mTC : na, title="Monthly TC", style=plot.style_circles,
color=color.blue, linewidth=2)
plot(showMonthlyTF? mR1 : na, title="Monthly R1", style=plot.style_circles,
color=color.green, linewidth=2)
plot(showMonthlyTF? mR2 : na, title="Monthly R2", style=plot.style_circles,
color=color.green, linewidth=2)
plot(showMonthlyTF? mR3 : na, title="Monthly R3", style=plot.style_circles,
color=color.green, linewidth=2)
plot(showMonthlyTF? mR4 : na, title="Monthly R4", style=plot.style_circles,
color=color.green, linewidth=2)
plot(showMonthlyTF? mS1 : na, title="Monthly S1", style=plot.style_circles,
color=color.red, linewidth=2)
```

```
plot(showMonthlyTF? mS2 : na, title="Monthly S2", style=plot.style_circles,
color=color.red, linewidth=2)
plot(showMonthlyTF? mS3 : na, title="Monthly S3", style=plot.style_circles,
color=color.red, linewidth=2)
plot(showMonthlyTF? mS4 : na, title="Monthly S4", style=plot.style_circles,
color=color.red, linewidth=2)
plot(showMonthlyTF? mH: na, title="Prev Month High", style=plot.style_
circles, color=color.black, linewidth=2)
plot(showMonthlyTF? mL: na, title="Prev Month Low", style=plot.style_
circles, color=color.black, linewidth=2)
```

Developing CPR

```
//@version=6
indicator('DEV_CPR', overlay = true, shorttitle = 'DEV_CPR')
plotDeveloping = input.bool(true, title = 'Plot Developing')

// Detect new day (works on intraday charts)
var float periodHigh = na
var float periodLow = na
isNewDay = ta.change(time('D'))
if bar_index == 0 or bool(isNewDay)
periodHigh: = high
periodLow: = low
periodLow
else
periodHigh: = math.max(periodHigh, high)
periodLow: = math.min(periodLow, low)
periodLow
fPP = (periodHigh + periodLow + close) / 3
fBC = (periodHigh + periodLow) / 2
fTC = fPP - fBC + fPP
plot(plotDeveloping? fPP: na, title = 'Developing Central Pivot', color =
color.blue, linewidth = 2)
plot(plotDeveloping? fTC: na, title = 'Developing Top Pivot', color =
color.blue, linewidth = 2)
plot(plotDeveloping? fBC: na, title = 'Developing Bottom Pivot', color =
color.blue, linewidth = 2)
```

Camarilla S3 and R3

```
//@version=6
indicator(title = 'Camarilla Pivot Points', shorttitle = 'CPP', overlay = true)
res = input.timeframe(title = 'Resolution', defval = 'D')
width = input.int(1, minval = 1)
xHigh = request.security(syminfo.tickerid, res, high)
xLow = request.security(syminfo.tickerid, res, low)
xClose = request.security(syminfo.tickerid, res, close)
H3 = 0.275 * (xHigh - xLow) + xClose
L3 = xClose - 0.275 * (xHigh - xLow)
plot(H3[1], color = color.new(#ff014a, 0), title = 'H3', style = plot.
style_circles, linewidth = math.max(1, width))
plot(L3[1], color = color.new(#004900, 0), title = 'L3', style = plot.
style_circles, linewidth = math.max(1, width))
```

BIBLIOGRAPHY

Mark B. Fisher, The Logical Trader: Applying a Method to the Madness

Franklin O. Ochoa, Secrets of a Pivot Boss

Ashwani Gujral, How to Make Money in Intraday Trading

TradingView: www.tradingview.com

www.ingramcontent.com/pod-product-compliance
Lightning Source LLC
LaVergne TN
LVHW052113210926
848482LV00025B/583

* 9 7 9 8 8 9 8 2 6 6 6 0 8 *